CW00434283

SUMPTUOUS AND RICHLY ADORN'D

The Decoration of Salisbury Cathedral

ROYAL
COMMISSION
ON THE HISTORICAL
MONUMENTS
OF ENGLAND

SUMPTUOUS AND RICHLY ADORN'D

The Decoration of Salisbury Cathedral

Sarah Brown

LONDON: The Stationery Office

First published 1999

ISBN 0 11 300096 0

British Library Cataloguing in Publication Data
A CIP catalogue record for this book is available
from the British Library

Published by The Stationery Office and available from:

The Publications Centre
(mail, telephone and fax orders only)
PO Box 276, London SW8 5DT
General enquiries 0170 873 0011
Telephone orders 0171 873 9090
Fax orders 0171 873 8200

The Stationery Office Bookshops
123 Kingsway, London WC2B 6PQ
0171 242 6393   Fax 0171 242 6394
68–69 Bull Street, Birmingham B4 6AD
0121 236 9696   Fax 0121 236 9699
33 Wine Street, Bristol BS1 2BQ
0117 9264306   Fax 0117 9294515
9–21 Princess Street, Manchester M60 8AS
0161 834 7201   Fax 0161 833 0634
16 Arthur Street, Belfast BT1 4GD
01232 238451   Fax 01232 235401
The Stationery Office Oriel Bookshop
The Friary, Cardiff CF1 4AA
01222 395548   Fax 01222 384347
71 Lothian Road, Edinburgh EH3 9AZ
0131 228 4181   Fax 0131 622 7017

The Stationery Office's Accredited Agents
(see Yellow Pages)

and through good booksellers

Printed in the United Kingdom for The Stationery Office
J43075 C15 3/99 039462

Contents

Full contents detailed overleaf

CONTENTS IN FULL

Illustrations

Figures

Colour plates

The Royal Commission is grateful to the various institutions and individuals who permitted the photographing of topographical material in their care and the reproduction of copyright material.

Sources of illustrations, other than photographs and drawings prepared by Royal Commission staff, appear by permission of the following: B T Batsford Ltd, Fig 54; The Bodleian Library, Oxford, Figs 9, 15, 17, 18, 19, 41, 126 and 127; The British Library, Figs 4, 14, 76 and 104; The Conway Library, Courtauld Institute of Art, Figs 143, 144 and 145; The Dean and Chapter of Salisbury, Fig 40; Mr A F Kersting, Fig 146; The Salisbury and South Wiltshire Museum, Fig 42 and Plates 4 and 5; The Society of Antiquaries of London, Fig 142 and Plate 6; The Board of Trustees of the Victoria and Albert Museum, Figs 10, 63, 68, 69 and 75; The Library of the Wiltshire Archaeological and Natural History Society, Plates 2 and 3.

Every effort has been made to trace copyright holders; the Royal Commission wishes to apologise to any who may have been inadvertently omitted from the above list.

Commissioners

Chairman's Foreword

In 1993 the Royal Commission published the first of our contributions to the study of Salisbury Cathedral, focusing on the foundation, design and history of the building. This, the second volume, concerns the equally important subject of the furnishing and decoration of the Cathedral from its foundation to the end of the 20th century. Opinion as to the value and interest of the interior and its decoration has been sharply divided in the past. In August 1635 the well-travelled Lt Hammond declared the Cathedral to be 'sumptuous and richly adorn'd', the equal of any in the land. Daniel Defoe was far less complimentary in the 1720s: 'it must be acknowledged that the inside of the work is not answerable in the decoration of things, to the workmanship without.' Since then the Cathedral has undergone two thorough restorations which have had a major impact on the interior: in the late 18th century by James Wyatt and in the 19th century by George Gilbert Scott. Now, in the late 20th century, the Cathedral is the subject of major conservation work, accompanied by renewed scholarly attention and careful archaeological recording. The work of our staff has contributed to and benefited from this activity. The Commissioners are grateful to Sarah Brown for collating the findings of earlier investigations with the results of recent work to form a valuable contribution to the study of the furnishing of the Cathedral which provided the backdrop to observance of the liturgy. Peter Spencer has continued his enthusiastic support and assistance and has provided further artwork.

The Commissioners also wish to acknowledge the work of four former members of staff, John Reeves, the late Norman Drinkwater and the late Nicholas Moore for investigation and Dr Bridgett Jones for documentary research; the late Ron Parsons, Tony Rumsey, Steven Cole, Peter Williams, Len Furbank and Mike Hesketh-Roberts for photography; Hugh Richmond and Dr John Bold for comments on the text; and Dr Robin Taylor, Hilary Walford and Rachel Brown for editorial advice and assistance. The index was prepared by Ann Hudson.

Work in the Cathedral would have been impossible without the continuing support and cooperation of successive Bishops of Salisbury, the Dean and Chapter and the Cathedral staff. In particular we thank the Cathedral Librarian and keeper of the Muniments, Miss S Eward, the former Cathedral Clerk of Works, Mr R O C Spring, and the Cathedral's Archaeological Consultant, Mr T Tatton-Brown.

Access to archive material outside the Cathedral has considerably enriched the record: Our thanks extend to the staff of the Diocesan Record Office, the staff of the Salisbury and South Wiltshire Museum, to the Wiltshire Archaeological and Natural History Society, Devizes Museum, in particular Mrs P Coleman, the staff of the Victoria and Albert Museum's Department of Prints and Drawings and its Archive of Art and Design, the Manuscripts Department of the British Library, and Mr Bernard Nurse and his staff in the library of the Society of Antiquaries of London. Individual scholars have supplied information and advice on a number of inventory sections and their generous assistance is acknowledged in the text.

The project archive, including the complete photographic record, can be consulted in the National Monuments Record, National Monuments Record Centre, Kemble Drive, Swindon SN2 2GZ; telephone 01793 414600.

FARINGDON
Chairman

Abbreviations

BL	British Library
BN	Bibliothèque Nationale
Bodl	Bodleian Library
FOSC	Friends of Salisbury Cathedral
JBAA	*Journal of the British Archaeological Association*
N&Q	*Notes & Queries*
PRO	Public Records Office
RIBA	Royal Institute of British Architects
Sarum D&C	Salisbury, Dean and Chapter
SJ	*Salisbury Journal*
V&A	Victoria and Albert Museum
V&A, AAD	Victoria and Albert Museum, Archive of Art and Design
VCH	Victoria History of the Counties of England
WANHS	Wiltshire Archaeological and Natural History Society
WAM	*Wiltshire Archaeological Magazine*
Wilts N&Q	*Wiltshire Notes & Queries*

· I ·

Historical Summary

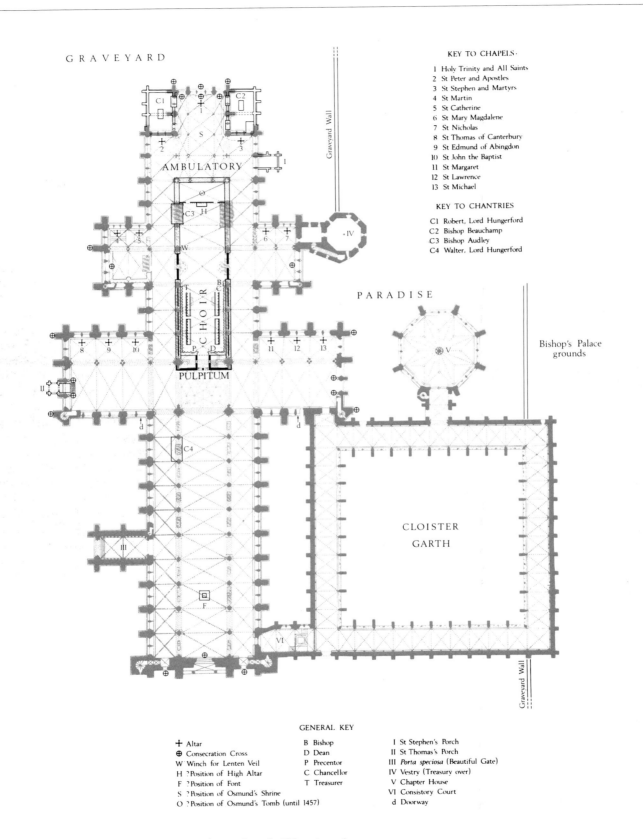

GRAVEYARD

AMBULATORY

CHOIR

PULPITUM

PARADISE

Bishop's Palace grounds

CLOISTER GARTH

KEY TO CHAPELS·

1 Holy Trinity and All Saints
2 St Peter and Apostles
3 St Stephen and Martyrs
4 St Martin
5 St Catherine
6 St Mary Magdalene
7 St Nicholas
8 St Thomas of Canterbury
9 St Edmund of Abingdon
10 St John the Baptist
11 St Margaret
12 St Lawrence
13 St Michael

KEY TO CHANTRIES

C1 Robert, Lord Hungerford
C2 Bishop Beauchamp
C3 Bishop Audley
C4 Walter, Lord Hungerford

GENERAL KEY

+ Altar	B Bishop	I	St Stephen's Porch
⊕ Consecration Cross	D Dean	II	St Thomas's Porch
W Winch for Lenten Veil	P Precentor	III	*Porta speciosa* (Beautiful Gate)
H ?Position of High Altar	C Chancellor	IV	Vestry (Treasury over)
F ?Position of Font	T Treasurer	V	Chapter House
S ?Position of Osmund's Shrine		VI	Consistory Court
O ?Position of Osmund's Tomb (until 1457)		d	Doorway

1   Features of the medieval interior superimposed upon the early 19th-century plan

The medieval context

IT is now extremely difficult to visualise the original context for those medieval furnishings and decorations that survive in Salisbury Cathedral. The effects of reformation, iconoclasm and misguided restoration have taken their toll, not only on the furnishings themselves, but also on the decorative environment in which they were designed to be seen. Some aspects of the Cathedral's medieval decoration survive only as vestiges; wall paintings, stained glass and tiles have all suffered badly. Of wooden sculpture and imagery nothing remains and figurative stone sculpture survives either heavily weathered (the west front), partially defaced (the pulpitum) or drastically restored (the Chapter House). The once sumptuous furnishings of the many altars, and the numerous vestments donned by the clergy officiating at them, are recalled only in the evidence of medieval inventories, of which several survive, providing valuable evidence of the contents of the Cathedral treasury at a number of key points in its history [Rich Jones 1884, 127–41; Wordsworth 1901, 160–84]. Despite the somewhat fragmentary nature of the picture, it is none the less possible to reconstruct in part the original context for which the furnishings were intended. Medieval ecclesiastical architecture was intended to create an appropriate setting for the liturgical function and to provide a backdrop to the decorative and figurative arts. Nowhere is this more the case than at Salisbury, where the sober decorum of the architecture provided a dignified but unassertive foil. The interiors of Westminster or Lincoln denuded of original colour and furniture are still richly textured and visually exciting. Salisbury stripped of its medieval finery is plain by comparison. An attempt to re-create the decorative environment in which its medieval furnishings were once installed serves two purposes – to make greater sense of what survives and to underline the importance of these embellishments to the impact of the original decorative scheme.

Accommodating the liturgy

The official reasons for moving from Old Sarum, as reiterated by Precentor William de Waude (dean from 1220), concerned the deficiencies of the site and the behaviour of the neighbours. In his *Historia Translationis veteris ecclesiae Beatae Mariae Sarum ad Novam* [Rich Jones 1884], the reasons were stated to be the cramped location, which was also noisy and windy, the shortage of water, the inconvenient proximity of the nearby garrison and the inadequate accommodation available for the canons. The underlying reasons were more likely to have been connected with the lack of what Peter Kidson has called the 'ecclesiastical amenities' [Kidson 1993, 37].

Although the canons undoubtedly benefited from the move to a site which allowed for the planning of commodious residences from the outset, the real improvements lay in the planning of the church. The general similarities of plan between the Cathedral at Old Sarum and the new Cathedral, under construction from 1220 onwards, have often been remarked upon. The inadequate space available at the east end of the old church was one of the reasons for the relocation to a new virgin site.[1] In the event, however, it was the nave, liturgically of lesser importance, that was to be considerably enlarged in the new building. However, while the actual space occupied by the eastern arm of the new church may not have been substantially greater than that occupied at Old Sarum, its disposition was significantly improved upon for the purposes of liturgical observance, offering a series of interconnecting spaces better suited to the requirements of the Use of Sarum [Draper 1987, 83–91; Draper 1996]. It was no coincidence that the Ordinal that codified the liturgical customs of Salisbury was revised at this time, probably the work of Richard Poore (dean 1198–1215 and bishop 1217–28), although Osmund was always credited with authorship [Greenaway 1996]. The most significant addition to the plan of the church was a second pair of transepts, immediately increasing the space available for chapels, and thus altars, at which mass could be celebrated daily. The Salisbury Chapter was the third largest in England, having been increased from approximately thirty-six to forty-two *c* 1150 and to fifty-two by 1226 [Greenaway 1991, Greenaway 1996, 5–6]. In addition to the high altar, dedicated to the Assumption of the Blessed Virgin, and a nave altar to serve the laity, the new Cathedral boasted thirteen altars, sufficient to allow the daily celebration of mass by the one-quarter of the Chapter required by the statutes to be in residence at any one time. The rectangular form of the Trinity Chapel, retrochoir chapels and two transepts allowed all the altars to be oriented east and all were at ground level, greatly facilitating their visitation by the processions that were a feature of the Use of Sarum [Wordsworth 1901]. The Sunday procession, for example, assembled first to asperge the high altar, proceeding then out of the choir by the north door, passed round the ambulatory into the south-choir aisle, thence to the west end of the nave, visiting each altar in turn. In the nave the continuous plinth or stylobate between piers is breached at those points where the processional route crossed from one side of the nave to the other or from the aisles into the main body of the nave. On special feast days such as Palm Sunday, the processions were considerably elaborated and took in the cloisters and the exterior of the building.[2] It has been demonstrated that in the planning of the west front

the liturgical requirements superseded aesthetic considerations [Blum 1986]. Quatrefoil openings (blocked in
the 19th century), accessed from an internal gallery,
allowed the choir to sing the *Gloria Laus et Honor* from
an elevated position (*pueri in eminenti loci*) to those
gathered below enacting the entry into Jerusalem, as
required by the Palm Sunday observance. As late as
1794 this usage was still recalled; the openings were
described as being 'at choir level'. They were only
blocked *c* 1870 when the new statuary was added to the
west front. Most medieval churches made do with the
erection of a temporary scaffold for this purpose [Duffy
1992, 24]. The procession then entered the church
under the west portal, the height of which had been
compromised by the internal arrangements servicing the
gallery. The Palm Sunday procession was one of the
most dramatic spectacles of the religious year. The building was, however, a stage on which religious theatre was
regularly performed; the earliest printed Salisbury processional contains diagrammatic plans of the positions
to be adopted by the priest, deacons and acolytes, closely resembling stage instructions [Wordsworth 1901].

The new building provided two cruciform churches
in one, for the community enjoyed the amenity of a second complete cruciform space to the east of the pulpitum. The choir of the new cathedral, located between
the western and eastern transepts, was effectively sited
further from the nave than was the case at Old
Sarum, withdrawing into a more secluded position.
Furthermore, a clear distinction between choir and presbytery could now be made, the latter defined by the eastern transepts which marked its entrance. The Cathedral
now had a clearly differentiated space in which the sacra-
ment could be reserved in seclusion and dignity.

To the east of the presbytery, the church extended
into a large halled space accommodating the chapel of
the Holy Trinity and All Saints. From the end of the 12th
century onwards, the observance of the daily sung mass
of the Virgin had been widely adopted by monastic and
secular communities, and new chapels were added to
existing buildings to accommodate this. In Salisbury the
new Cathedral was provided with a spacious and elegant
space for this observance; the Trinity Chapel was commonly referred to as the Lady Chapel and was the site of
the daily mass of the Virgin. The Trinity Chapel altar was
also frequently referred to as the *Salve* altar, after the
words of the antiphon *Salve, Sancta Parens* (Hail, Holy
Parent). It is possible that the work on the east end of
Winchester Cathedral, begun under Bishop Godfrey de
Lucy *c* 1204 and continued under his successor, Bishop
Peter de Roches (1205–38), and barely 25 miles from
Salisbury, served as a model for such treatment [Draper
and Morris 1993]. The chapel needed to be of sufficient

size to accommodate the resident canons attending the
daily mass of the Virgin, but it has also been suggested
that the eastern chapel was originally planned as a
memorial chapel for Osmund [eg Kidson 1993, 56], a
function that has also been suggested for the retrochoir
at Winchester. Recent research has shown, however, that
at Winchester, where the Dean and Chapter already had
in Swithun a fully validated saint, together with a considerable collection of other relics, the equivalent space
was not, in fact, used to accommodate the principal
shrine until the 15th century [see Crook, 1993*b*]. The
documentary evidence for the exact location and nature
of Osmund's first burial place in the new Cathedral at
Salisbury in the period between the transfer of his body
from Old Sarum to the new Cathedral in 1226 to his
canonisation and translation to a new shrine in 1457
leaves a number of questions only partially answered.
The protracted delay in securing the canonisation may
also have necessitated a rethink of any original plan for
Osmund's commemoration.

Osmund and the new Cathedral

Osmund had long been revered by the Cathedral community as its ancient benefactor and most illustrious
bishop, and his chasuble and broken staff were preserved in the Cathedral treasury [Wordsworth 1901, 173,
175]. There is plenty of evidence to suggest that those
members of the Chapter intent upon relocating the
Cathedral, particularly Richard Poore, had decided to
harness Osmund's prestige in this cause. Indeed, it was
hoped that his reputation for sanctity would soon
receive papal sanction. As early as 1222, he was referred
to as 'saint' in the Cathedral register [Rich Jones 1884,
55], and miracles were already taking place at the tomb
at Old Sarum. It was intended that the new Cathedral
would be regarded as Osmund's cathedral, and the very
forms of liturgical observance practised by the Chapter
on a daily basis were attributed to his authorship.

On 25 September 1226, the vigil of St Michael, Dean
William de Waude's account of the building of the new
Cathedral records the consecration of the three altars in
the easternmost part of the new building: the altar of the
Holy Trinity in the Trinity Chapel, that of St Peter and
the Apostles in the northern retrochoir and that of St
Stephen and Martyrs in the equivalent position on the
south side [Rich Jones 1884, 55]. A few days later the
bodies of Osmund and Bishops Jocelin and Roger were
brought from Old Sarum *ad novam fabricam*, together
with the stones that covered them. William does not
record exactly where they were laid to rest, however,
although it must be assumed that all three were rein-
terred somewhere in the Trinity Chapel or adjoining
chapels, the only part of the new building complete at

2   The Trinity Chapel, looking north-east [BB71/2312]

that time. Recent research [Stroud 1984, 1993] has shown that two monuments surviving in the Cathedral, the Purbeck marble table tomb with pierced sides and the Purbeck marble slab with effigy and elaborate biographical verses (monuments 90 and 69), can be associated with Osmund's first burial in the new Cathedral. In 1228 the first (unsuccessful) attempt to secure Osmund's canonisation was initiated with the gathering of witness testimony [Malden 1901, 1–45].

3   12th-century effigial slab (monument 69), attributed to St Osmund [BB73/7070]

The close similarity of form between the Salisbury Purbeck marble tomb base (monument 90) and Becket's first tomb in the crypt at Canterbury, depicted in the Becket miracle windows in the choir ambulatory, has long been noted. Both are of the form defined as a 'tomb-shrine' [Crook 1990]. The earliest reference to the 13th-century Purbeck marble table tomb which clearly associates it with Osmund is found in the witness testimony gathered in 1424, as the second, and ultimately successful, attempt to secure Osmund's canonisation gained momentum. The event described probably took place *c* 1380, when John Bemyster, seized of a fit, placed his head and hands in the holes (*foramina*) of the tomb, and was cured. A further description of the tomb base is found in Leland's account of the Cathedral made in 1542 [Chandler 1993, xxvii], not long after the destruction of the 15th-century shrine in 1539. He described the monument as 'S. Osmundes first tumbe... whil the shrine was a makyng', and it was at that time raised on the stylobate between the Trinity Chapel and St Stephen's chapel [Toulmin Smith 1964, 264]. It remained there until the late 18th century, when it was drawn by John Carter [BL Add MS 29,925, fol 128], and is shown with one side against the wooden screen that separated the two chapels.

The tomb base conforms to a type which allowed the pilgrim to place part of his or her body inside the openings of the base in order to get closer to the body of the saint within, in the manner illustrated in the Canterbury stained-glass images of Becket's original tomb and in the Westminster manuscript of *La Estoire de Saint Aedward le Rei* [Cambridge University Library MS Ee 3.59]. It has also been established that the mid 13th-century tomb-shrine over the original grave of St Swithun at Winchester included a base with apertures [Crook 1990].[3] Recent re-examination of the 12th-century effigial slab with verse inscription (monument 69) has concluded that it commemorates Osmund, was brought from Old Sarum in 1226 and may have rested on top of the Purbeck marble table tomb [Stroud 1993, 113–17]. What is not clear, however, is whether the table tomb was made *c* 1226 to receive the slab on its transfer to the new Cathedral or had been part of the tomb at Old Sarum. While a date of *c* 1226 is acceptable for the form of the Purbeck marble base, comparison with the Becket tomb at Canterbury in use *c* 1170–1220 and the illustrations of the St Edward shrine in the Westminster *Estoire*, illuminated *c* 1250–60, shows that bases of this type were being commissioned over a long period. It cannot be discounted, therefore, that the base had been part of Osmund's tomb at Old Sarum; in 1216 a miracle that took place at Old Sarum describes a boy tied to the tomb of Osmund, which would have been achieved more

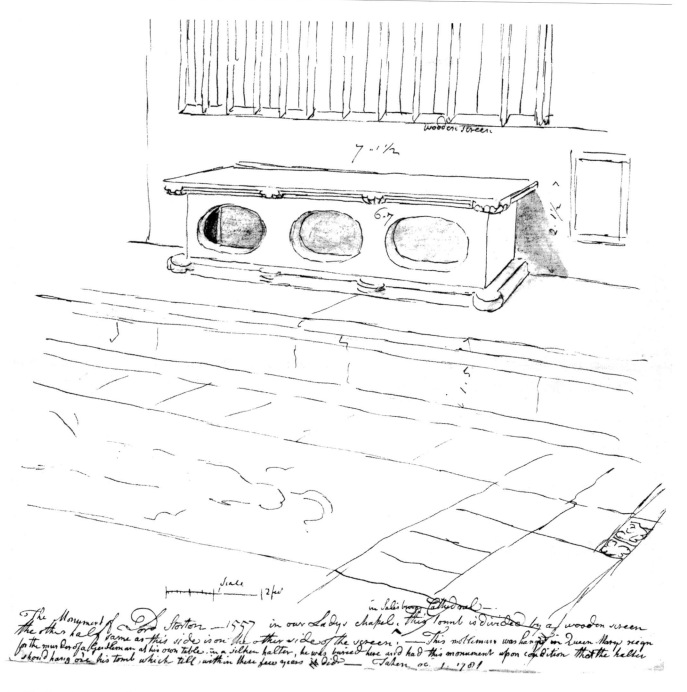

4   *John Carter's drawing of St Osmund's tomb base (monument 90) in 1781, positioned on the stylobate between St Stephen's chapel and the Trinity Chapel [BL Add MS 29,925, fol 128]*

easily if the tomb base had holes in it [Malden 1901, 45; Stroud 1984, 51]. In attributing the verse epitaph on the effigial slab to Osmund and accepting that it was first composed at the time of his death in 1099, Stroud has recognised that the style of the sculpture dates it to the second half of the 12th century, suggesting that the

tomb at Old Sarum underwent some refurbishment at that time, the period in which the earliest recorded miracles were taking place [Malden 1901, 35, 36].

It might also be questioned whether the table tomb had originally been placed where Leland saw it in the early 16th century and Carter saw it in the late 18th century. The description of John Bemyster's experiences describes the tomb as being *'in capella beate Marie'*, where he heard the mass of the Virgin; a position on the south-western stylobate seems to be rather peripheral to deserve such a description. Furthermore, the form of the tomb base, with holes pierced in both of its long sides, suggests that it was designed to be accessible from both sides, and for this purpose a location on the plinth between two chapels, with one side against a screen (see Figs 4, 14 and 15), was hardly ideal. This line of reasoning could be dismissed if it could be established that the base had been made for Old Sarum rather than the new Cathedral. On balance, however, it seems safer to assume that, as William de Waude states, it was the stone slabs alone that were translated to the new Cathedral, suggesting that the Chapter provided a simple Purbeck marble base to mark the burial place of Blessed Osmund in his new Cathedral, originally occupying a position that allowed the circulation of the faithful and access to the *foramina* in the long sides. In 1226 any arrangement would have been regarded as a short-term expedient, intended to be superseded by the construction of an appropriately splendid shrine.

The simplest explanation for the stylobate position for the tomb base recorded by Leland and Carter is that it was moved there from a more central site at the time of the construction of the new shrine in 1457. That the tomb was dismantled can be inferred from the payments made in 1457 for a new coffin of 'tymbre' [Malden 1901, 217]. It was perhaps at this time that the effigial slab became detached from the base, for Leland saw it, together with the slab here identified as that of Bishop Roger, in the south aisle of the nave. It is strange, however, that the slab and its base were not reassembled together; at Canterbury, Winchester and York, for example, the earlier tombs of the translated saints continued to be venerated by pilgrims.

Over two hundred years separated Osmund's first burial in the new Cathedral in 1226 and his canonisation and translation to a new shrine in 1457. While the documentary evidence for the veneration of St Osmund relates only to the Lady Chapel, there is some circumstantial evidence to suggest that the space behind the high altar may also have served as a focus for commemoration. The evidence for this is discussed more fully below (p 13). New arrangements for Osmund's commemoration, perhaps made in the 1240s as the presbytery and choir, unavailable in 1226, neared completion, offer an alternative point at which effigial slab and tomb base could have been separated. The arrangements of 1226 had, after all, been made in the confident expectation of Osmund's canonisation and were not necessarily convenient as a long-term expedient.

The 13th-century decoration of the Trinity Chapel

The 19th-century repainting of the Trinity Chapel and retrochoir vaults, instigated by Scott, offers a fairly accurate impression of the original 13th-century decoration, although Scott was not entirely happy with the results, having failed to supervise the work owing to ill health [Stamp 1995, 479–80]. In addition to the articulation of ribs and mouldings, triangular 'wedges' of foliage ornament radiate from intersections of the ribs. This treatment once extended into the choir aisles and western transepts, although only in the Chapter House vestibule does this type of decoration survive in anything like its original condition (see Fig 128). Although the general effect was thus far richer than that sought by the 18th-century 'improvers', who covered the entire interior with a buff wash, it was one in which the play of light and dark suggested by the architecture itself, where light masonry contrasts with the darker Purbeck marble accents, is echoed by the polychrome effect.

It was in the Trinity Chapel and retrochoir, with their restrained painted decoration, that stained glass was used to great effect. For much of the Middle Ages the most substantial areas of bright colour in the Trinity Chapel would have been supplied by its windows. While the inventories reveal the wealth of textiles, plate and ornaments that ornamented the altars of the medieval Cathedral, many of these items would have been on display at only certain times of day or on special feast days. The permanent and most impressive decoration of the Trinity Chapel would thus have been its stained glass. This is the only part of the Cathedral other than the Chapter House for which there is any substantial evidence for figurative glazing, although destruction of so much glass in the post-Reformation period makes any reconstruction of the glazing of the eastern arm of the church rather speculative (see pp 80–6). Visitors to Salisbury in the 17th and 18th centuries commented upon the historiated glass in the eastern arm. The Jesse Tree fragments now in the south aisle of the nave would fit both physically and iconographically into the east window of the Trinity Chapel, which was *de facto* a Lady Chapel, although by the end of the 18th century the glass had been moved first into the north transept and then into the nave [Carter 1845, I, pl LXXIX; Winston 1865, 108]. This glass, even in its damaged state, gives some impression of the rich effect once conveyed by the windows. Other figurative glass in the Cathedral together with fragments removed to the parish church of Grately in Hampshire in the 18th century, can be attributed to windows above the altars in the retrochoir and eastern chapels (see Fig 1).

Further enrichment was provided by pavements of

5 *The 19th-century painted decoration of the Trinity Chapel vault, by Clayton and Bell, in imitation of the medieval original [BB93/16206]*

two-colour tiles arranged in geometric patterns. Vestiges of original medieval flooring survived into the 18th and 19th centuries; Francis Price noticed pavements of 'inlaid brick' in 'many of the chapels' [Price 1753, 65], and in 1781 John Carter drew a small section of surviving pavement in the Trinity Chapel [BL Add MS 29,925, fol 129]. This has since disappeared, a victim of Wyatt's 'improvements'. The decorative effect of these long-lost pavements can best be appreciated from the surviving pavement in the Muniment Room or from the closely related, albeit slightly earlier, Clarendon Palace pavement now in the British Museum.

The Trinity Chapel was also a place of burial, although some of the earliest memorials were of a simple nature; that of Bishop Nicholas Longespee (d 1297) in the middle of the chapel before the *Salve* altar, for example, was in the form of a ledger slab with brass and inscription. According to Leland, Bishop Robert de Wickhampton and Bishop Henry de Braunstone (d 1284) lay on either side of him [Toulmin Smith 1964, 264]. William Longespee, earl of Salisbury (d 1226), was the first completely new burial in the Cathedral and was commemorated in a more conspicuous manner. His wooden tomb chest surmounted by his Tournai marble effigy was originally located on the plinth in the north-west corner of the Trinity Chapel, in a position appropriate to one who had laid one of the foundation stones. Recent conservation of William Longespee's effigy and tomb chest has revealed the extent of the rich polychrome that once adorned it.[4] Bishop Richard Poore, so instrumental in promoting the move from Old to New Sarum, was not buried in the Cathedral church owing so much to his vigorous organisation, although an inscription in the Trinity Chapel, recorded by Leland, acknowl-

6   Monument of William Longespee (d 1226), south-nave aisle (monument 96). Moved from the north side of the Trinity Chapel in the 18th century [BB74/4671]

edged his achievements [Toulmin Smith 1964, 262–3].

Later burials in the Trinity Chapel were concentrated in the area before the *Salve* altar (see Figs 14 and 15), although the monument to John Montacute was positioned on the northern plinth with that of William Longespee. The monuments of both Longespee and Montacute were moved westwards in the 15th century to accommodate the entrance to the new Hungerford chantry chapel, inserted in what had been the original northern exterior wall of the Trinity Chapel. They were subsequently moved to the nave in the 18th century.

The presbytery and choir

In 1228 the translation of Bishop Poore to Durham seems to have removed from the Salisbury scene the one person most determined to promote Osmund as a saint. The initial canonisation initiative foundered, mainly from lack of interest and determination among the Chapter. The documentation assembled in support of the process was apparently never forwarded to Rome [Malden 1901].

New priorities emerged and attention shifted to the task of completing and enriching the presbytery and choir, the heart of the community's devotional life. In 1246 the St Albans chronicler Matthew Paris attributed the furnishing of the choir, the provision of stained glass and the choir stalls and the covering of the roof of the eastern arm with lead to Poore's successor, Bishop de Bingham (1229–46) [Madden 1869, 260], and it is probably de Bingham who was buried in the position reserved for a founder on the north side of the high altar (monument 10). Matthew's testimony is supported by recent reconsideration of the chronology of the building [Blum 1991; Simpson 1996, 10–20]. The establishment of a date of 1236 for the construction of the choir stalls is of particular importance [*Cal Close* 1234–7, 279], not only confirming that Salisbury preserves the earliest surviving choir furniture in England, but also establishing a date for the pulpitum against which they abut. Furthermore, this provides a context for the provision of ornaments and vestments for the Cathedral in the early

7   *General view of the presbytery, looking east [BB71/3252]*

8   Painted decoration of the presbytery and choir vault, executed in 1872 by Clayton and Bell, in an attempt to re-create the medieval scheme of c 1230–40 [BB93/22091]

1240s; in March 1244 King Henry III paid for the making of a pyx (*cuppam*) for the reservation of the host at the high altar, a commission supervised by Elias de Dereham [*Cal Lib*, 1240–5, 222], and in February 1245 Henry ordered that a silk cope be purchased for the Cathedral, or, if one could not be found, a suitably ornamented one be made [*Cal Lib*, 1240–5, 291]. As the choir stalls and pulpitum projected into the main transept space and the former abutted the pulpitum, it can probably be assumed that the eastern arm and main transepts are of the same date. A tree-ring date of 1250 has been established for the floor of the lantern over the crossing, confirming the documentary evidence [Simpson 1996].

The original position of the high altar within the presbytery remains uncertain. Its present location, at the extreme east, is unlikely to be original. The enrichment of the capitals at the crossing of the chancel and the eastern transepts, and the positioning of the painted Christ in Majesty immediately above, on the vault of the crossing bay, prompted the suggestion that this bay once housed the high altar [Rich Jones 1878; 1883, xxxii–xxxiii], although this position is problematic for a number of practical reasons. First, this was the point at which Scott uncovered (and then reinstated) the original entrance to the choir from the aisle. A high altar here would have impeded entrance to the choir, would have allowed very little space in front for liturgical observance and would have left an enormous space behind it. On the northeastern pier of the eastern crossing bay is a windlass handle which marks the position of the Lenten Veil, lowered to obscure the altar and presbytery during Lent. The high altar must have been to the east of this. There is also evidence of steps, an insertion of perhaps *c* 1300, which cut across the pier bases at this point and suggest the introduction of chancel steps and perhaps some rearrangement of the presbytery at this time.[5] It seems likely, therefore, that the high altar originally stood at least one bay to the east of the eastern crossing and that the enrichment of the capitals at this point was intended to mark the entrance to the presbytery as a whole. The position of the high altar in the early 16th century can be demonstrated to have been to the east of the eastern crossing, for the Audley chantry, founded in 1520, was inserted in the central northern bay, with an internal altar dedicated to the assumption of the Virgin, a dedication it shared with the high altar, and an Easter sepulchre incorporated into its southern elevation. In the late Middle Ages extra windows were inserted in the south triforium, opposite the Audley chantry chapel, presumably to shed more light on the high altar. They were removed by James Wyatt *c* 1790. Leland provides further corroboration, describing the high altar as being level with the weathered Mottram inscription (see p 188)

(see p 188)

on the exterior of the south-west buttress of the ambulatory [Toulmin Smith 1964, 265].

The siting of the high altar at the eastern end of the central bay of the presbytery would still have left a very considerable space behind it. The secular nature of the 13th-century roundels painted on the vault above, which depict the Labours of the Months, prompted Rich Jones to suggest that this area was reserved for the use of the laity [Rich Jones 1878]. This is an implausible suggestion, however, as this is the area normally reserved for an important tomb or for the shrine of a saint. At Canterbury, Westminster Abbey, St Albans, Winchester and York, for example, the principal shrine was behind the high altar.[6] Nor would the decoration of the Salisbury presbytery vault have looked inappropriate for a sacred space to the medieval eye. At Canterbury, for example, the pavement of the Trinity Chapel in the vicinity of the original location of Becket's shrine is decorated with roundels depicting Labours of the Months and signs of the Zodiac – a subject often paired with the Labours of the Months in the decoration of a manuscript calendar [Toke 1930].

It has been suggested that the tomb of Osmund was located beneath the central arch of the gable wall of the presbytery, 'the geometrical centre from which the whole construction eastward was generated' [Kidson 1993, 75, Fig 1]. This was the location later occupied by the tomb of Bishop Blythe, in a monument with a north–south orientation, an unlikely orientation for a saint's burial, although in the 1960s an east–west tomb cavity was discovered nearly underneath the original site of the Blythe tomb.[7] The Blythe tomb had originated as a small chantry chapel founded by Bishop Beauchamp and was once surmounted by a wooden superstructure, described by Leland and Price. It was Beauchamp who was the force behind the final and successful stages of the second attempt to secure Osmund's canonisation. The wooden loft surmounting the chapel could have served as a watching loft for the space behind the high altar, a position traditionally associated with the burial of saints and the veneration of relics and a location with ample space for the accommodation of a tomb-shrine [Tracy 1992, 104–5]. Beauchamp was eventually buried in a chantry chapel to the south east of the Trinity Chapel and it was Bishop Blythe who was buried in the chapel at the east end of the presbytery. Beauchamp's new chantry, entered from the Trinity Chapel, was thus closer to the shrine of the saint whose canonisation he had done so much to secure, and his change of plan may be indicative of the eastwards shift in the veneration of St Osmund.

Further circumstantial evidence for the presbytery as a focus for the veneration of Osmund is found in a 15th-century addition to the instructions for the washing

9   Jacob Schnebbelie's 1789 drawing of the medieval decoration of the presbytery vault before its obliteration [Bodl MS Gough Maps, vol 32, fol 56ʳ]

of the altars on Maundy Thursday, which places the altar of St Osmund immediately after the washing of the altar of the assumption of the Virgin Mary, the high altar [Wordsworth 1901, 74]. As the text is organised in the order to be followed by the procession, with the visit to the altar of Osmund sandwiched between the washing of the high altar and an instruction for the procession to exit on the north side and go next to the altars of St Martin and St Catherine (both in the north-east transept), it is difficult to see how Osmund's altar was anywhere but in the presbytery.

Unfortunately no light can be shed on the problem of the original location of the high altar by the position of the sedilia (the group of three seats for the use of the clergy officiating at mass) or the piscina (for the ablution of sacred vessels during and after mass), as nothing now survives of either. Francis Price describes the choir enclosure in the vicinity of the altar (which by the 18th century stood in the middle of the easternmost bay of the presbytery) as being adorned on its interior face with 'niches, marble pillars and tender ornaments on top' [Price 1753, 65]. As the easternmost bays on the north side were filled by the Audley chantry and the Bingham monument, it is possible that in Price's few lines we have our only glimpse of the sedilia. The southern side of the 13th-century presbytery enclosure was destroyed by the insertion of the Radnor family pew in 1779 and the removal of the rest by Wyatt as part of his eastward extension of the choir.

The decoration of the presbytery and choir

The interior of the Cathedral was originally painted and, in some places, gilded. The rendering and painting of masonry were a common feature of most churches and Salisbury was no exception. The vault webs and the walls throughout the church were decorated with red lines in imitation of ashlar, but the richest effects were achieved in the eastern arm, where the vault ribs and mouldings of the triforium arcade and clerestory windows were also picked out in red, green and black.

The richest painted decoration was reserved for the interior of the choir, presbytery and eastern transepts, with its rich figurative scheme on the vaults and its sumptuous foliage decoration in the spandrels of the main arcade and on the eastern wall, marking out the choir as the heart of the Cathedral's devotional life (see pp 161–6). Twenty-four figure medallions, depicting Christ in Majesty, the Evangelists, Prophets, Patriarchs, Apostles, and Sibyls, decorated the choir vaults, with the Labours of the Months over the presbytery and an angelic host in each of the eastern transepts. To what extent this richness would have been visible to anyone outside the choir is debatable, although its splendours were hint-

ed at by the painted and gilded pulpitum which effectively shielded the choir from view from the nave. The figural scheme recreated by the firm of Clayton and Bell in the 1870s was, in fact, only partially accurate [Horlbeck 1960].

It is unlikely that the clerestory windows of the choir or presbytery were glazed with coloured historiated glass; in 1849 Winston saw unpainted grisaille still *in situ* in clerestory windows [Winston 1865, 121] and it is likely that the triforium windows were glazed in the same way.[8] Unpainted grisaille glass would have allowed the vault decoration, of considerable iconographic importance, to be properly illuminated.

There is no evidence for the original appearance of the windows of the choir aisles. Until the 1950s, painted grisaille remained in window nV, and, despite Wyatt's activities in the late 18th century, a surprising quantity of grisaille has survived, the largest amount now assembled in the south-east transept. Although figurative medallions could have been combined with plainer grisaille, it is more likely that grisaille alone was used in a purely ornamental manner, as seems to have been the case at Lincoln [Morgan 1983, 39]. There is no evidence to suggest that the surviving grisaille panels at Salisbury ever accommodated figure panels, and it is quite possible

10 *Drawing of 13th-century grisaille glass by Octavius Hudson (1843) [V&A, Dept of Prints and Drawings, B3a]*

that, outside the Trinity Chapel and the windows above the altars in the retrochoir and transept chapels, grisaille used on its own played a major role in the Salisbury glazing, as in the slightly later Five Sisters window in the north transept of York Minster. In this respect the stained glass would have echoed the restrained chromatic effect established by the architect.

This is further evidence of the careful thought that went into the planning of the decorative scheme of the eastern arm as a whole; in the choir and presbytery, lit by relatively small clerestory windows (views of the choir-aisle windows should have been restricted by the choir enclosure), the chief decorative medium was paint. In the Trinity Chapel and retrochoir chapels, each with a large window, and with altars positioned below a number of them, stained glass was the more prominent medium and painted decoration played a subsidiary role. A balance, both aesthetic and iconographic, was achieved.

In considering the original arrangement of the choir, it is easy to overlook the 13th-century choir stalls, which are of a simple and unassertive character, somewhat obscured by the 19th-century additions to the choir

furniture. They survive *in situ* and virtually intact. Omitted in the earliest literature on the subject, they have now been identified as the earliest complete set to survive in England [Tracy 1987, 5]. The choir of the cathedral church at Old Sarum is thought to have been furnished only with benches [Hope 1917b, 115–16]. The new Cathedral was provided in 1236 with substantial stalls and desks, provision attributed by Matthew Paris to the patronage of Bishop de Bingham (1229–46) [Madden 1869, 260]. The choir furniture shares many of the motifs of the surrounding architecture. The seats of the dignitaries and the stall ends have ornamentation including human heads (eg the elbow of the precentor's seat), although the bulk of the ornament is foliate, reminiscent of the architectural capitals and roof bosses. Originally the stalls did not have canopies, as they do today, but were backed simply by the stone screens that once enclosed the choir and separated it from the aisles. Price realised that the choir had once been fully enclosed by a wall plain to the aisles and ornamented on its interior face [Price 1753, 65]. Scott found traces of the enclosure behind the stalls during his restoration of

11   Misericord, c 1236. [BB74/2730]

the choir [Scott 1870, 7]. He described it as having been 'a wall of considerable thickness'. These traces have since been obscured. The interior face of these screens may have been draped with hangings as at Westminster Abbey [Binski 1991, 85–100], or painted as in the re-created scheme in the choir at Rochester Cathedral, where the stalls themselves have been far more heavily restored [Tracy 1987, 5]. Either medium might have provided a vehicle for a hagiographical cycle devoted to Osmund, which is otherwise absent from the Cathedral.[9]

The choir and presbytery were, like the Trinity Chapel, originally paved with two-colour tiles arranged in radiating geometric patterns, into which several brasses and burial ledgers had been set by the end of the Middle Ages, notably the large brass to Bishop de Wyville. What remained of the medieval choir pavement was replaced in two paving campaigns in the 17th century (see p 168).

The presbytery, soon to emerge as a favoured location for episcopal burial, contained monuments of an architectural nature, structures that also served as the enclosure of the choir. In the north-east corner is the reconstructed tomb traditionally associated with Bishop Poore, but here attributed to Bishop de Bingham (d 1246).[10] Two bays west, on north and south sides, are the canopies with grilles of Bishops Simon de Gandavo (d 1315) and Roger de Martival (d 1330). Bishop de Wyville's splendid brass (d 1375), now in the north-east transept, was originally in the centre of the presbytery pavement. This concentration of early episcopal burials in the three eastern bays of the presbytery is further compelling evidence for the location of the high altar to the east of the crossing of choir and eastern transepts. Those seeking a more ambitious and assertive monument, such as Bishop de Bridport (d 1262), preferred locations outside the choir. In the 16th century the presbytery enclosure was breached on the north side by the construction of the chantry of Bishop Audley (d 1524) which completely fills the second bay from the east, but continued the tradition for functionality established in the 13th century, providing the high altar with an Easter sepulchre as part of the chapel's south elevation.

Paint was an integral part of the decoration of most medieval monuments, a decoration the impact of which is now almost impossible to envisage. Carter did not record any paint on the de Bingham monument, already in a poor state when he examined it, and no pigment survives on the de Gandavo and de Martival monuments; the de Bridport tomb in the south-choir aisle was almost certainly painted, although only minute traces of paint now survive. The later medieval monuments were certainly richly coloured. Traces of considerable quantities of paint and gilding can still be seen on Bishop Medford's tomb, also in the south-choir aisle (see Plate 2) and on the Audley chantry, although only the pigment on the interior of the chantry is medieval. That on the northern exterior elevation is modern.

The medieval treasury

The permanent decoration of the Cathedral interior was enriched further by movable and more ephemeral works, of which the altar furnishings were the most costly. An impression of their splendour is conveyed in the surviving treasury inventories. Osmund had been a generous benefactor to his cathedral [Malden 1901, 53; Wordsworth 1901, 183]. His successors had augmented the treasury considerably, and its contents on the eve of the translation of the community to the new Cathedral can be glimpsed in the records made by Treasurer Abraham de Winton (1214–22) [Rich Jones 1884, 127–41; Wordsworth 1901, 169–82]. Thus, on 28 September 1225, when the first three altars at the east end of the new Cathedral (the *Salve* or Trinity altar, and those of St Peter and the Apostles and St Stephen and Martyrs) were dedicated by Bishop Poore, the Cathedral treasury already possessed a quantity of liturgical vessels, ornaments and vestments. The lists include four gold cruets, two crystal ones, a silver crown, three silver chains and a silver dove, to be hung before the high altar at the eucharist, jewelled crosses containing relics, a processional cross, nine enamelled candlesticks, several feretories and a number of vestments. One chasuble was said to have been Osmund's, and three copes and a jewel-encrusted chasuble had been given by Bishop Roger. Altar cloths given by King Richard and Queen Eleanor are also described, together with an eagle desk and a number of curtains, hangings and silk embroideries. To this number were added two palls (probably meaning altar cloths) given by King Henry III and two given by Bishop Poore on his enthronement (c 1217), together with further silver vessels, one for the eucharist, given by Bishop Herbert Poore (d 1216) and two silver cruets given by Dean Adam (d 1220).

The Cathedral treasury was enriched further at the time of the translation of the community to its new church [Rich Jones 1884, cxx–cxxii]. On the day of the dedication of the three altars in the new Cathedral, Bishop Poore offered for service at the altar of the Trinity Chapel two silver candlesticks and two silver ewers bequeathed by Gundreda de Warren and gave 10 marks per annum out of his own purse for the maintenance of lights around the altar. Four days after the community's ceremonial entry into the church, on 2 October 1225, King Henry III, attended by Hubert de Burgh, offered a piece of costly silk and 10 marks in

12   *Monument of Bishop Roger de Martival (d 1330). North-choir aisle (monument 13) [BB71/3285]*

13 Silver-gilt chalice recovered in the 18th century from the tomb of Bishop Nicholas Longespee (d 1297) [BB73/5789]

silver, while the justiciar promised to present a jewelled Gospel book. At Christmas 1225 the king revisited the Cathedral, offering a gold ring decorated with a ruby and a gold cup. The ring was to be used to augment the decoration of Hubert de Burgh's Gospel book, presented at the altar of the Trinity Chapel on the same day. In the 1240s the completion of the choir prompted further royal generosity, for Henry was often at nearby Clarendon, the scene of a great deal of building and decorating work, and no doubt followed the progress of the Cathedral's construction with great interest. A pyx was ordered in 1244 and in 1246 a large piece of purple samite was offered at the high altar [*Cal Lib*, 1245–51, 61]. The following year 100*s* were spent on fabric for copes [*Cal Lib*, 1245–51, 135], and in 1249 copes of red samite decorated with a gilded clasp and silver bells were ordered [*Cal Close* 1247–51, 143, 166, 201]. The treasury already possessed furnishings for an altar dedicated to St Thomas Becket, and in 1246, when Edmund Rich, Archbishop of Canterbury and former canon and treasurer of Salisbury, was canonised, an altar in the adjoining chapel in the north transept could be allocated to him.[11] By 1266 the Cathedral was complete and in 1267 Treasurer Robert de Knareville made provision in his will for the purchase of fourteen gold cruets, so that each altar would have a pair.

An inventory of 1536 made by Treasurer Thomas Robertson [Wordsworth 1901, 160–8] reveals that the original contents of the treasury had been considerably augmented in the intervening centuries. Images of the Virgin given by Treasurer Stratford (*c* 1336) and Chancellor Norton (1362–1401), and a chalice and paten given by Dean Gilbert Kymer (1449–63), are evidence

of the continued prosperity and generosity of the Cathedral's clergy, although numerous vestments and pieces of plate are attributed to the generosity of lay people such as Lady Hungerford, who in the 1470s made a gift of four pairs of censers. Of these sumptuous gifts, nothing remains. Individual chantries were also generously endowed; an inventory for the Hungerford chantry made in 1472 describes an enormous collection of textiles [Jackson 1869, 334–9]. Of these movable treasures a single medieval silver-gilt chalice and paten and two episcopal rings, all recovered from burials disturbed in the 18th century, comprise the full complement (see pp 68–69). The only medieval vestment surviving in the Cathedral treasury is of uncertain provenance (see pp 172–173).

The impact of the furnishings and decoration was no doubt heightened by the fact that they were viewed by the faithful in a series of relatively enclosed spaces, illuminated by flickering candles ensuring that even semiprecious materials looked exotic. Each chapel in the eastern arm was separated from the adjoining one by a screen (see Figs 14 and 15). Thus, the medieval cathedral interior was made up of a series of enclosures, each one more or less self-sufficient in a liturgical sense; the chapels are well served with aumbries and piscinae. The altar of each chapel may have been furnished with some sort of altarpiece, although there is scant evidence for this. No complete medieval reredos of wood or stone has survived, although traces of a 13th-century painted one survive on the eastern wall of the chapel of St Martin and a defaced sculpted example depicting the Assumption of the Virgin remains in the Audley chapel. In addition, suitable textile furnishings and perhaps a stained-glass window depicting the saint to whom the

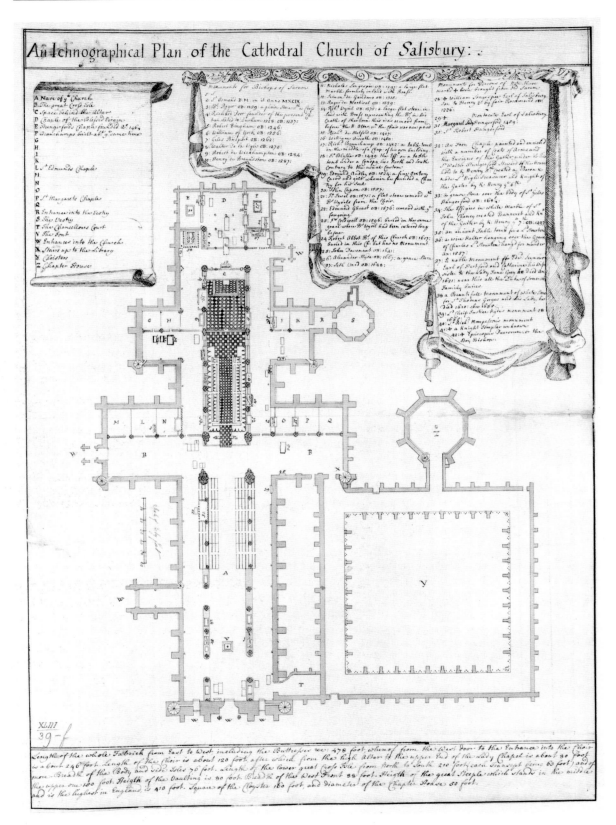

14   Plan of Salisbury Cathedral before 1745 [BL Maps, King's Top Coll XLIII, fol 39]

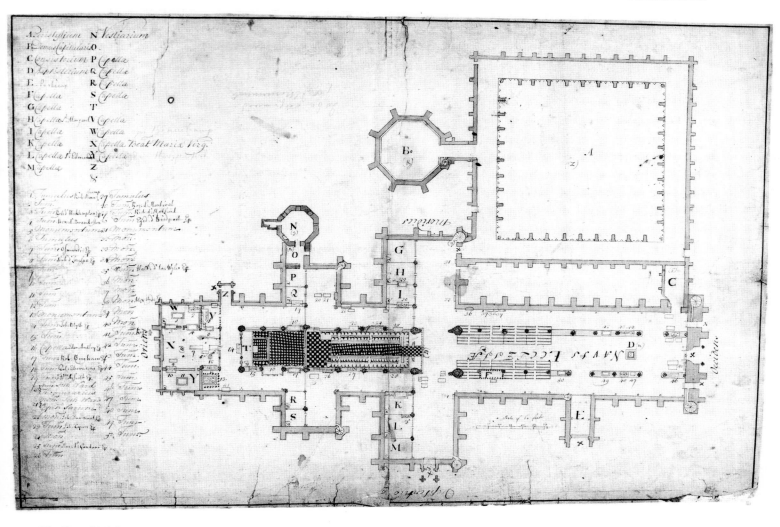

15   Plan of Salisbury Cathedral c 1789 [Bodl MS Gough Maps, vol 32, fol 63ᵛ]

altar below was dedicated may have adorned each chapel. The ornaments provided by the Dean and Chapter and great lay benefactors were augmented by the *ad hoc* offerings made by the faithful. Some impression of these is provided by Bishop Shaxton's 1538 injunctions, forbidding night watches and the 'decking of images with gold, silver, cloths, lights or herbs'. Offerings included 'candles, oats, cake-bread, cheese, wool' [Frere 1910*b*, 59]. East of the choir stalls, monuments sufficiently high and solid to serve as screens obscured the choir from view from the aisles and retrochoir, until Wyatt's removal of the altar screen and the Bingham monument and enclosure on the south side. The enclosing screens in the retrochoir and transepts, creating these decorative 'capsules', were all removed by Wyatt, although they had survived into the 18th century. They are shown on the pre-Wyatt plans of

the Cathedral (Figs 14 and 15) and one can be seen in John Carter's 1781 drawing of the 13th-century feretory (monument 90) [BL Add MS 29,925, fol 128], then positioned on the plinth between the Trinity Chapel and St Stephen's chapel. The open vistas of the retrochoir are an 18th-century invention, perpetuated in the 20th by the removal of Scott's reredos and choir screen.

The canonisation of Osmund and the construction of the 15th-century shrine

In the 15th century the Chapter renewed its efforts to secure the canonisation of Osmund. In 1424 the testimony of witnesses was gathered once more, augmenting the evidence assembled in 1228, but, interestingly, revealing that direct contact with the tomb of Blessed Osmund had become less important as part of the miraculous intercession of the putative saint. After more than two decades of concerted effort and the expenditure of £731 13s [Malden 1901, xxxii], Salisbury was at last successful in getting Osmund recognised as a saint. The pope confirmed this in a letter written on 13 December 1456, which arrived in Salisbury on 15 January 1457; 1 January 1457 was fixed as the day of canonisation [Malden 1901, 167]. A letter of 3 January 1457 requested that the body of the saint be moved to a shrine in a more prominent place and specified how the offerings at the shrine were to be used [Malden 1901, 215–17]. That this entailed the removal of the body from the original tomb can be inferred from the payments for a new coffin of 'tymbre' [Malden 1901, 217]. Work on the shrine was still under way when the prebend of Horton was sequestrated for its making on 11 April 1458 [Rich Jones 1881, 394]. Little is known of the appearance of the new shrine, although comparison with other 15th-century saints' shrines offers a useful idea of what a 15th-century pilgrim would expect to see. Parts of the late-15th-century shrine of St William of York survive, sufficient to allow a reconstruction to be suggested [Wilson 1977, 18]. A substantial architectural base of polished limestone with three canopied niches on either side was surmounted by a silver-gilt feretory, covered by a protective wooden canopy, which could be raised to reveal the feretrum at appropriate times. A small altar stood at its western face, with two smaller altars to north and south. Images of this shrine in the St William window in York Minster (window nVII) illustrate the custom among pilgrims of leaving behind some tangible reference to the affliction for which a cure was sought in the form of models of diseased or disabled limbs, made of wax, wood or some more precious material. That Osmund's shrine had some sort of architectural base must be supposed, although no fragments of it survived the Reformation. A fragmentary description of the jewelled feretory survives in the Cathedral archives [Malden 1901, 217–19]; that it included some sort of sculptural image of the saint can be concluded from the memorandum of expenses 'for Saynt Osmundis hede with garnyshyng' and 'for xx grete stonys for the mytre and fote' [Malden 1901, 217]. This is probably the 83 oz (2.35 kg) image of St Osmund mentioned in Treasurer Robertson's inventory of 1536 [Wordsworth 1901, 160]. The translation to the shrine took place in July 1457 [Wordsworth 1901, 219], and royal gifts were generous, including 'unam tabulam auream'. The time taken to dismantle the shrine in 1539 suggests that care was taken to salvage the valuable materials [Fletcher 1938].

Not only is the form and appearance of the shrine uncertain; it is by no means clear where it was located, for the 15th-century references to Osmund's translation do not shed any light on the geography of the event.

Most writers have assumed that it was located in the Trinity Chapel [eg Stroud 1984; Cocke 1993, 13]. Certainly by the beginning of the 17th century the stone with the date of Osmund's death (monument 4) had been placed in the middle of the Trinity Chapel, marking what was erroneously believed to be the location of the saint's bodily remains [Bodl MS Gough Eccl Top 55, fol 272]. It has been suggested [Stroud 1984] that this represented a Marian attempt to recreate the shrine. This is borne out by the fact that when Symonds saw this stone in 1644 he concluded that the date had been cut only recently [Long 1859, 130]. The 18th-century plans of the Cathedral (Figs 14 and 15) indicate the shrine in this position. We do not, therefore, have any firm indication of the position of the shrine earlier than 1601. Comparisons with the locations of 15th-century saints' shrines elsewhere offer contradictory information; in Winchester the shrine of Swithun was moved from behind the high altar to a more accessible location in the retrochoir in 1476, while at York the shrine was remodelled c 1472 and remained in the relative seclusion of the area behind the high altar. The significance of the reference to the altar of St Osmund in the 15th-century processional mentioned above remains problematic, especially as the area behind the high altar would have been an equally appropriate location. Perhaps it is the renewed interest in the Trinity Chapel as a place of burial in the 15th century that finally clinches the argument in favour of the chapel as the location of the 15th-century shrine. Bishop Beauchamp, in whose episcopacy the canonisation had finally been achieved, had originally intended to be buried within a stone monument with a wooden superstructure that was aligned north–south against the eastern face of the presbytery screen [Toulmin Smith 1964, 264]. He changed his mind some time after 1457, however, constructing instead a separate chantry chapel added to the south-east corner of the Cathedral, matching one constructed on the north-east side by the widow of Robert, Lord Hungerford. These two structures were of considerable size and magnificence and attest to the attraction of a saint's shrine, an amenity denied Salisbury for so long.

The Hungerford and Beauchamp chantry chapels

The 15th-century chantry chapels added to the eastern ends of the choir aisles were substantial additions to the medieval fabric of the Cathedral. Both were of three bays, with large windows, although the Beauchamp chapel, with its ogival eastern gable, was higher than the Hungerford chapel. Both were entered by doors pierced in the side, formerly exterior, walls of the Trinity Chapel, which resulted in some reorganisation of monuments already occupying these areas. Both entailed the partial

16 Interior of the Hungerford chantry chapel, looking east, recorded by Jacob Schnebbelie in 1789 and published in 1796 in vol II of Richard Gough's Sepulchral Monuments in Great Britain *[BB69/6613]*

blocking of the 13th-century east windows of the chapels of St Peter and St Stephen.

Robert Hungerford (d 1459) asked to be buried at the altar of St Osmund, but his wife Margaret (Botreaux), who survived him, had more ambitious plans, and the chantry chapel appears to have been constructed at her behest, at a cost of £497. Her tomb chest, originally with surmounting brass, stood in the centre of the chapel, with Robert's chest and alabaster effigy located in a canopied niche in the south wall. The fragment of a dedication inscription supported by an angel was recorded by Symonds, although the date of dedication was incomplete – 14 October 'A.D. M.CCCCLX…' [Long 1859, 131]. The contemporary inventory of the chantry's treasury, valued at £250, made in 1472, describes the chapel as 'late founded and stablisshed by the saide Lady', who joined her husband in the chapel in 1477. It was richly

furnished with plate, textiles and books through the generosity of Lady Hungerford [Jackson 1869] and was served by two priests with a house in the Close. The chapel was remarkable for the richness of its painted mural decoration, including heraldry of both Hungerford and Botreaux families and their connections, together with figurative paintings of St Christopher, the Virgin and Child, and Death and the Gallant with admonitory inscriptions. They were described by Symonds in the 17th century [Long 1859, 131] and drawn by Schnebbelie in the late 18th century, although by that time the chapel had fallen into a very poor state of repair and demolition had already begun.

The chantry built on the south side by Bishop Beauchamp was founded at his death in 1481, and in his will Richard Beauchamp left directions to be buried in the centre of it. Four chaplains were provided supported

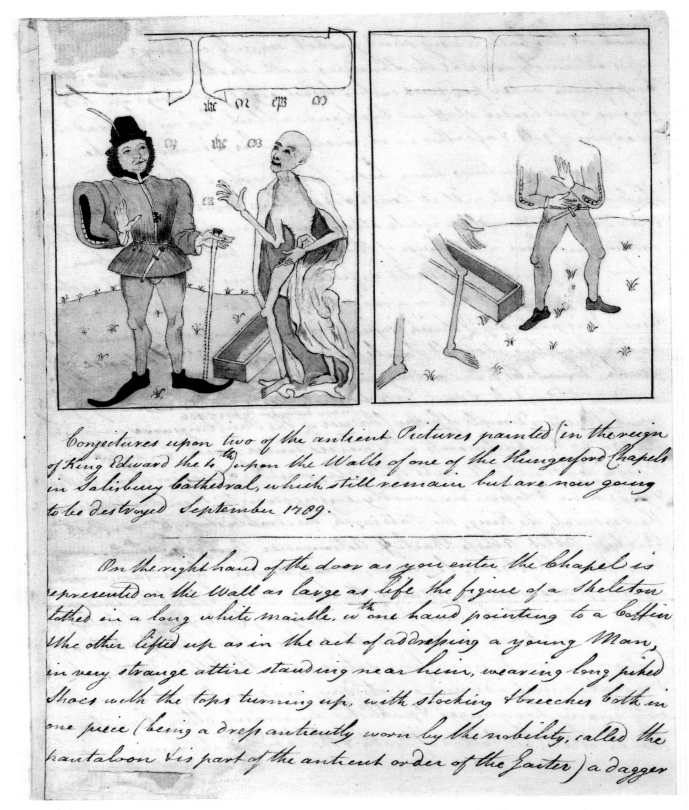

Conjectures upon two of the antient Pictures painted (in the reign of King Edward the 4th) upon the Walls of one of the Hungerford Chapels in Salisbury Cathedral, which still remain but are now going to be destroyed September 1789.

_____

On the right hand of the door as you enter the Chapel is represented on the Wall as large as life the figure of a Skeleton bathed in a long white mantle, w.th one hand pointing to a Coffin the other lifted up as in the act of addressing a young Man, in very strange attire standing near him, wearing long piked Shoes with the tops turning up, with stocking & breeches both in one piece (being a dress antiently worn by the nobility, called the pantaloon & is part of the antient order of the Garter) a dagger

17   Detail of the wall painting of Death and the Gallant on the south wall of the Hungerford chantry, drawn by Jacob Schnebbelie in 1789. [Bodl MS Gough Maps, vol 32, fol 53v]

by a property valued at £50 per annum, although the number of clergy officiating at the chapel quickly declined. The decoration of the chapel was sculptural rather than painted [*VCH* III, 181], with a great deal of heraldic display which appealed to Symonds [Long 1859, 132–3]. A description of 1635 by Lt Hammond reveals that the coffered ogival vault was of 'curiouslie carv'd Irish wood' [Legg 1936, 62]. Symonds was unable to identify Beauchamp's tomb chest in the centre of the chapel, as, like so many other monuments in the cathedral, it had lost its brass. The two tombs in the recesses in the north walls were said by Lt Hammond to be of his two brothers [Legg 1936, 62] and by James Harris to be of the bishop's parents [Harris 1825, 112]. Harris attributed a brass in the pavement to Richard Beauchamp's brother, Lord St Amand. In the south-west corner of the chapel was the canopied monument of Sir John Cheney (d 1509), said to have been one of the bishop's executors

[Fletcher 1938, 171]. Sir John was a Knight of the Garter (the Order of which Richard Beauchamp had been Chancellor), sometime chaplain and superintendent of building work at St George's Chapel, Windsor.

By 1505 Bishop Beauchamp's chapel was already in a poor state of repair [*VCH* III, 181]. Both chapels were badly dilapidated by the end of the 18th century and it was argued that they were endangering the stability of the Trinity Chapel against which they had been built. An appeal to the heirs to assist in their repair came to nothing and the chapels were dismantled in 1790. The monuments fared badly. Margaret Botreaux's monument has disappeared and her husband's effigy survives under the south nave arcade without its original chest and canopy (monument 84). Bishop Beauchamp's monument has also been lost, although John Cheney's alabaster effigy has survived (monument 51). Some of the carved stone of the Beauchamp chapel remains in the Cathedral,

18   *Interior of the Beauchamp chantry chapel, looking east [Bodl MS Douce G Subt 25(2), page 1]*

applied to the north and south walls of the Trinity Chapel, while the door that formerly connected the Trinity Chapel with the Beauchamp chapel is now located in the north-east transept, between two sections of the displaced pulpitum (see p 189). Of the plate and furnishings that once adorned the chapels, nothing remains, although Bishop Beauchamp's episcopal ring was retrieved from his coffin. His bodily remains fared less well.

The nave

In the layout of the new Cathedral it was the nave that was to be considerably increased in size in comparison to the old Cathedral at Old Sarum. This is perhaps surprising, as the nave was liturgically of secondary importance, reflected in the fact that throughout the Middle Ages it attracted far fewer patrons of the decorative and figurative arts. The size of the nave can perhaps best be explained as a manifestation of the Chapter's confident expectation of the growth of the new town of Salisbury, developing at the Cathedral's door; it is significant that, despite the great screen-like west front, the principal entrance into the Cathedral for the laity was through the substantial north porch, facing directly into the town. The documentary evidence for the construction of the nave suggests that the momentum was maintained under the new Bishop William of York (1247–56). Credited with 'having taken much pains in finishing of the building of his church', William introduced a new works administration, including Radulphus of York as *custos fabrice* and Master Nicholas of York, called *Il Engingnur*. Leland, quoting from the martyrology, attributed the covering of the whole church with lead to William of York's successor, Bishop Giles de Bridport (1257–62), who presided over the consecration of the Cathedral in 1258 in the presence of Archbishop Boniface and the king and queen [Toulmin Smith 1964, 266, 268].

The physical separation of the liturgically important parts of the church, to the east, and those parts to which the laity might be admitted, to the west, was effected by the pulpitum, which projected slightly westwards of the line of the eastern aisle of the main transept (see Fig 1). This differentiation between the nave and all those parts east of the pulpitum was reinforced in architectural terms; a single-pier type is employed in the nave, while greater variation is found east of the crossing. The plinth level to the east of the crossing is higher, and, as we have seen, the presbytery was further distinguished from the choir by a rise in floor level and by the use of foliage capitals at its entrance. However, these architectural distinctions are of a very understated nature.

The nave, practically half of the building, was, compared to the eastern parts of the church, relatively plainly decorated. Although the 'wedges' of foliage ornament decorating the vault of the Trinity Chapel, retrochoir and choir aisles were continued into the nave and can still be discerned through the 18th-century over-painting, they do not occur in the nave aisles, where simple imitation ashlaring prevailed, large areas of which survive. The nave was also sparsely furnished. In common with all medieval cathedrals, there was no fixed seating in the nave until the 17th century. There were, however, a number of altars. The altar of St Andrew and St George stood on the north side of the nave, with the altar of St Denis on the south side. In the 15th century there was also an altar somewhere in the north aisle dedicated to St Ursula and the Eleven Thousand Virgins [Wordsworth 1901, 187–205]. There is no surviving physical evidence of the arrangements made to accommodate these altars, however. No traces of reredoses painted on the nave piers (like St Albans) or sculpted tabernacles (as at Gloucester) are discernible.

The east end of the nave was dominated by the pulpitum between the eastern crossing piers and the rood, the 'great cross' mentioned in so many Salisbury documents. The pulpitum, in position *c* 1236, the remains of which are now located in the north-east transept, was originally approximately 4 metres deep, projecting slightly westwards of the eastern crossing piers [Hope 1917a, 46–56]. Entrance into the choir was made by way of a double door, flanked on either side by five shallow niches containing statuary of kings, now lost [Hope 1917c]. Each niche had a pointed head, triple Purbeck marble shafts and stiff-leaf capitals. The spandrels contain angels with outstretched wings bearing symbols that echo the iconography on the eastern transept vaults. Above was a shallow parapet panelled in twelve divisions. The pulpitum, on which considerable traces of paint and gilding can still be detected, would have been the most dramatic feature in the nave. Gough's plan shows that the top was reached via stairs on either side of the central doors, and the Gospel and Epistle were read from this gallery. On Christmas Day Christ's genealogy was sung from here and an eagle desk was provided for the reader. The pulpitum was also included in the route of the Sarum processions and is clearly visible, surmounted by Renatus Harris's organ of 1710, in James Biddlecombe's view of the nave of 1754 (Fig 19). Of the rood that was once supported on the beam that probably spanned the western crossing piers with a screen beneath, cut down by Wyatt, no visual record survives.[12]

The nave was also a place of burial for richer laymen, and for priests and the less prominent members of the Cathedral community. The nave pavement must have been disturbed to accommodate these burials relatively

19   The nave, looking east (J Biddlecombe 1754). The 13th-century pulpitum, Renatus Harris's organ of 1710 surmounting it and the font of 1661 have all been removed. [Bodl MS Gough Maps, vol 32, fol 47ʳ]

frequently; in March 1468 John Goldryng, vicar choral, was buried under a marble stone at the east end of the north nave aisle. In January of 1473 Walter Maschall, senior altarist of the chapel of St Thomas, was buried near the small north door and in May of the same year Master William Cook, advocate of the Consistory Court, was buried beneath a marble stone on the west side of the font [Malden 1904, 30, 32]. For the most part these nave burials were commemorated by flat ledger stones alone, although there were exceptions. The notable structure in the nave by the close of the Middle Ages was the chantry chapel of Walter, Lord Hungerford, of 1430 [Shortt 1970, 2–6]. The ledger stones (originally surmounted by brasses) of Walter and his wife Catherine were set into the nave pavement and were once enclosed

by the iron grilles that now form the Radnor pew. They were raised onto their present chest in 1789. A number of burials in the nave, shown on Gough's plan (Fig 15), were obscured, if not disturbed, by Wyatt's repositioning in the nave of monuments from the eastern arm, and recent examination of the displaced monuments has uncovered traces of these earlier burials [Spring 1979].

There is very little evidence for the nature of the nave glazing in the Middle Ages. The medieval glass presently located in the nave windows has been relocated from elsewhere in the Cathedral, although one panel of grisaille in window s33 is of a more developed type than the other grisaille that can be assigned to the choir. It does not, however, belong to the later Chapter House windows, and might therefore represent an original nave grisaille design.

The Chapter House

The chronology of the Chapter House has been the subject of considerable debate. Earlier writers, struck by its close similarities to the Westminster Chapter House, completed by 1253, concluded that its construction had followed closely upon the completion of the church dedicated in 1258 [Webb 1965, 98]. This view has the virtue of practicality. The community at Old Sarum had been served by a Chapter House, and, despite evidence for a temporary structure on the new site as early as 1227, it seems unlikely that the Chapter would have been content to manage without such an important amenity for very long.

A date close to that of Westminster Abbey for the Salisbury Chapter House seemed to be borne out by the 14th-century transcript of a 13th-century document in the Cathedral's *Liber Evidentiarum B* (fol 141[r]), which records a grant of land 'in nostro anno primo' by Bishop 'W' with the consent of the dean, Lord Robert, for the enlargement of the cloister. Assuming this to mean Bishop William of York and Dean Robert de Hertford, the commencement of the campaign to complete the cloisters and construct the chapter house was placed in the year 1248. Dr Blum has pointed out that this reference could equally apply to Bishop Walter de la Wyle and Dean Robert de Wickhampton, placing the commencement of the campaign in 1263 [Blum 1991]. This redating makes sense of the continued provision of timber into the early 1260s, after the consecration of the church in 1258 [*Cal Close*, 1259–61, 337, 407], suggesting that the cloisters were not completed until the 1260s [Tatton-Brown 1995*b*].

Dr Blum's redating of the Chapter House campaign to after 1280 has, however, received less support. Her case rests on the record of a discovery in the 19th century of pennies of the reign of Edward I in those parts of the Chapter House requiring underpinning [Burges 1859]. This has been claimed as objective evidence for the building's date, as the first coinage of Edward I was only minted in December 1279. This case cannot easily be tested, however, as the coins themselves have not survived and the exact location in which they were found was not recorded.[13] In the meantime, tree-ring dating of the Chapter House roof timbers appears to support the interpretation that the documentary reference to the completion of the 'church of Sarum' by March 1266 refers not only to the cathedral but also to the Chapter House and cloisters [summary in *Vernacular Architecture* 1996, 79, 81]. The heraldic evidence contained in the glazing of the Chapter House [Shortt 1958], together with the style of the grisaille glass and the tiled pavement, all support this chronology.

The original 13th-century decorative scheme of the Chapter House survived, albeit damaged, into the 19th century. Some damage as a result of 16th-century reforming zeal might be inferred from the spate of repairs, especially to windows, recorded in the fabric accounts for the 1560s and 1580s [Fabric Accounts]. More serious damage, particularly to the sculpture, can be attributed to the use of the Chapter House for meetings of Parliamentary Commissioners during the Civil War [Blum 1978, 70]. *Ad hoc* repairs (including the removal of medieval glass in the early 19th century) accounted for further damage to the integrity of the medieval decoration. The Chapter House was not, however, included in the 18th-century 'improvements', and in 1855 William Burges was able to study vestiges of all aspects of the medieval decoration [Burges 1859], as a thoroughgoing restoration was undertaken, involving the restoration and repainting of the sculpture, reglazing of the windows and the replacement of the pavement with a somewhat inaccurate replica (see pp 168–169).

The iconography of the English medieval Chapter House has yet to receive extensive scholarly scrutiny. Studies of individual buildings have suggested a diversity of iconographic emphasis from place to place [Wilson 1983] and the most recent study of Westminster Abbey has suggested that there is little evidence for consistent iconographic programmes in English Chapter Houses of the 13th century [Binski 1995, 187]. The unpublished study of the Salisbury Chapter House [Blum 1978] has, however, proposed the existence of an integrated scheme presided over by the (restored) tympanum figure of Christ flanked by the Evangelist symbols, the image of the Book of Revelation (4: 2–8), the Christ of the Apocalyptic Second Coming.

There is reason to believe that the scheme was an eclectic mix of themes, some derived from existing Salisbury programmes and some elements drawn from further afield. The building is entered via a doorway decorated with figures of the triumphant Virtues, trampling figures of the vanquished Vices. In this Salisbury is quite unlike Westminster Abbey, where the entrance is dominated by a Marian theme (the Annunciation). The Virtues, derived from the *Psychomachia*, were a relatively unusual subject at this date. The subject supports the Apocalypse theme proposed by Blum, for the triumphant Virtues were used to decorate commentaries on the Apocalypse of the period, notably the Lambeth Apocalypse (Lambeth Palace, MS 209) [Morgan 1990], but also suggests a link with Westminster and the art of the 1260s. It was the Palace rather than the Abbey church where the subject could be seen, perhaps by 1267, for the Triumphant Virtues decorated the window splays of Henry III's Painted Chamber [Binski 1986, 41–2]. The two schemes are not identical, but serve as a

20   *The interior of the Chapter House before the removal of the Ward and Hughes west window in 1967 [B36/2033]*

21   *The canons' stalls and the sculpted arcade in the Chapter House [BB73/3161]*

reminder that Clarendon Palace, the scene of so much building work throughout Henry III's reign, provided an alternative conduit for Westminster influence at Salisbury.

The stained-glass windows were closer in their visual message to the imagery of the cathedral church. The main tracery opening contained images of kings and bishops standing beneath simple canopies, with the smaller tracery openings filled with medallions showing angels carrying symbolic objects such as a palm, crown, crescent moon, censers and books. The main lights were filled with a cool, silvery foliage grisaille and, in the east window at least, with shields of arms that have prompted comparison with the windows of Westminster Abbey [Lethaby 1925, 238–9]. The angels in medallions are close in design and attributes to the angels painted on the choir vault, which also has an image of the Christ of the Apocalypse vision at its heart. The disposition of the windows can also be compared to the sculptural scheme on the pulpitum, with its figures of kings in niches and angel figures with very similar attributes in the span-

drels. The identity of the bishops and kings in the windows cannot now be established with any certainty, but figures significant in the history and benefaction of the Cathedral and diocese may be assumed. The heraldry below related to Henry III, his family and nobles closely associated with his court. The glazing would thus be a fitting backdrop to the daily reading of the martyrology and obits that took place in the Chapter House.

The high level of transmitted light admitted by the large, grisaille-filled windows provided ample illumination for the appreciation of the richly coloured Old Testament sculptural frieze in the spandrels of the blind arcade below. Depicting sixty scenes from the books of Genesis and Exodus, recounting the history of the world from the Creation to the granting of the Commandments to Moses, the figures, picked out in pale colours, were displayed against alternating blue and red grounds [Burges 1859, 10]. The backs of the prebendal stalls were draped with fictive curtains, thought by Burges to have been 'pink, diapered, edged with yellow, and lined with green' [Burges 1859, 22]. The name of each prebend was displayed above in square frames. Mouldings and capitals were also coloured, so that the eye would have been drawn to the arcade. The vault above was, in comparison, very restrained in its decoration, the vault ribs being accentuated by flanking wedges of foliage ornament [BL Add MS 29,939, fol 80ʳ] so that the building grew lighter as the eye travelled upwards. The decoration of the Chapter House was completed by the provision of a tiled pavement in a radiating design [Norton 1996, 95–7] (see Plate 6). Burial beneath the floor in the Chapter House was therefore no longer an option, making the commemoration of the revered dead in visual and verbal ways all the more important.

22   The Chapter House vault with painted decoration restored under the direction of William Burges c 1855, in imitation of the medieval original [BB89/3027]

From the Reformation to the Restoration

For the fabric of a secular cathedral like Salisbury, the early stages of the Henrician reformation had little immediate effect. The canons were, of course, affected by the prohibition of pluralism and non-residency, but, for the most part, the measures of the late 1530s concentrated on the fate of the monastic institutions, which were dissolved from 1538 onwards, or were devoted to political and constitutional issues, which, despite their far-reaching implications, had a limited impact on the everyday life of the secular cathedrals and their clergy. However, the participation of the entire congregation in religious observance meant that in cathedrals like Salisbury the choir, formerly reserved for the cathedral clergy, now also served the laity. Bishop Shaxton, Salisbury's first reforming bishop, concentrated on measures intended to improve the quality of diocesan clergy and their parochial ministry. Emphasis was placed upon regular residence and the use of English [Frere 1910b, 53] and the provision of an English Bible in each church [Frere 1910b, 59]. The observances of the Reformed Church were to involve the active participation of all members of the congregation, which in practice meant greater use of the choir, formerly reserved for the use of the Cathedral clergy.

The most immediate way in which the Henrician reforms affected Salisbury Cathedral was in the matter of images. In 1538 Thomas Cromwell issued injunctions against religious imagery, ordering the removal of superstitious images without delay. Many of the jewelled images described in Treasurer Robertson's Inventory of 1536 [Wordsworth 1901, 160–8] were probably destroyed as a result. The 83-oz (2.53 kg) image of St Osmund, in silver gilt and covered with stones of various colours, and the 74-oz (2.09 kg) image of the Trinity are unlikely to have survived this first spate of iconoclasm. Relics and shrines were attacked as idolatrous; Bishop Shaxton's 1538 injunctions for the Salisbury diocese ordered that all 'stinking boots, mucky combs, ragged rockets, rotten girdles, pyled purses, great bullocks horns, locks of hair and filthy rags, gobbets of wood … and such pelfrey beyond estimacion' be delivered to the episcopal residence at Ramsbury for examination, and if necessary for confiscation and destruction as fraudulent and idolatrous [Frere 1910b, 59–60]. The Cathedral's medieval faithful had assembled a collection of over 360 relics [Wordsworth 1901, 33–41]. This collection included relics of Christ's Passion, the Virgin Mary, the Disciples, the Martyrs and two of the Holy Innocents. The treasury contained relics of St Catherine enclosed in a silver head brought from Rome in the 13th century and an arm reliquary of St Thomas Becket [Wordsworth 1901, 160]. All were disposed of at this time.

The most serious casualty was, of course, the 15th-century shrine of St Osmund, to which his remains had been translated in July 1457. St Osmund was apparently not of sufficient celebrity to attract immediate attention. Canterbury, Winchester, Chichester and Lichfield all suffered despoliation of their medieval shrines in 1538. Salisbury's turn came early in 1539, when St Osmund's magnificent shrine was stripped of its gold and jewels. In January and February two men were employed for nine days and four men were employed for one day on this task. In May two men were employed for a further fifteen days [Fletcher 1938]. The Dean and Chapter of Salisbury had waited two centuries to secure papal recognition of Osmund's sanctity, and the shrine they built to commemorate this had lasted barely ninety years. By the time Leland visited the Cathedral in 1542 [Chandler 1993, xxvii], the work of destruction had been completed, although the 13th-century Purbeck marble tomb base remained in the retrochoir [Toulmin Smith 1964, 264]. The effigial slab (monument 69), which had probably surmounted it, had been moved into the nave, where its association with the saint was either forgotten, or, more likely, deliberately kept from the inquisitive Leland, who merely described it [Toulmin Smith 1964, 265].

These early attempts at reform certainly met with resistance in the Close [VCH III, 185–6]; in 1537 the bishop's chaplain reported that the pope's name was still to be found in the Cathedral missal, and an image of the Virgin Mary, perhaps one of the two 14th-century images described in the 1536 inventory, survived until 1644, when it fell prey to Parliamentarian looters [Benson and Hatcher 1843, 397].

Apart from attacks on the imagery of Catholicism, the Cathedral continued to worship according to the Use of Sarum; indeed, the use of the Sarum Breviary was compulsory throughout the Canterbury province, and the Latin mass continued to be said, although there was an increasing emphasis on the use of the vernacular for at least part of the service. This was soon to be reinforced by royal decree; in 1541 all cathedrals were ordered to set up an English Bible for public consultation and a lesson was to be read from it at Matins and Evensong on all holy days. Although their altarpieces may have been defaced or destroyed, the chantries survived, and Cromwell's injunctions had, in fact, countenanced the preservation of some images as long as the clergy explained to their flock that they were merely to serve as books of instruction for the unlettered [Lehmberg 1988, 103]. By the end of Henry's reign, however, there were some signs that more thoroughgoing reforms, particularly of the liturgy, were not far off. In 1544 the king ordered that Cranmer's English Litany, the forerunner of the new Prayer Book, was to be used everywhere. As long as Henry lived, however, the traditional services much beloved by the king continued to be the basis of religious observance. The accession in 1547 of Edward VI, educated by a Protestant tutor and advised by Protestant counsellors, was to herald a period of dramatic change, destined to have an enormous impact on the interior of churches.

Within six months of his father's death, the new king had ordered the complete destruction of all shrines, candlesticks, pictures, paintings or other monuments of idolatry. Only the high altar was to be lit with candles – all other lights were prohibited [Aston 1988, 246-7]. The English Litany, to continue in use while a new prayer book was prepared, was not to be said in procession, but while the clergy knelt in the nave, in order to facilitate audibility and comprehension [Lehmberg 1988, 1091]. In a cathedral designed to accommodate the processional requirements of the Use of Sarum, this change alone must have had a considerable impact. The Epistle and the Gospel were to be read in English and all cathedrals were instructed to establish a library containing specified patristic texts and a grammar school, if either was lacking, and to make annual inventories of vestments plate and ornaments [Frere 1910b, 135-9]. The enforcement of these injunctions was to be ensured by a series of visitations by crown nominees.

The dissolution of the chantries, passed by parliament late in 1547 and implemented in the course of 1548, was to be one of the most destructive measures of the new reign. Their abolition undermined the financial and social structure of the Cathedral, as the saying of chantry masses and obits had been an important source of income for the canons and their abolition considerably reduced the need for officiating clergy. Chantry chaplains with no other cathedral duties were now redundant. The abolition also led to the dispersal of vestments, altar vessels, ornaments and furniture supplied by the chantry founders, which, as the Hungerford inventory reveals, could be considerable [Jackson 1869, 334-9], and a new phase of iconoclasm was ushered in. The damage to Bishop Audley's chantry probably dates from this time. In 1548 the plate from the chantries was purchased by Thomas Chaffyne [Wordsworth 1901, 199 n 1]. Financial difficulties prompted the king to order further confiscations of plate. In 1549 the Dean and Chapter were ordered to supply plate to the value of 2,000 marks to the mint at Bristol. The defunct chantries no doubt helped to fulfil this demand.

In 1549 Cranmer's new English Prayer Book, based at least in part on the Use of Sarum, was introduced throughout England, providing the basis for liturgical uniformity for the first time in the history of the English Church. The use of Latin was banned, and on Christmas Day 1549 all service books, graduals, antiphoners, processionals and missals were ordered destroyed. The Cathedral library preserves a medieval gradual and antiphoner, two of the small number of pre-Reformation service books to have escaped this destruction [Frere 1894; 1902]. The wearing of vestments was also affected by the new liturgy; the priest administering Communion was to wear 'a white albe plaine, with a vestment or cope' and, at a service where no celebration followed, the priest was to wear an alb or surplice with a cope. The richly decorated vestments and apparels described in Treasurer Robertson's inventory of 1536 are not itemised in Treasurer Sprint's inventory of 1583, no doubt having been destroyed because of objectionable imagery, cannibalised for repairs to other textiles in the Cathedral, or adapted for other uses. The introduction of the new Prayer Book and the abolition of the chantries drastically reduced the number of observances being held in the Cathedral, together with the numbers of clergy required to observe them, emphasising a trend already in train on the eve of the Reformation.

The 1549 Prayer Book unequivocally rejected the theory of transubstantiation and the concept of the Eucharist as a sacrifice. The full participation of the congregation was assumed, although this presented difficulties where the choir was of insufficient size to admit the entire congregation. The more zealous reformers confronted the problems of how to accommodate everyone in an ecclesiastical interior divided by screens that reduced visibility and audibility; Bishop Hooper of Gloucester, for example, ordered the destruction of all screens and divisions separating clergy and laity. Together with Bishop Ridley of London, he led the movement to abolish stone altars in favour of tables. The Council finally recognised this, and in November 1550 Bishop Salcote received orders to destroy the Salisbury altars, which were to be replaced with plain tables [Wordsworth 1901, 306]. The Prayer Book of 1552, a less ambiguous work than its predecessor, required that Communion, now perceived in terms of an act of commemoration, be administered at a table covered with a plain linen cloth, by a priest wearing a plain white surplice. The Prayer Book did not specify the exact orientation of the table, but, by ordering the celebrant to stand at the north side, assumes that it was positioned table-wise, with its short ends facing east and west, with the communicants assembled around it. Location was to depend upon the convenience of the minister and his congregation, glossing over the difficulties of accommodation in medieval churches still, for the most part, divided by screens [Addleshaw and Etchells 1948, 22-9]. These more radical changes were to be

23   12th-century Tournai marble coffin lid (monument 4), incised with
ANNO MXCIX (1099), the date of St Osmund's death [BB73/7067]

short-lived, however, for Edward died in July 1553, and
a desire to preserve the legitimate succession proved
stronger than allegiance to the Protestant religion, for
Catholic Queen Mary came to the throne.

Salisbury appears to have been little affected by the
worst aspects of the Marian reaction. Mary restored
Peter Vannes to the deanery, while his reforming usurper,
Thomas Coles, fled to the Continent [VCH III, 306].
Attempts were made to recreate the ecclesiastical setting
of the restored Latin mass and the shrines of the saints
were restored. It has been suggested that the date 'ANNO
MXCIX', cut into the marble ledger stone now on the stylobate in the south-west corner of the Trinity Chapel,
represents the attempt to rehabilitate the shrine of
Osmund, using some small relic that had escaped the
desecration of 1539 [Stroud 1984, 50–4]. Leland, who
visited the Cathedral in 1542, made no mention of this
stone, which by 1601, now firmly associated with
Osmund, was to be found in the middle of the Trinity
Chapel, where it was erroneously believed to cover the
bodily remains of the saint [Bodl MS Gough Eccl Top 55,
fol 272]. This might explain why, in 1644, Symonds
described the date as 'newly written' [Long 1859, 130].
It remained there until the 18th century (Figs 14 and
15). Altars were reinstated and vestments restored to
use. The results of Mary's efforts remained superficial,
however. The chantries, for example, were not restored,
for she wisely held back from attacking the interests of
those who had benefited from the dispersal of the associated lands and properties. The return to Catholic
orthodoxy was, however, reflected in two clerical monuments of the period. Those of Bishop Capon and
Chancellor Bennett (monuments 128 and 14) conform to
standard late medieval patterns.

The accession of Queen Elizabeth marked the
renewal of efforts to reorder the interior of the Cathedral
in line with Protestant ideals, and it was the Elizabethan
settlement that determined the form of the Anglican
cathedral interior. Despite the queen's own preference
for the more conservative customs current at the end of
her father's reign, she was forced to rely on the return-
ing Marian exiles, and it was the 1552 liturgy that prevailed in 1559. Initially, this meant a further spate of
destruction. The clerk of works' accounts for 15 August
1559 list payments for the 'taking down of aulters', and
in October of the same year altar stones were being laid
in the pavement [Wordsworth 1901, 306]. There were
further sales of jewels, ornaments and copes [VCH III,
185]. Further destruction of imagery in stained-glass
windows also followed Elizabeth's accession. The Fabric
Rolls for 1558 list payments for the boarding-up and new
glazing of windows throughout the church [Fabric
Accounts]. The Elizabethan Church countenanced the

continuation of the fundamental division between choir and nave, effected by the pulpitum, although the Royal Order of 1561 specified the removal of the rood and its loft [Addleshaw and Etchells 1948, 30]. At Salisbury Cathedral the rood loft was still in use in 1562 [Fabric Accounts].

In 1560 the queen prohibited the further defacing of monuments and tombs [Lehmberg 1988, 145]. The visitation carried out in 1562 found the Cathedral to be in a deplorable state [Frere 1910c, 123]; the church was said to be 'in great ruin', requiring £2,000 worth of repairs. A combination of iconoclasm and neglect had taken their toll. Bishop Jewel (1559-71) made serious efforts to put the building in good order, beginning with his statutes of Pentecost 1560, when provision was first made for the collection of funds for the repairs to the fabric [Wordsworth and Macleane 1915, 386-8]. The Fabric Rolls for 1558 and 1562 record numerous repairs to windows and work done to the pavement in the church and renewal of marble pillars in the cloister. In 1567 Bishop Jewel's arms were made for a window on the south side of the church and Symonds noticed Jewel's name and the date of 1569 in many of the north windows of the nave [Long 1859, 140]. As late as 1571, however, a painter was paid 6d 'for washinge oute of imagery in the church' [Fabric Accounts]. The work of restoring the fabric continued to the end of the century, with references to repairs made in both Bishop Gheast's visitation of 1574 [Frere 1910c, 367-9] and Bishop Cotton's of 1607 [Everett 1943, 178].[14] Archbishop Laud's visitation of 1634 found 'noe fault in any of the p'ticulars mentioned in the article... saving the pavements of the church and cloister are somewhat defective, and some other small defects' [Wilts N&Q, I (1893), 21], testimony to the enormous improvements since 1560.

To Bishop Jewel's episcopate can be attributed the development of closer relations between the Cathedral and the city, with strenuous efforts made to improve the pastoral and instructive role of the Cathedral clergy. A preaching rota was introduced in 1560 [Wordsworth and Macleane 1915, 386] and it was at this time that the nave was provided with the fixed seating mentioned in Laud's visitation of 1634 [Wilts N&Q, I (1893), 23]. The mayor and corporation attended Cathedral services every Sunday, and quarrels between the city wives and those of the clergy erupted over questions of precedence [VCH III, 188]. These seats, criticised for the irregularity of their height and the noise made by their occupants on opening and closing the doors during sermons, remained in place until the visitation of 1634, when their removal was ordered by Archbishop Laud. Thereafter only movable seats were to be used, and were to be put out only when required for the sermons [VCH III, 188,

23]. That the Cathedral was somewhat rehabilitated in the minds of its local community can be inferred from the renewed secular patronage; the inventories of 1601 and 1624-5 reveal the acquisition of a quantity of plate and a large number of curtains, velvet cushions and altar cloths [Wordsworth 1915, 30-6]. In the first half of the 17th century two major secular monuments were erected on the sites of the altars formerly in the chapels of St Peter and St Stephen - the Gorges and Hertford monuments. This period was also one in which the music of the Cathedral prospered. In 1635 the great organ was enlarged, and was gilded in the following year [Matthews 1989, 4]. Since 1625 Sundays and holidays had been celebrated with sackbutts and cornetts in addition to the organ [Wordsworth and Robertson 1938, 221-7].

The advent of Civil War once more threatened the life of the Cathedral and its Close, although Salisbury suffered very little compared with Durham, Lichfield or Peterborough. In recognition of changing attitudes, the organ was dismantled in 1643 [Matthews 1989, 5], a sad event in a cathedral renowned for its music in the 1630s.[15] The only serious damage resulted from the actions of parliamentary forces in 1644, who sacked the treasury. Between 5 and 12 August a quantity of plate, a number of copes, surplices, tippets, hoods and an image of the Virgin Mary were taken away. Parliament examined the loot and ordered the restoration of the plate and an altar cloth - the rest of the booty was destroyed [Benson and Hatcher 1843, 397]. The city was the scene of serious fighting in 1644 and 1645 and the parliamentarians entrenched themselves in the Close. Forced to retreat, they left a small rearguard barricaded in the belfry, prompting the royalists to set fire to the belfry door [Firth 1894, I, 107-12].

Cathedral documentation for the period of the Commonwealth is sparse, for in 1643 the Fabric Accounts cease and in 1648 Parliament abolished all deans, chapters, vicars choral and choristers, although many canons had already been ejected for their support of the royalist cause [VCH III, 192]. It is clear, however, that, in general, the Cathedral fabric continued to be maintained, responsibility being taken by the city government and by the local gentry, particularly members of the Hyde family. In 1653, 289 Dutch prisoners of war were held in poor conditions in the Cathedral cloisters. They caused much damage to the pillars of the cloister and the windows of the library and it was Mayor Thomas Ray who wrote to Parliament requesting their removal. It was also Ray who was entrusted with the task of assessing the extent of the damage [Benson and Hatcher 1843, 397-400; Eward 1983, 21].

The Restoration of the monarchy in 1660 was accompanied by the reinstatement of the institutions of the

24   The Gorges monument (monument 1), 1635, erected on the site of the altar in the chapel of St Peter and the Apostles [BB71/2377]

Anglican Church and, after twenty years of neglect and some iconoclasm, the Cathedral was once again in need of repair and adornment. Salisbury had fared better than many cathedrals. When Bishop Ward (1667–89) arrived in Salisbury in 1667 he found that, contrary to his expectations, the Cathedral 'did not want much reparation, for to the eternal honour of the loyal gentry of that diocese ... during the whole of the time of the Civil Wars, when there was neither bishop or dean to take care of it, they employed workmen to keep that magnificent pile in repair' [Pope 1697, 65]. None the less, Ward, himself a distinguished scientist and founder member of the Royal Society, commissioned a report on the structure from his friend Christopher Wren in the summer of 1668. Wren's principal recommendations concerned the structure of the spire, which was in need of strengthening [Wren Society 1934, 21–6]. He also prepared specifications for the repair of the cloisters and the western half of the nave roof, all of which was executed according to his instructions and remain to this day.[16]

Some attempts had already been made under Ward's immediate predecessors to restore the Cathedral and its furnishings. Bishop Duppa (1641–60), for example, had given £500 towards the work in c 1662 [Wordsworth 1915, 37]. The great organ, gilded and enlarged in 1635 and dismantled in 1643, was reinstated by Thomas Harris in 1661 [Matthews 1989, 5], and new song books were purchased [Wordsworth 1915, 40]. New altar rails had been made in 1660–1 at a cost of £7, and were gilded in the following year [Wordsworth 1915, 40]. In 1662 a new font was purchased in London. Several pieces of plate in the Cathedral's treasury were acquired at this time.

Under Bishop Ward every effort was made to ensure that the Fabric Fund was placed on a proper financial footing; in the Convocation of 1668, each canon undertook to pay one-fifth of his prebendal income into the Fund and in 1669 the Master of the Fabric was empowered to employ the appropriate workmen [Dodsworth 1814, 172]. In the beautification of the Cathedral's interior, Ward took a personal interest and made a significant financial contribution [Pope 1697, 66]. At Ward's expense, the east walk of the cloister, connecting the bishop's private garden with the church, was repaved. The choir was refurbished in 1671–2 in a campaign for which Wren acted as adviser and designer and to which Ward also contributed financially. It was enclosed with a wooden screen in white and gold, painted with floral wreaths [VCH III, 300]. The choir stalls were extended, repaired and embellished. Alexander Fort was engaged in 1671, provided with designs supplied by Wren [Eltringham 1958, 56–63]. Although Fort was the son of a Salisbury man, Thomas Fort, he had flourished as a

25   The 1662 font (J Biddlecombe 1754)

prominent member of Wren's circle of craftsmen, in the employ of royal and aristocratic patrons. The medieval stalls were raised above those of the singing men and new desks and stall backs were provided. The singing men's seats were also raised and provided with kneeling benches. The work was decorated with shields, friezes and vases of flowers. Fort was also directed to construct 'the Deanes seate very Decent and Handsome' [Eltringham 1958, 58], and it is this seat, with its punning device on Brideoak's name, that is the principal survivor of his work in the Cathedral, although part of Alexander Fort's work has been reused as panelling in No. 9 The Close [RCHME 1993b, 82–3, pls 49 and 50]. The greatest expense was lavished on a new bishop's

throne, paid for by Ward himself, and commissioned in 1672 [Eltringham 1958, 61–3]. Fort was also commissioned to pave the floor around the stalls with white Purbeck marble [Eltringham 1958, 59]. The paving of the choir as a whole was completed at the expense of Robert Townson in 1684, at which time the memorials to Bishops Wyville, Gheast and Jewel were moved to the north-east transept (see p 158).

The new work was set off by a set of sumptuous purple velvet altar hangings with gold fringes and a panel of cloth of gold, the gift of Edward Hyde, earl of Clarendon, valued at £170 in 1676 [Wordsworth 1915, 37]. This was the most notable of a number of Hyde benefactions to the Cathedral, and supports the widely-held local belief that it was the Hydes who had taken a hand in maintaining the fabric during the Commonwealth. The inventory of 1685 reveals that the Cathedral's depleted collection of plate was also replenished in this period and many of the vessels remain in the Treasury (see pp 68–9). The high altar and choir altars were

27   *Dean Brideoak's stall of 1671, the work of Alexander Fort [BB74/2733]*

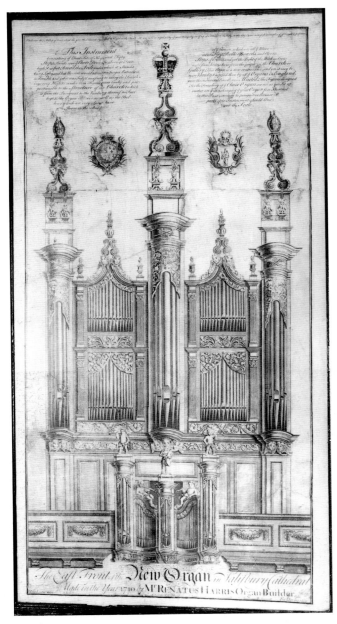

28 *John Lyons's 1745 engraving of Renatus Harris's organ of 1710*
[BB71/2595]

inhabitants of the Close [Wordsworth 1915, 46–52]. Under Ward the Cathedral is said to have been kept spotlessly clean: 'anyone who had occasion for dust to throw on the superscription of a letter, he would have a hard task to find it there' [Pope 1697, 66].

Ward's choir furnishings were later to be attacked for their inappropriately showy display. Daniel Defoe, who first visited the Cathedral in the 1720s, found the decoration of the choir 'mean, and more like the ordinary method of common drawing room, or tavern painting, than that of a church; the carving is good, but very little of it' [Defoe 1928, I, 190]. Another commentator, frequently quoted and erroneously identified as Defoe, but as yet unidentified, stressed the inappropriate theatricality of Bishop Ward's decorations: 'each stall hath the arms of its holder in gilt letters on blue writ upon it, and the episcopal throne with Bishop Ward's arms upon it would make it fine theatrical decoration, being supported by gilt pillars and painted with flowers upon white all over' [*VCH* III, 200]. The nave was soon to be dominated by the new organ, commissioned from Renatus Harris, son of Thomas, in 1710. This magnificent instrument, the first in England to have four manuals, was depicted in an engraving printed and sold by John Lyons in 1745. Visible in Biddlecombe's 1754 view of the nave, it was larger than its predecessor, requiring more men to work the bellows. Their salary was increased in acknowledgement of their greater efforts [Matthews 1983, 8–11].

The 18th century

The early 18th-century Chapter included a number of able, active and learned men, in contrast to the reputation for complacency and worldliness of cathedral clergy elsewhere. Considerable efforts were made to improve the Cathedral library; a librarian was appointed and the catalogue of manuscripts was revised [*VCH* III, 199]. Thomas Tanner and Richard Rawlinson made extensive studies in the muniments and in 1723 the latter published his *History and Antiquities of the Church of Salisbury*. In Bishop Sherlock (1734–48) Salisbury had yet another bishop who took an active interest in the Cathedral fabric. When George Vertue visited Salisbury in 1740, Sherlock showed him the manuscript of William de Waude's history together with Wren's survey and details of Sherlock's own repairs [Walpole Society 1937–8, 129]. He also displayed the new plan of the Cathedral he had prepared. The works initiated by Sherlock seem to have concentrated on structural matters. It was through his intervention that Francis Price became clerk of works and undertook his survey of the Cathedral [Cocke 1993, 24–5]. In Francis Price, clerk of

more than adequately supplied with vessels and were furnished with frontals, hangings, carpets and cushions [Wordsworth 1915, 43–6; Beddard 1971, 147–55]. The richly draped altar with its flanking candlesticks attracted the admiring attention of Cosmo III, duke of Tuscany, who visited the Cathedral in 1669 [Magalotti 1821, 153] and by Celia Fiennes later in the century [Morris 1995, 37]. Nor was the nave neglected; it was repaved where necessary and new seating was introduced in 1676–7, with orders of seating issued for the works 1743–53, the Cathedral had one of the most able surveyors of the day [Ferriday 1953, 327–8] and *A Series of Particular and Useful Observations... upon... the Cathedral Church of Salisbury* [Price 1753] is a landmark in the serious study of Gothic structure. It was followed in 1774 by a posthumously revised and expanded edition, *A Description of that Admirable Structure the Cathedral Church of Salisbury*. In the second half of the century the fabric was in less safe hands.

As early as 1758 the decision was made to demolish rather than attempt to repair the southern range of the library. The spire and tower of the belfry were to be dismantled as being 'neither useful nor ornamental' [Chapter Acts, 25 Nov 1758, fol 131]. In 1777 five out of the eight bells were sold [Fletcher 1937, 612]. Further works were initiated during the episcopate of Bishop Hume (1766–82), directed by Clerk of Works Edmund Lush, and his son William, although little is known of their nature and extent [Dodsworth 1814, 177]. The Cathedral was closed from 1777 to 1779 [*SJ* 26 May 1777; *SJ* 27 Sept 1779] to allow the removal of the

pulpit and seats from the nave [Dodsworth 1814, 177]; henceforth the sermon was to be delivered in the choir, which was lengthened towards the Trinity Chapel by 20 feet (6.09 m). Wren's stall backs were removed and the choir was enclosed with a new screen, painted in imitation of oak, and galleries reached by stairs from the aisles were erected behind the prebendal stalls [Benson and Hatcher 1843, 532]. Those occupying the galleried pews had little, if any, view of the choir below and little light to see by [Smith 1980, 13]. Lush's work included the widening of the entrance into the choir through the pulpitum, the original door of which was removed; in this respect Lush anticipated to some extent the later desire for open vistas.[17] Jacob, second Earl Radnor, donated £200 towards the works, and in 1778 the railings of the cage-like chantry chapel of Walter Lord Hungerford were removed from the nave to the choir to form part of a new Radnor pew, decorated internally with heraldry and Georgian Gothic motifs [Cocke 1993, 25]. In November 1778 the Chapter considered the earl's designs for a new east window [Chapter Acts, 7 Nov

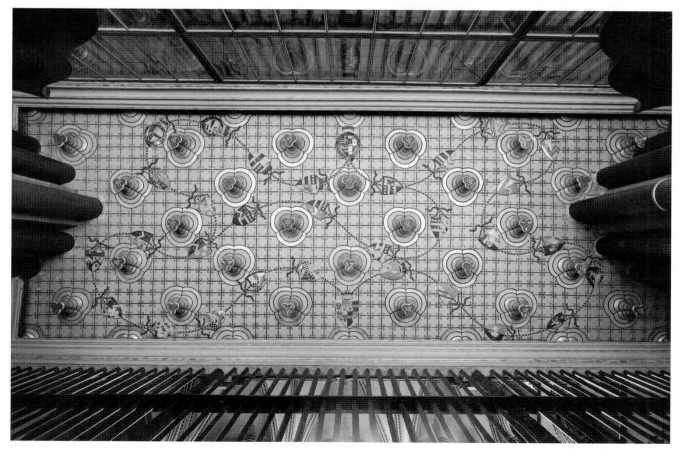

29   *Interior decoration of the Radnor pew, 1778 [BB71/2496]*

30 *The choir clerestory east window, made by James Pearson after a painting by J H Mortimer, installed in 1781, the gift of the earl of Radnor [BB93/22059]*

1778, fol 251], and in 1781 the glass, depicting Moses and the Brazen serpent, designed by John Hamilton Mortimer and executed by James Pearson, was installed. The window, which originally contained the earl's arms at its apex, was praised for its ingenious construction, for the iron armatures holding it in place were bent in such a way that they did not interfere with the design.[18] Elsewhere in the Cathedral, glass was destroyed in this period. The glazier John Berry's oft-quoted letter describing the stripping of medieval glass for its lead was penned in 1788 (see p 97).

The work of the 1770s was but a prelude to the more drastic 'improvements' initiated by Bishop Shute Barrington (1782–91), prompted by the desire to create a picturesque vista within the Cathedral, a principle also guiding the tidying-up of the burial ground around the Cathedral, creating a park-like setting for the church, immortalised by Constable. Barrington, who took the lead in the funding of the work, secured the services of James Wyatt, who undertook a survey of the building in 1787 [Dodsworth 1792, 25–30], during which he repeated the experiments carried out by Wren and Price, expressing renewed concern for the stability of the crossing. More extensive proposals were considered and approved by the Chapter on 26 August 1789, with further major aspects of the work approved on 6 October 1789, 12 November 1789 and 5 February 1790, at which it was agreed that the free-standing belfry be demolished. These accounts, while describing the main 'improvements' that were to be implemented over the next three years, convey no impression in their deceptively bland words of the true extent of the upheaval, or, indeed, of the furore that was to ensue in certain circles. The Cathedral was closed on 1 October 1789 [Chapter Acts, 26 Aug 1789], to be reopened only in September 1792 [SJ 10 Sept 1792]. It is interesting to speculate whether the strict orders forbidding the admission of unauthorised persons to the Cathedral in the meantime were a health and safety measure or a precaution against critical intervention in the progress of Wyatt's work [Chapter Acts, 26 Aug 1789].

In preparing his survey, Wyatt had been mindful of the findings of Christopher Wren and, more recently, Francis Price. His final plan proposed to 'rebuild and make good the Walls and Butterasses to the church' and 'to alter and enlarge the organ loft' [Chapter Acts, 12 Nov 1789]. The pulpitum was thus regarded as being principally a form of buttress to the crossing, while the Beauchamp and Hungerford chantry chapels were considered to weaken the structure of the Trinity Chapel. Lord Radnor, one of the most influential supporters of the 'improvements', whose advice Bishop Barrington sought, agreed that the function of the screen was to brace 'the legs of the steeple', and so, although a supporter of the 'open-vista' concept, he reluctantly accepted the necessity of continuing the division of choir and nave by means of a choir screen. The earl took a considerable personal interest in the Cathedral and provided financial support for work of which he approved [Hollaender 1958-9; Frew 1984]. In the presentation of the cases for and against the 'improvements', it is clear that in the discussion of structural matters both sides were hampered by an imperfect understanding of Gothic structure. While lamenting the destruction of the chantry chapels, and repeating Richard Gough's earlier criticisms of the Chapter for allowing them to become so run down, Bishop John Milner, one of Wyatt's sternest critics, found himself unable to refute with absolute confidence the view that they were weakening the Trinity Chapel, although he did suggest an alternative way of strengthening it without demolishing them [Milner 1798, 39]. [19]

Although Lord Radnor accepted both the liturgical and structural necessity of maintaining the division between the choir and the nave, his own design for a new screen and organ would have allowed a less restricted view of the choir [Hollaender 1958-9, 22-6]. The screen, made out of fragments of the medieval chantry chapels, installed by Wyatt in place of the pulpitum, was, in fact, shallower than its medieval predecessor, but higher, thereby supposedly more effective in bracing the crossing. Renatus Harris's organ of 1710 was removed, to be lost almost without trace, and King George III donated a new one (costing 1,000 guineas) by Samuel Green of Isleworth. This was larger than the one it replaced [Britton 1801, 61, Matthews 1989, 11-15] and effectively blocked any vista into the choir, quite the opposite of Radnor's intention. In addition to removing the medieval pulpitum, the rood beam, condemned as useless in providing support for the building, was 'sawn asunder and taken down for inspection' [Dodsworth 1814, 180-1].

The decision to remove the screen behind the high altar, thereby lengthening the choir and creating an open vista into the Trinity Chapel, was primarily an aesthetic one, although it also created a unified space capable of accommodating the congregation. The choir was opened up further by the demolition of the easternmost bay of the choir enclosure on the north and south sides. On the north side this meant the demolition of Bishop Bingham's monument. The floor levels of the presbytery were lowered to allow unimpeded passage throughout the enlarged choir. The extended choir was fitted with a new pulpit and bishop's throne, and new canopies were added to all the stalls [Britton 1801, 59-60; Dodsworth 1814, 177, 180]. Using medieval fragments from the demolished Beauchamp and Hungerford chapels, Wyatt

31   *The nave looking east, c 1860, showing James Wyatt's choir screen and Samuel Green's organ, both removed*
by George Gilbert Scott in the restoration of the 1870s [BB85/2187b]

constructed a reredos against the eastern wall of the Trinity Chapel. The new altar was formed out of a stone discovered when the old Trinity Chapel altar was removed. Of this construction, visible in the illustrations in Britton [1801] and Dodsworth [1814], only the cornice and panelling taken from the Beauchamp chapel and placed under the north and south side windows of the Trinity Chapel remain. The floor level of the Trinity Chapel was raised a few inches to give an ascent from the choir, and a suitably mysterious light was shed by the enamel painted window of the Resurrection designed by Joshua Reynolds and executed by Francis Eginton. The remaining medieval glazing was removed and replaced by 'mosaic painted glass to give effect to the painting, and throw on this part of the building that sober light which befits a place of devotion' [Dodsworth 1814, 179]. The windows of the presbytery triforium, inserted in the late Middle Ages, were blocked up. Finally, the remaining glass was 'painted of a dark colour with common paint' to increase the sepulchral quality of the illumination [Chapter Acts, 23 June 1792].

The extensive 13th-century paintings on the choir vault, described by Dodsworth, Wyatt's most eloquent defender, as 'the efforts of a wretched taste, which, in

32 *The choir looking west c 1850, showing Wyatt's choir furniture and the altar table introduced c 1830 [BB57/1506]*

attempting to ornament, had deformed the edifice' [Dodsworth, 1814, 183], were covered over with a wash, as were those in the eastern transepts. Dodsworth and other Wyatt supporters argued that these paintings were not coeval with the choir, although in 1789 the Society of Antiquaries had believed them of sufficient interest to warrant commissioning Jacob Schnebbelie to record them (see Fig 9). The remaining medieval tiles in the Trinity Chapel were swept away in favour of blue stone paving in squares made of cut-up gravestones [Chapter Acts, 26 Aug 1789].

The demolition of the Beauchamp and Hungerford chantry chapels had already begun when Schnebbelie began to record them in September 1789. Although the chapels had clearly fallen into a deplorable state of repair, they were widely admired for their wall paintings and fine tombs, having excited the interest of both Leland and Symonds. In dismantling the chapels, Wyatt may have felt he was preserving as much as possible by reusing fragments in his Trinity Chapel decorations and choir screen. Of the monuments, he took little care; Bishop Beauchamp's was lost, together with those of his mother and father and his brother, Lord St Amand. The Cheney tomb chest and effigy, formerly in the south-west corner of the chapel, were moved into the nave, but lost their canopy. The present tomb chest of Robert, Lord Hungerford, which was moved to the nave, is made up of fragments from the demolished chapels.

The splendid canopy of the original was destroyed. His wife's tomb, formerly in the centre of the chantry, has disappeared.

The reordering of the Trinity Chapel occasioned further disruption. Tombs that had been there since the foundation era, and in particular that of William Longespee (d 1226) were moved arbitrarily to the nave. Bishop Barrington also allowed some of his illustrious predecessors to be decanted unceremoniously into the nave. Nicholas Longespee (d 1297) and Bishop Blythe (d 1499), for example, were both moved from the east end. Bishop Wyle (d 1271) was moved from the north transept and his effigy now lies on a chest made up of reused material. In the 19th century a number of these tombs were opened and found to be empty, suggesting that the earthly remains of the original occupants had not received careful handling during their perambulations, despite the Chapter's orders that 'such human bones as have been discovered, be deposited as near as may be to the monuments to which they respectively belong' [Chapter Acts, 26 Aug 1789]. In repositioning the choir monuments in the nave, a number of burials of less illustrious persons were effectively obliterated.

The carelessness with which the tombs and their occupants were handled certainly fuelled the criticism. Milner described the use of the north-eastern transept as a 'lumber room' for the 'heterogeneous articles and ornaments which could not be made use of at the late alterations' [Milner 1798, 25 and n 3] and records the way in which tomb slabs were cut up for paving. A number of slabs, together with rings, chalices, patens, croziers and pieces of textile found in the opened tombs, were displayed in the vestry for the edification of the curious [Milner 1798, 29]. Carter recalled picking through the antiquarian debris dumped in the cloister [Carter 1803, 642–3]. While Wyatt cannot be held personally responsible for every piece of damage – John Britton blamed the destruction of Bishop Beauchamp's tomb on Mr Lush [Britton 1801, 90] – it could be argued that the work was poorly and negligently supervised. In March 1792 Edmund Lush was replaced as clerk of works by Richard Morris. No explanation was given for his dismissal [Chapter Acts, 24 Mar 1792]. No official record was kept of the movements of tombs, considerably exacerbating present problems of identification. John Carter's scandalised account of the nave after the 'improvements' remains the most useful record of these activities [Carter 1803, 1021–3].

The Cathedral was reopened in September 1792 in the presence of King George III, the queen and six princesses [VCH III, 200]. Wyatt's efforts were widely and warmly welcomed by the majority of his contemporaries; Prince Puckler-Muskau was enthusiastic in his praise:

> The interior of this magnificent temple is in the highest degree inspiring, and has been improved by Wyatt's genius. It was an admirable idea to remove the most remarkable old monuments from the walls and obscure corners and to place them in the space between the great double avenues of pillars. . . Nothing can have a finer effect than these rows of Gothic sarcophagi. [Robinson 1979, 66]

Wyatt's greatest apologist was undoubtedly the verger William Dodsworth, who hastened to produce a laudatory account of the 'Improvements' in 1792, with a longer and more considered account published in 1814. The reopened Cathedral attracted a number of new guide books [Britton 1801; Easton 1825; Harris 1825; Storer c 1820], all of them praising Wyatt's taste and his new 'Gothic' furnishings. Wyatt's critics, despite their considerable eminence, failed to persuade the world at large that his Salisbury 'improvements' were detrimental to the Cathedral. Richard Gough, director of the Society of Antiquaries and author of Sepulchral Monuments in Great Britain (1796) had been alerted to the imminent washing-over of the vault paintings in the choir, by Jacob Schnebbelie, there to record them for the Society. He had written an impassioned letter to the Gentleman's Magazine in October 1789 in which he deplored the destruction of paintings 'that would do honour to the Italian school' and the 'capricious displacement of the

monuments' with no regard for the remains of the illustrious personages buried there [Gentleman's Magazine 1789]. The controversy continued long after Wyatt's departure from Salisbury and was considerably fuelled by his subsequent activities in Durham Cathedral, also undertaken for Shute Barrington, translated there in 1795.

The debate is of particular significance for an understanding of the emergence of an archaeological approach to the study and appreciation of medieval buildings when it is understood that battle was joined within the rooms of the Society of Antiquaries, where the arguments were rehearsed before a more than averagely well-informed audience [Evans 1956, 207–11]. Criticism of Wyatt's treatment of Salisbury Cathedral was aired when he was proposed for election to the fellowship of the Society in 1797. Richard Gough, director of the Society, led the anti-Wyatt party and at the first ballot held on 18 May 1797 Wyatt was black-balled [Evans 1956, 207; Crook 1995, 24–5]. Milner's Dissertation was prepared to be read to the Society on the eve of the second ballot in December 1797. In the event, the Council declined to allow Milner to read his paper and Wyatt was elected fellow by a considerable majority. Gough resigned in protest and Carter's appointment as draughtsman to the Society was terminated. Carter continued to make embittered attacks on Wyatt (notably in the Gentleman's Magazine), but the taste of the majority of his contemporaries and the as-yet imperfect understanding of Gothic structure meant that his diatribe largely fell on deaf ears. Wyatt's furnishings remained in place until the 1870s and his vision of the interior has left a permanent mark on modern perceptions of the Cathedral.

The 19th and 20th centuries

Within a very short space of time, Wyatt's arrangement of the choir was found to be liturgically inconvenient; the Trinity Chapel altar, slightingly described by Milner as 'a diminutive object' [Milner 1798, 38], was found to be far too distant from the main body of the choir to be practical. Accordingly, an altar table was reintroduced to the choir some time after 1814, occupying the position of the former high altar; it was 'draped and unadorned'. The choir and Trinity Chapel continued to operate as a single unified space. By 1830, however, the unsatisfactory nature of these arrangements led to calls for reordering, with a restoration of a physical division between choir and Trinity Chapel [Gentleman's Magazine 1830]. It was suggested that this could be effected by the installation of a low screen in 13th-century style, according to a design by J C Buckler [Gentleman's Magazine 1830].

This screen would completely enclose the choir but would not entirely impede a view of the architecture of the Trinity Chapel beyond. In the event, the design was never executed. By 1838 it was felt that 'a regard for propriety had dictated a restoration of the choir to something like its former state' [Garland and Moule 1838, 11], anticipating the views of the Cambridge Camden Society, founded in 1839. The enamel painted glass, praised so fulsomely by Britton in 1801, provoked derogatory remarks, the Pearson window described as 'of very ordinary merit' and the Reynolds window criticised for its colours, which were not 'sufficiently resplendent' [Garland and Moule 1838, 14]. In 1854 it was removed and replaced by a Clayton and Bell window in 13th-century style dedicated to Dean Lear [Fletcher 1930a, 248]. The 18th-century 'mosaic glass' in the side windows was to survive into the 1880s. Despite the dissatisfaction expressed in the 1830s, no drastic changes were made until the 1870s and thus Wyatt's choir survived well into the age of photography.

The Chapter House had largely escaped Wyatt's attentions, but by the 1850s was in a dilapidated state. The remaining medieval stained glass had been removed c 1819. Sargent's 1852 watercolour (Plate 4) shows it mainly plain-glazed, with a window partially boarded up and the 13th-century tiled pavement broken in a number of places. By 1843 restoration of the Chapter House was identified as a priority and a survey was made by T H Wyatt. The central pier had shifted out of the perpendicular and, according to the architect William Burges, the building 'had got a twist' [Burges 1859, 6]. Bishop Denison had restored the badly dilapidated cloister, although this had attracted criticism for its use of Chilmark instead of Purbeck marble for the renewed shafts [Murray 1861, 101] and after his death in 1854 it was decided that the Chapter House should be restored in his memory. Work was directed by the Cathedral architect Henry Clutton, assisted by William Burges. Clutton concentrated on correcting the structural faults, rebuilding the central shaft (which included the replacement of its sculpted base) and underpinning the walls. During this operation 'sundry pennies of Edward I in those parts of the foundations requiring underpinning' were found [Burges 1859, 6]. Work then began on the vestibule, including the restoration of the portal sculpture and the laying of a new mosaic pavement, designed by Burges. The extent of the restoration can be appreciated from Cockerell's account of the sculpture prior to restoration [Cockerell 1851] and from Frederick Pepys Cockerell's drawings in the RIBA drawings collection [Green 1968]. Burges's tiled floor has been replaced. However, it was as iconographic adviser in the restoration of the Chapter House sculptures that Burges was

most influential [Crook 1981, 181–3]. The iconographic scheme was reconstructed with reference to the 14th-century cycle in the Queen Mary Psalter, and Burges's careful notes on the surviving traces of polychromy, and his comments on the medieval stained glass then remaining in the Chapter House, continue to be the most valuable record of the original appearance of the interior [Burges 1859]. The restoration of the sculpture was executed by J B Philip with painting by Octavius Hudson. Colour and a decorative background to the sculptural frieze itself were restored, and the wall arcade below was filled with a frieze of fictive drapery hanging from rings. The medieval pavement was replaced with a Minton replica and the vault was repainted. The polychromy of the medieval table was also restored under Burges's direction.[20] New glazing by the firm of Ward and Hughes, broadly following the medieval scheme, albeit without the heraldic elements advocated by both Burges and Winston, was installed in 1860.

While a few anxious voices questioned the advisability of executing such an extensive and thoroughgoing re-creation of a medieval scheme,[21] the Chapter House restoration was almost universally applauded [Crook 1981, 182–3]. Burges's scholarship was widely praised and his restoration of both the iconography of the sculptures and the base of the column accepted as completely accurate. Approbation was forthcoming from *The Builder*, the *Ecclesiologist* and the *Gentleman's Magazine*, in the pages of which so much criticism of earlier Salisbury restorations had found expression. This sumptuous programme was short-lived, however, for by 1874 Hudson's painting was beginning to deteriorate and by 1900 the Chapter House had been scraped clean. In 1967 two of the Ward and Hughes stained-glass windows were removed, although public outcry was sufficient to stop the removal of any more. One has since been replaced with glass designed and executed by the Cathedral glaziers.

The later stages of the Chapter House restoration were carried through under the direction of Sir George Gilbert Scott, for in 1856 Clutton's conversion to Roman Catholicism led to his resignation as Cathedral architect. Until his death in 1878, Scott went about repairing the Cathedral and recreating a Gothic interior, sweeping away all traces of Wyatt's work. In this he was provided with generous financial support. In 1862 a grant of £10,000 was arranged with the Ecclesiastical Commissioners and when this proved insufficient, further funds were raised by public subscription; over £82,000 was spent in total [*VCH* III, 204]. External and structural repairs, which included the provision of new statuary for the west front, were Scott's first priority, but in 1869 he began to reorder the choir. This work was

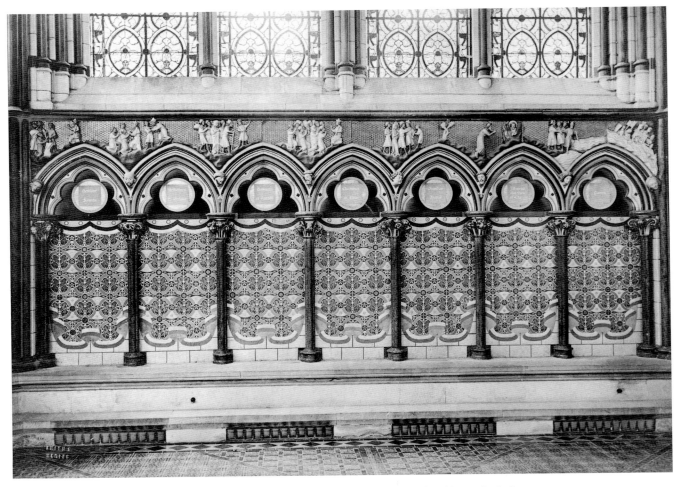

33   *The Chapter House after the 1855 restoration of the sculpture by John Birnie Philip and the addition of polychrome by Octavius Hudson [BB92/25072]*

undertaken in memory of Bishop Hamilton, whose monument, designed by Scott, is situated on the south side of the choir (monument 149).

Scott outlined his scheme to the Chapter in November 1869 [Scott 1870], estimating that at least £15,000 would be required. His intention was to recreate a Gothic interior, as accurate as liturgical convenience would allow. Once again, the architect was faced with the problems of reconciling a flexible liturgical space with the archaeological and aesthetic demands of a Gothic cathedral. While arguing for the retention of a choir screen, desirable for visual reasons and essential to support the organ, Scott advocated an open screen which would allow a nave congregation to see into the choir. He proposed a double screen supported by marble columns. The organ would be positioned on top of it, with some parts of it hidden in the aisles or triforium. The 18th-century choir furniture and screens would be removed, uncovering the monuments of Bishops de

Martival and de Gandavo. Likewise, screens obscuring the monuments of Bishops Bridport and Medford would be cleared out of the transepts. Scott appreciated the importance of the 13th-century choir stalls, proposing that they be provided with new desks and canopies. The choir enclosure was to be restored through the re-creation of Bishop de Bingham's monument (Scott firmly believed it to be that of Richard Poore) and the installation of a reredos behind the high altar. Here Scott revealed his ambivalence in the screens-versus-vistas debate, for, while the bay behind the altar was effectively to be filled, the spaces either side would be occupied by openwork grilles, allowing views into the Trinity Chapel. In one important respect his plans were not realised, for his original intention was to remove the Radnor pew, restoring the structure to the Hungerford monument in the nave, and replace the former with a re-creation of the lost sedilia using the remains of the 13th-century pulpitum [Scott 1870, 15].

In the event, Wyatt's choir screen was dismantled, as was Mr Green's organ. Fragments of this screen, in effect bits of the late medieval chantry chapels, are now preserved in the lapidarium above the presbytery roof. Scott's original design for a stone screen had to be abandoned, however, for Dean Lear's widow, who commissioned it as a memorial to her husband, refused to meet the expense, preferring to pay £1,000 for an iron screen by Francis Skidmore of Coventry [Stamp 1995, 487].[22] Even then, Scott believed Skidmore to have subsidised the real cost of the work. East of the new screen, the 18th-century furnishings were removed, revealing the original side entrances to the choir, which were reinstated. The choir stalls were cleaned of paint and augmented with desks (canopies were added later). A new bishop's throne was commissioned from Earp of Lambeth and a marble choir pulpit designed. The tomb believed by Scott to be that of Bishop Poore was re-created using Carter's drawing and 'some beautiful fragments recently discovered', affording Scott considerable personal satisfaction [Stamp 1995, 307–8]. The equivalent position on the south side was to be occupied by the monument to Bishop Hamilton designed by Scott, although not unveiled until 1881 [Wheeler 1901, 4]. The vista into the Trinity Chapel was cut off by the marble reredos, the gift of Earl Beauchamp, in memory of Bishop Beauchamp, designed by Scott and executed by Farmer and Brindley at a cost of £1,800. Scott found Beauchamp's personal interest in the commission irksome [Stamp 1995, 487]. Some controversy surrounded the positioning of the high altar [Armfield 1873; Scott 1876], but Scott had his way. An iron grille separated choir from retrochoir. The choir pavement was laid with tiles by Godwin [Victoria and Albert Museum 1971, 173–4]. From 1867 Gurney stoves replaced the smoky charcoal braziers which had formerly heated the choir alone [Smith 1980, 13].

34 *Scott's choir with choir screen of 1870 by Francis Skidmore of Coventry. Erected as a memorial to Dean Francis Lear (d 1850) [BB71/2962]*

The interior was cleaned of whitewash and an attempt was made to recover something of the painted decoration of the vaults; the firm of Clayton and Bell was entrusted with the task. In the winter of 1870–1, the paintings on the Trinity Chapel vault were restored, although through illness Scott was not on hand to supervise work and was not satisfied that it had been done accurately [Stamp 1995, 304]. Early in 1871 the choir vault was examined and tracings were made of the 13th-century paintings faintly visible beneath Wyatt's buff wash. Scott was initially under the impression that Clayton and Bell's scheme was a faithful copy of the medieval originals. His own investigations in 1877 convinced him otherwise [Stamp 1995, 305]. In the event, Clayton and Bell seem largely to have made up the content of those medallions which they were unable to

35   The medieval choir stalls with (in the foreground) poppy heads added by Scott [BB93/22090]

36   Scott's presbytery with reredos by Farmer and Brindley and gasoliers designed by Sir Arthur Blomfield [BB94/6961]

37 Bishop Moberly's monument in the south-choir aisle (monument 151). Designed by Sir Arthur Blomfield and executed by Thomas Nicholls, it was unveiled in 1888 [BB93/16191]

discern, basing their work on English manuscript models rather than on their own tracings or on the Schnebbelie drawings [Horlbeck 1960, 119]. The tracings, which were exhibited in London at the Society of Antiquaries in 1876, have been lost [Armfield 1873; Borenius 1932]. The spandrels of the eastern wall were repainted, as was the south-west bay of the choir arcade. The scheme never was completed and plans to 'recover' the paintings in the eastern transepts never realised.

Scott's work in the Trinity Chapel was less extensive. Wyatt's reredos and altar were removed, although the panelling applied to the north and south walls remained. The marble slab incised with the date of Osmund's death was moved to the south-eastern stylobate. No attempt was made to reinstate the monuments displaced by Wyatt, although the Trinity Chapel and retrochoir once

again became the resting place of bishops, with Bishop Wordsworth's monument on the north side and Bishop Moberly's in a recess in the south-aisle wall, obscuring the door to the canon's cemetery, blocked by Wyatt.

Scott, who died in 1878, was succeeded as Cathedral architect by George Edmund Street, under whom the work of restoring the interior continued, albeit at a slower pace. Street's most ambitious plan to reinstate the medieval pulpitum never was realised. He designed the organ case and supervised the restoration of the north porch as a memorial to Bishop Hamilton, paid for by his widow; the doors, gates, boot-scraper and chandelier are all to his designs [White 1921, 32; Spring 1987a, 41]. He was also responsible for the fine mosaic tomb to John Henry Jacob in the south-transept aisle (monument 120). New furnishings continued to be provided; in 1882 the

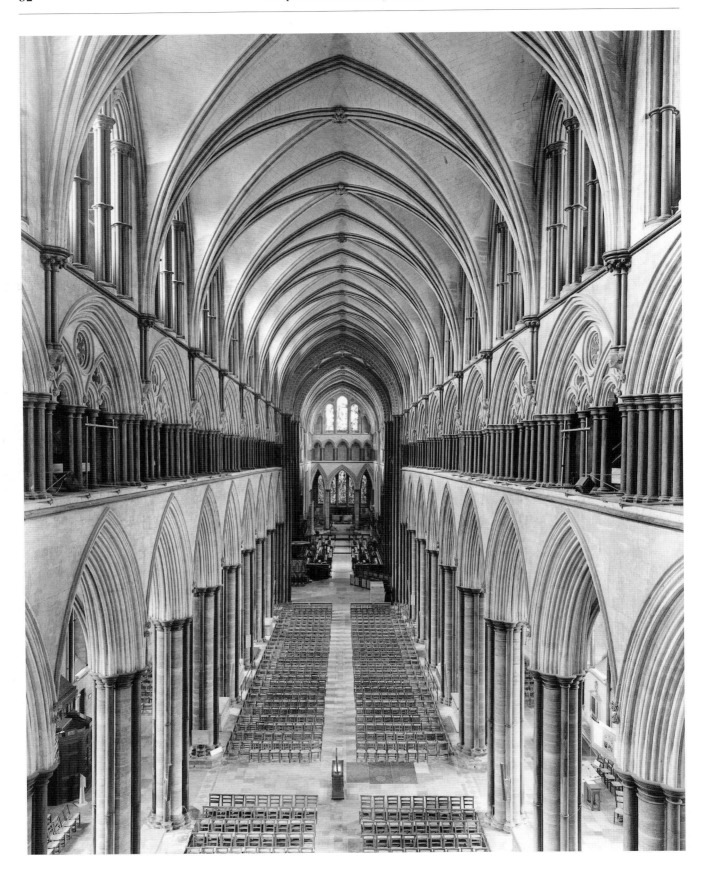

choir was lit by splendid gasoliers designed by A W Blomfield, which were described thus: 'the bases are of foreign walnut and the whole surface is richly decorated with embossed and saw-pierced solid silver' [Brown 1882, 46]. Blomfield also designed the new triptych for the Trinity Chapel, installed in 1896 [Wheeler 1901, 71].[23] In 1913 a new set of choir-stall canopies was designed by C E Ponting, in memory of Bishop Wordsworth, although the First World War delayed their completion until 1925. Throughout both Scott's and Street's periods of stewardship the windows of the eastern arm and transepts were gradually filled with stained glass, with many of the most important Victorian firms represented. In the closing years of the century the great gable windows in the north and south transepts were filled with grisaille in imitation of the original 13th-century glass. Attempts were made to restore surviving medieval glass.

The period after the First World War witnessed the addition of a number of memorials to the fallen and the transformation of the aisle of the south transept into a Victory chapel, dominated by Reginald Bell's powerful window in the south wall. The memorials of the Second World War are also predominantly in glass. The only other significant addition has been the provision between 1938 and 1948 of eleven sculpted saints in niches on the strainer arches and the screen wall in the south-choir aisle.

By the 1950s the tide of taste had turned again; it was heralded by the decision immediately after the war not to reinstate Dean Lear's window in the Trinity Chapel. The next casualty was Scott's choir pulpit, replaced in 1950 by one by Randol Blacking. Scott's other pulpit, at the crossing, survives. Lord Mottistone's plans for a completely open cathedral interior revived the smouldering controversy of screens versus vistas, fanned into flames by the removal, literally overnight, of the Skidmore choir screen [Mount 1960],[24] to be followed a year later by Scott's reredos.[25] Between 1959 and 1962 Scott's choir was effectively destroyed; his pavement was replaced with one of Purbeck marble[26] and his altar table was replaced in 1984 after fire damage. The new altar makes use of stone from Old Sarum. The vista at the close of the 20th century is yet another version of the Salisbury interior, unfamiliar to medieval designer, 18th-century improver and 19th-century restorer alike (Fig 38).

The contribution of the last quarter of the 20th century to the fabric of Salisbury Cathedral has, of necessity, concentrated on the preservation of the building, with few resources for furnishings. The major acquisitions of these years have included Elizabeth Frink's *Walking Madonna*. Inside the Cathedral the uninterrupted vista is dominated by the overwhelming blue of Gabriel Loire's 'Prisoners of Conscience' window, the latest occupant of the Trinity Chapel east wall. Conservation has replaced restoration as the theme for the 1980s and 1990s; the monuments have undergone careful stabilisation, providing an opportunity for further study [Spring 1979]. The necessary renewal of stonework in the south-east transept has provided the catalyst for a stained-glass conservation programme, and the west front is once again the subject of major conservation. A new ethos and new protective legislation[27] make dramatic change far less likely in the foreseeable future.

38 View of the nave in 1995, looking east [BB95/5287]

Notes to Part I

1 The early 20th-century excavations of the cathedral church at Old Sarum have never been fully published. A report was included in *Proceedings of the Society of Antiquaries*, 1913, 1914, 1915 and 1916. The findings of Lt-Col Hawley's excavations were incorporated into the RCHME account [RCHME 1980]. For a recent reassessment, see Gem 1990.

2 'The Palm Sunday procession was, by the end of the Middle Ages, the most elaborate and eloquent procession of the Sarum Rite' [Duffy 1992, 23–7].

3 The tomb-shrine, with apertures, was probably located in the 'memorial court', the area around St Swithun's original grave in the middle of the west work of the old Minster at Winchester, a location that continued to attract considerable veneration even after the removal of the saint's remains to the area behind the high altar from the mid 12th century onwards [Crook 1993b, 59].

4 The monument was restored by Anne Ballantyne in 1972 and detailed records of surviving paint traces were made. A watercolour showing a reconstruction of the original appearance of the monument is on display in the Cathedral.

5 Both 18th-century plans of the Cathedral show steps at this point and around the high altar. Both are believed to be medieval by Tim Tatton-Brown, Consultant Archaeologist to the Dean and Chapter. I am grateful to him for his advice on this and many other points.

6 The shrine of St Swithun was only moved into the retrochoir in 1476 [Crook 1993b, 64]. At York St William was translated from the nave to a position behind the high altar in 1284. In *c* 1472 he was moved to an enlarged shrine which remained in this position in the new choir [Wilson 1977].

7 Information supplied by Mr R O C Spring, former Cathedral clerk of works.

8 Window STri13, in the south transept, contains panels of unpainted grisaille that have been releaded (in the 19th century?), but which may be *in situ*.

9 Abbot Berkyng's tapestries, given *c* 1246, depicted Gospel scenes (hung on the south side) and scenes from the life of St Edward the Confessor (on the north side) [Binski 1991].

10 Both Carter and Scott believed the monument to be that of Poore, although this view is contradicted by the inscription recorded by Leland [Toulmin Smith 1964, 262]. Bingham, on the other hand, is known to have been buried on the north side of the presbytery [Malden 1912, 343] and was acknowledged by Matthew Paris to have been the principal benefactor of the choir furnishing scheme [Madden 1869, 260].

11 At Chichester St Edmund's friend Bishop Richard de Wych (himself canonised in 1262) established altars to both archbishops at about the same time [Hobbs 1994, 20].

12 This position, paralleled at Canterbury, solves the problem of the location of the Holy Cross altar, which would have been immediately west of the screen. I am grateful to Tim Tatton-Brown for this suggestion.

13 No record of their discovery can be traced in the *Numismatic Chronicle* (information provided by the Department of Coins and Medals, the British Museum).

14 The eastern half of the nave roof and that of the south-west transept was probably rebuilt in the Elizabethan period. I am grateful to Tim Tatton-Brown for this information.

15 In the early 1630s, for example, the poet George Herbert frequently visited the Cathedral to enjoy the music [*VCH* III, 189–90].

16 Information supplied by Tim Tatton-Brown.

17 This explains the disappearance of the original door of the pulpitum. *SJ* (27 Sept 1779) provides the only documentary evidence of this work; 'And, the entrance [to the choir] being much enlarged, gives a grand and pleasing view of St Mary's chapel.'

18 Britton [1801, 55–6]. The window was exhibited in London at the Pantheon, where its novel construction excited the interest of an Italian traveller, the architect Giannantonio Selva [de la Ruffinière du Prey 1982, 25]. Other Pearson windows have been found to use this type of support-system (eg the portrait of George III from Windsor Castle, dated 1793 and copied from the painting of 1780 by Joshua Reynolds; now on loan from the Collection of HM the Queen to the Stained Glass Museum, Ely.

19 John Milner (1752–1826), bishop of Castabala and vicar-apostolic of the western district of England. Trained at the English College at Douai, ordained priest in 1777 and in 1779 appointed pastor of the Roman Catholic community of Winchester. The Roman Catholic chapel built at Winchester in 1792 was claimed to be the first ecclesiastical edifice built in the Gothic style since the Reformation. While in Winchester, Milner pursued his antiquarian studies, publishing an account of antiquities in the city [Milner 1798–1801]. In 1790 he was elected a Fellow of the Society of Antiquaries on the recommendation of Richard Gough.

20 The table had already undergone partial restoration in the 1820s, when its original top was replaced. See *Gentleman's Magazine* [1833, 297–9]. For Burges's work, see Crook [1981, 294].

21 The full extent of Philip's work is charted in Blum 1978 and 1996. Some criticised the extent of the restoration: 'in the new frieze there – which, by the way, has not more than half the figures of the old one gave the impression' reported *The Builder*, XXVI (1868), 473–4.

22 Scott had estimated that a stone screen built to his design would cost between £3,000 and £3,500, to include the remodelling of the organ [Scott 1870, 17].

23 This has now been moved to the chapel of St Edmund Rich in the north transept.

24 The screen was sold to Mr B Shergold of Salisbury in 1959 and was sold off in parts [Victoria and Albert Museum 1971, 59]. Part of it now forms the altar rails at nearby Alderbury church. The cross from above the central gable was retained by the Dean and Chapter. The gates are preserved in the Victoria and Albert Museum, forming the entrance to the bookshop (V&A, M4&a-1979).

25 Pevsner and Metcalf [1985, 279]. Parts of Scott's reredos were buried along the south wall of the cloister, where they were uncovered during drain excavations in 1986, together with parts of the screen [Spring 1987a, 102]. Further fragments were recovered outside the south wall of the cloister in 1994.

26 The Godwin tiles are said to have been buried in the grounds of the Bishop's Palace [Spring 1987a, 102].

27 Principally the *Care of Cathedrals Measure* of 1990.

· II ·

The Decoration and Furnishings of Salisbury Cathedral

Furniture and movable fittings

Altarpieces

The Cathedral was once rich in altar images. Treasurer Robertson's 1536 inventory, made on the eve of the Reformation, lists only the most important, but the list includes 'An image of God the Father, with our Saviour, young, of silver and gilt with gold, ornate with red stones' weighing 74 oz (2.09 kg), two images of the Virgin and Child, one perhaps a statue rather than a two-dimensional image and 'a grate ymage of the holy Seynt Ousmund, all of silver and gilt, ornate with stones of divers colours' weighing 83 oz (2.35 kg) [Wordsworth 1901, 160]. These three-dimensional images were probably reliquaries, serving a processional function as well as being revered on an altar.

Evidence for static stone or wooden altarpieces is scant. On the E wall of the chapel of St Martin is the faint trace of a painted 13th-century Crucifixion. The chantry chapel of Bishop Audley has the much defaced remains of a sculptural reredos of the Assumption of the Virgin Mary, to whom the chantry was dedicated.

Scott's marble reredos, executed by the firm of Farmer and Brindley at a cost of £1,800 [White 1921, 57–8], the gift of Earl Beauchamp in memory of Bishop Beauchamp, was destroyed in 1960 (see Fig 36) and the only surviving altarpiece of note is the triptych designed by Sir Arthur Blomfield with paintings by C E Buckeridge, originally made for the Trinity Chapel, where it was installed in 1896 [Wheeler 1901, 71] but now located in the chapel of St Edmund Rich.

39 The Trinity Chapel altarpiece, designed by Sir Arthur Blomfield and C E Buckeridge [BB95/5295]

Altars

The 13th-century Cathedral provided for chapels for thirteen altars (see Fig 1), a higher than average number for a secular cathedral, sufficient to allow the daily performance of mass by each of the thirteen canons whose regular residence was compulsory (a quarter of the full number of fifty-two). The exact positions of the high altar and nave altar are uncertain [Scott 1876; Armfield 1878; Rich Jones 1878], although it is likely that the high altar stood east of the Lenten veil, at the eastern end of the middle bay of the presbytery. The medieval Processionals reveal the existence of numerous subsidiary altars, dedicated to chantries, guilds, etc [Wordsworth 1901, 277–306]. The Beauchamp, Audley and two Hungerford chantries also contained altars. The medieval altars survived the Henrician phase of the Reformation, but their destruction was ordered in November 1550, their place to be taken by a simple communion table. They were restored in the reign of Queen Mary, but on the accession of Elizabeth were once again removed; in August 1559 payments were made for their dismantling. The altar stones were laid in the pavement in October of the same year [Wordsworth 1901, 307–8].

As part of his reorganisation of the Trinity Chapel, Wyatt lined the walls of the chapel with fragments from the demolished Hungerford and Beauchamp chantry chapels, using part of one of the tomb chests with a stone top as a new altar. This altar was found to be inconveniently far from the choir and was superseded by a draped table further W (Fig 32). In the 1930s the Wyatt altar in the Trinity Chapel was replaced, and the displaced 'altar', after a sojourn in the cloisters, was reinstated as the altar in the church of Fordington St George, Dorset [FOSC 1971, 8–10].

Scott provided the choir with a new high altar as part of his medievalising of the choir. This was replaced in 1984, having been badly damaged by arson [Spring 1987a, 102].

Only two medieval altars have survived; in St Lawrence's chapel, Purbeck slab (2.2 m x 1.0 m), with hollow chamfered N, S and W edges and roughly chamfered E edge. In the fifth bay of the S nave arcade, reused to form the top of a 15th-century table tomb (monument 83), reset in 1789, Purbeck slab (2.1 m x 0.8 m), but originally larger, with consecration crosses. The present high altar, designed by Alan Rome, former Cathedral architect, has a Purbeck altar slab, resting on Chilmark supports, the central one with carved decoration.

Barometer and thermometer

For many years a rare, very early 18th-century barometer and thermometer has hung in the vestry at Salisbury Cathedral. It used to hang on the W wall of the outer

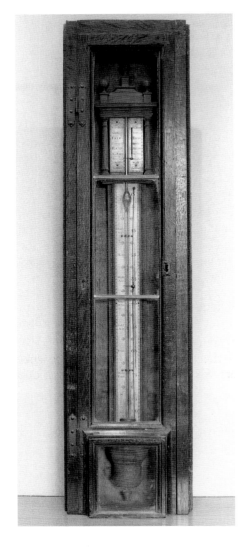

40   The early 18th-century barometer/ thermometer now in the inner vestry [Sarum D&C]

vestry, but was moved to the inner vestry some years ago for greater safety.

The barometer/thermometer is in its own case (almost certainly purpose-built for it, at the time of acquisition), which has a glass front door. The hinges to this door also suggest an early 18th-century date. The back of the case projects, and at the top is an iron staple for attaching it to a hook that was possibly originally set in a vertical slot in the wall. All the timber appears to be oak.

The barometer/thermometer itself is a 'portable barometer' which is similar to the barometers being made in London in the first decade of the 18th century by John Patrick. (The instrument appears to have no maker's name.) It has a portable cistern at the bottom, probably with a leather bag, and there is a screw device at the base to adjust the mercury level. This device was first used in c 1701, having possibly been invented by Patrick himself.

The scale for the barometer is marked in tenths between 28 and 31 inches (0.78 m and 0.96 m) in the usual way, and has its original sliding pointer. On either side are the now well-known weather indications, which go back to at least 1688. There are acanthus designs above and below, and the style is similar to other Patrick barometers.

On the front of the barometer is a sealed alcohol (coloured red) thermometer. It is marked in the very early 'Royal Society' scale, that predates the introduction of the Fahrenheit first scale in c 1709. At the top is 0°, marked 'Extream Hott' and the bottom 90° 'Extream Cold'. In between at 5°, 15°, 25°, etc are: 'Sultry – Hott – Warm Air – Temperate Air – Cold Air – Frost – Hard Frost'.

The top of the barometer is surmounted by three round ball-finials (not a more elaborate pediment design as in some Patrick portable barometers), and at the bottom the cistern cover is very much in the Patrick style. The instrument was probably made between 1701 and 1710.

John Patrick styled himself the 'Torricellian Operator' and was the first instrument-maker to specialise in barometers. Sir Nicholas Goodison points out

the scarcity of surviving barometers by Patrick and the great importance of his work [Goodison 1969].[1]

Bells

The ringing of bells was the means by which the Cathedral regulated its religious observance. Osmund himself stipulated their use and entrusted their care and maintenance to the treasurer [Rich Jones 1883, 12–13]. Bishop de Martival's statutes of c 1319 include instructions for the more regular ringing of the bells, the poor observance of which had had detrimental effects on the regularity of divine worship [Wordsworth and Macleane 1915, 360–2]. They were housed in the free-standing belfry that once stood to the NW of the church. In 1531 there were at least ten bells [Fletcher 1937, 610], although by 1771 the number in the peal had been reduced to eight [Walters 1927, 169].

Very little is known about the medieval bells of the Cathedral; a clock bell, morning bell and St Osmund's bell are all mentioned [Harding 1895], the latter possibly that for which 3s 4d was paid to Thomas Grey and John Brente in 1480 [Walters 1927, 173]. The former bishop's bell, hung in the S transept, with its recorded inscription '+IESUS NAZARENUS REX IUDEORUM' [Lukis 1857, 99;

41   *The Cathedral from the north-east, showing the 13th-century belfry demolished in 1790 [E Easton, 1761, Bodl MS Gough Maps, vol 32, fol 46ʳ]*

Walters 1927, 167 and illus], is the only one about which anything is known. It was replaced in 1854.

By the early 17th century the medieval bells were in poor condition and required attention. In the visitation of 1607, it was admitted that 'the officers of the church have not of late p'formed theire dewty by reason of the newe casting of our bells' [Everett 1943, 182]. In 1630 the tenor bell was recast [Harding 1895, 113] and at the Restoration the Salisbury bell-founder William Purdue made the sixth bell (see below). He received £362 for bell metal for those bells disposed of [Fletcher 1937, 611], suggesting that it was at this date that the medieval peal was reduced in size. In 1671 the seventh and eighth bells were reported to be cracked [Fletcher 1937, 611]. but nothing was done about it until 1680, when Clement Tosier and Elizabeth Fflowry were employed to recast them [Walters 1927, 173].

By the 18th century the bells were once more in need of repair. By 1746 two more bells were cracked and the peal was suspended until this had been rectified [Walters 1927, 174; Fletcher 1937, 612]. By the mid-18th century the belfry was surrounded by houses and shops and the ground floor had been turned into an ale house. The belfry, with its third storey intact and cluster of houses at its base, is clearly illustrated in the view from the NE, drawn by G B Jackson, engraved by John Fougerson and published by E Easton in 1761. The rowdy behaviour of the tavern's clients did nothing to endear the dilapidated tower to the Dean and Chapter, and in 1758 the third storey of the belfry was taken down [*VCH* III, 200]. In 1762 an unsuccessful application was made for permission to sell the bells, only three of which remained suspended, the other five being cracked and having been brought down to the ground floor [Walters 1927, 169; Fletcher 1937, 612]. A faculty for the sale of the five cracked bells was finally granted in 1777 and they were sold early in 1778 for the sum of £647 17s [Walters 1927, 169; Fletcher 1937, 612].

In March 1790 the sixth bell and the medieval clock were removed from the belfry, and were relocated in a new bell-frame in the central tower. The belfry was then demolished [Chapter Acts, 5 Feb 1790]. Early in 1793 the remaining two bells (numbers 1 and 4) were sold for the sum of £105 [Walters 1927, 169].

The surviving bells include William Purdue's service bell, 1.47 m in diameter, inscribed and dated

> FVSA ANNO REGIS CAROLI 2DI XIIIO AOQ DN1 1661 IMPENSIS ECCLESIAE WILLIAM PVRDVE R.T.:H.H.

which is mounted on the bell-frame of *c* 1790 in the third stage of the central tower.

Also in the central tower are the quarter bells 1–4 by J Taylor and Co of Loughborough, 1884. The Bishop's bell of 1854 is by C & G Mears of London.

Bishop's throne

Nothing is known of the appearance of the medieval bishop's throne. In 1672 Bishop Seth Ward agreed to pay Alexander Fort £60 for a new throne, according to a design by Christopher Wren [Eltringham 1958, 61–3]. Unlike the dean's stall, the throne does not survive, but was clearly highly decorative, carved with vases and palms. It is not clear whether the throne was removed during the choir restorations of 1777–9 or those of 1789–92; the latter is more likely. Wyatt's improvements certainly included a new throne (see Fig 32), praised by Britton: 'The bishop's throne, the pulpit and the canopies of the prebendal stalls, are all, but more particularly the first, beautiful pieces of workmanship, imitating what is termed the florid gothic style, and imparting a richly ornamental effect to the appearance of the choir' [Britton 1801, 61].

The present oak throne, with arcaded desk, diapered throne back and canopy gable decorated with Christ in Benediction, was designed by Scott and made by Thomas Earp of Lambeth in 1877, at a cost of £590.

Chests

Treasurer Abraham's inventory of 1214 includes six chests, of which one, iron-bound, was for the safe-keeping of charters and relics. Two other iron-bound chests are specified; one had been formerly used for the storage of the golden super-altar and another was in the treasury [Rich Jones 1884, 136]. In the 14th century, the Fabric Fund was stored in a chest in the treasury, under the control of two masters of the fabric; each master held a key to the chest and both had to be present to open it. In 1440 the procedure was tightened up and the dean and treasurer joined the masters of the fabric in joint responsibility for the contents of the chest [Edwards 1949, 234–5]. Hall's 1834 view of the Muniment Room shows that several of the chests described below once served to secure the medieval Cathedral's valuables; only the adaptation of the Muniment Room for use as a choir practice room disrupted this medieval arrangement.

There is no documentary evidence for the construction of any of the remaining chests at Salisbury, although in 1245 a silk cope was commissioned by King Henry III for the newly completed choir [*Cal Lib* 1240–5, 291]. This is an acceptable date for the surviving oak cope chest, in the N transept. The semicircular chest is 4 m in diameter and 0.8 m high. The curved frontage is formed of three main planks, with a much shorter one added to make good the length required. The three front legs are octagonal; two have shaped capitals, one is decorated with foliage. There are pulley blocks to lift the lid. It is the only surviving semi-circular cope

42   The interior of
the Muniment Room
(the medieval
treasury). Original
watercolour by
P. Hall, 1834
[Salisbury and
South Wiltshire
Museum]

43   13th-century
cope chest
[BB77/10044]

44   13th-century (?) iron-bound chest [BB73/7072]

chest in England [Hewitt 1988, 111–12 and figs. 10–13].

Also in the N transept are two iron-bound chests. The first (1.8 m x 0.7 m x 0.6 m), probably from the 13th century, has seven hasps, three locks, four padlocks and four links for carrying poles. The second (24 m x 0.7 m x 0.9 m), of oak, is possibly 14th century. The end styles are prolonged as legs. Both were formerly in the Muniment Room.

In the SE transept is another chest probably from the 13th century. Its original surfaces have been reworked. The oak styles are shaped at the base to form arcuated legs with pendants. There is also a panelled, 17th-century chest.

In the vestry is a cast-iron register chest, with panelled sides with lion-mask bosses, from the Bramshaw Foundry in 1813.

A medieval iron-bound chest (0.8 m x 0.6 m x 1.9 m) is chained to the NE wall of the Muniment Room; it has three hasps and staples. Also in the Muniment Room is an upright oak press (2.1 m x 0.6 m x 1.9 m), probably medieval, with ten doors hung on iron strap hinges. There are two other similar presses, but these are 19th century.

Clock

The earliest reference to a clock at the Cathedral is found in a settlement of disputes between the bishop and the citizens in August 1306. No person was to purchase flesh, fish or victuals before the clock of the Cathedral had struck one [Beeson 1971, 16]. Other articles in the same document describe how the striking of the clock marked a morning period for the transaction of market business. This is one of the earliest references to an equal-hour striking clock in Europe. It is not clear whether this clock is the same as the one described in a deed of January 1385–6 leasing a shop to Reginald Glover and his wife Alice on condition that they maintain the clock in the belfry of the canon's cloister [Duley 1989, 3]. This and the Salisbury clock's close similarity to the movement of the Wells Cathedral clock, first mentioned in 1392 [Duley 1989, 22], has generally been interpreted as supporting a late 14th-century date for the Salisbury clock, although some means of measuring the passage of time would always have been important to the Cathedral community required to observe the canonical hours. It has even been suggested that the

45   *The medieval clock. Probably late 14th century, perhaps as early as c 1385, the clock was originally housed in the detached belfry (see Fig 41). It was removed to the central tower in 1790 and remained there until 1931. It was restored to working order in 1956 [BB77/10057]*

appearance of a clock at Wells is a result of the translation of Bishop Erghum to Wells in 1388, and that the Wells clock, which also strikes the quarter hours, may be the work of the same clock-makers.

Until 1790 Salisbury's medieval clock was located in the belfry, where it chimed the hours, attached to the 'clock bell', the number six of the peal [Lukis 1857, 8]. In 1613 it had also acquired a dial [Harding 1895]. In 1790 it was moved into the central tower, where it remained in working order until 1884, when it was superseded by a modern clock. In 1931 it was removed from the tower and put on display in the N transept. In 1956 the Friends of the Cathedral, in consultation with antiquarian horologists T R Robinson and R P Howgrave-Graham, initiated the restoration of the clock by the firm of John Smith and Sons of Derby [Duley 1989, 4–8]. It now stands in the N-nave aisle.

The mechanism, made of wrought iron, is without a dial. The clock was designed with a verge and foliot escapement, although it had been converted twice to a pendulum escapement in the post-medieval period. The verge and foliot escapement was restored in 1956. It is now attached to the Bishop's bell and once again chimes the hours.

Doors

In the NE transept, at the foot of the NW stair (masked by the former pulpitum and accessible only from above), is a door with upright oak planks nailed to an inner layer of horizontal planks. The centre plank has a quatrefoil spy-hole. The door is probably 13th century, but the cover fillets may be later. There is a similar door in the SE transept.

The doorway from St Nicholas's chapel to the treasury vestibule, has inner and outer oak doors with upright planks nailed to a framework of diagonal intersecting battens. It is probably 13th century. At the foot of the treasury stair is a similar 13th-century door; its iron cog-bolt is perhaps of a later date.

There are two similar 13th-century doors at the head

46   *13th-century door at the head of the treasury stair [BB71/2618]*

of the treasury stair. The door into the Muniment Room retains its original latch plate, two original sliding bolts and a box lock with medieval key.

In the S transept, at the foot of the SW stair, is a 13th-century door with overlapping upright planks nailed to horizontal inner planks and with a later quatrefoil spy-hole.

The entrance to the library has a 15th-century oak door with keeled upright planks and hollow chamfered cover fillets.

At the W end of the nave are large doors with an intersecting framework from the 13th century. Exterior planks probably later. Engraved brass lock-case with crest of Bouverie, perhaps of secular origin, lock mechanism inscribed 'Taylor fecit 1722'.

At the W end of the nave aisles are similar but smaller doors, probably 13th century. See also *Piscinae and Aumbries*.

Hatchment

Reset in the S aisle of the chancel, immediately over monument 145 (to Mary Barnston), is a framed wooden panel (0.8 m x 0.7 m), painted with the arms of Barnston quartering Manning, differenced by a crescent argent, dated 1645.

The hatchment commemorates John Barnston [Dorling 1894, 314–16], canon residentiary, husband of Mary, whose monument is below. On his death, the crest above her tablet was knocked off to accommodate the hatchment, and the inscription on her tablet was altered accordingly. Both monument and hatchment were on the N wall of the Trinity Chapel until 1789 [Price 1774, 72]. The hatchment was removed to the triforium in the restoration of 1863–79 and was restored to the chancel aisle only *c* 1894.

47 13th-century doors at the west end of the nave, with lock-case of 1722 [BB73/7507]

48   Hatchment commemorating John Barnston (d 1645), reset over monument 145, to his wife Mary Barnston [BB73/5799]

Lectern

In the Middle Ages, reference is made to an eagle lectern located on the medieval pulpitum [Hope 1917a, 47]; no trace of this survives today. Price describes a lectern, made by Mr Sutton of London, given in 1714, at a price of £160 [Price 1774, 29]. This can be seen in Biddlecombe's view (Fig 19). The present brass lectern was the gift of the family of Dean Francis Lear (c 1850).

Organ

In the Middle Ages, there were organs in the choir, nave and Trinity Chapel. By 1539 the 'Great Organ' was positioned over the entrance to the choir. In 1635 John Burward was commissioned to extend the Great Organ and add a choir organ to it. It was this instrument that was dismantled in 1643, in anticipation of the Commonwealth Act requiring the demolition of organs (1644). At the Restoration it was reinstated by Thomas Harris and continued in use until 1710, when the Dean and Chapter commissioned a completely new organ from Renatus Harris, the first in England to have four manuals. On the evidence of the contemporary drawing of it by John Lyons (engraved by Francis Denning), it was also the most artistically distinguished of Salisbury's organs (Fig 28). Like so much else, Harris's masterpiece was to be a casualty of the restorations directed by Wyatt. In 1792 it was replaced by an organ made by Samuel Green of Isleworth, the gift of King George III in his capacity as a gentleman of Berkshire, then in the Salisbury diocese. It is now in the church of St Thomas [RCHME 1980, 30]. The location of the new organ in an alternative position was urged by Lord Radnor, in the interests of creating a more satisfactory vista, or failing that the commissioning of an organ with a less obstructive silhouette [Hollaender 1958-9]. In the event, however, the conviction that a substantial choir screen was necessary to reinforce the defective crossing prevailed, and the new organ was positioned on the top of Wyatt's new choir screen (Fig 31).

The present organ of 1876 is by 'Father' Henry Willis, the gift of Miss Chaffyn Grove of Zeals, with cases designed by G E Street and carved by Alfred Robinson. The problem of how to blow the organ prompted a lively debate, and serious consideration of a proposal to site a water tank in the roof. In the event, the structural engineer declared the weight to be too great, and a system of gas and air pumps was designed instead [Sarum D&C, Scott Papers, bundle 2]. It was altered in 1883 and 1892 by Sir Arthur Blomfield.

A small 18th-century chamber organ by Johannes Schnetzler was given to the Cathedral in 1958. Its case was made by the Cathedral works department in 1961. In 1986 the Cathedral was presented with a chamber organ by Peter Collins of Redbourn, Hertfordshire, with a carved limewood screen designed by John Roseaman and executed by Siegfried Pietszch.[2]

Plate and seals

Plate

The principal pieces of medieval plate include a chalice and paten of silver, parcel gilt. The chalice is 11.7 cm high, and was recovered c 1789, probably from the grave of Bishop Longespee (d 1297) at the W end of the Trinity Chapel (Fig 13). The chalice has a plain shallow bowl with tapered stem with knop. The base is partially missing, but was clearly decorated with foliage. The paten is decorated with the hand of God issuing from clouds. There are also two damaged pewter chalices, 9 cm in diameter, medieval, presumably recovered from graves.

17th-century vessels in use include a pair of silver-gilt cups and cover-patens without assay or maker's mark, c 1600. There is a silver-gilt London flagon of 1606, with a bulbous body and domed lid with ball-finial and thumb-stop. On the body are engraved the arms of the See. On the lid are the initials 'IL' for the donor, John Lowe, and his arms. Also on the lid is a worn maker's mark, a lion between a dot and a pellet, within a shield outline. A pair of large London flagons of 1610 are

49   *Silver-gilt cup and cover paten, c 1600 [BB73/5797]*

50 Silver-gilt London flagon of 1606, the gift of John Lowe [BB73/5790]

51 Silver London flagon of 1610, the gift of John Barnston [BB73/5785]

52 Silver-gilt alms dish, London, 1672 [BB73/5781]

inscribed with the arms of the See and those of John Barnston, the donor; they bear the inscription 'X dono Mr I Barnston Pbday de bishopston quem^m Rob Johnson bons senex istmnto dtavit'.

Two silver stand-patens of 1661, with London marks, are inscribed on the base of the foot 'Ex Dono Jacobi Hyde'. Two silver-gilt candlesticks, 66 cm high, with assay marks of 1663, have the inscription 'Ex dono Roberti Hyde Militis Capitalis Justiciai ad Placita Corum Rege Carolo 2° tinend Anno 1663'. A silver-gilt alms dish, 57 cm in diameter, has a London assay mark of 1672 and a maker's mark of initials 'T.L.'. Underneath is the inscription 'It weighs 80 1/2 ounces, whereof 20 lb was the gift of Dr Selleck, Prebendary, AD 1672, the rest was an old basin of ye church'. The treasury also possesses a continental chalice, perhaps German, of *c* 1600. It is silver-gilt, with a maker's mark P within a shield; it has a sexfoil bowl on an elaborate stem with three scrolled handles.

From the 18th century there are three silver-mounted vergers' wands; they are unmarked, but one has an inscription of 1712.

53   Seals and matrices
[BB76/7134]

Seals and matrices

There are seven silver seal matrices and one of brass: *S. sce. Marie sarebiriensis eccl. ad peticiones et ad cas.*, probably 13th century; *S. comune vicarorum eccles ..e sbriens*, original common seal of the Vicars Choral, first half of the 13th century; *Sigillum deccani et capitli Well ad causas*, 13th-century seal of the Dean and Chapter of Wells; *Sigillu. officii decani Sarum*, black-letter, 15th century; *Sigillum officialitatis iurisdiccionis deconaatus Sarum*, black-letter, worn, 15th century; *Sigillum officii peculiaris de Gyllingham 1664*; *Sigillum Thomae Ieames thesaurarii* (Thomas James, treasurer 1679–87); *James Stirling Samber subdean of Sarum 1759* (brass).

Screens

The pre-Wyatt plans of the Cathedral (Figs 14 and 15) show that screens were once a dominant feature of the interior, creating a compartmentalised interior quite unlike the present one, which still bears the stamp of Wyatt's attempts to create a series of open vistas. Gough's plan of the interior marks the position of the wooden screens that divided the retrochoir and transeptal chapels and suggests that the entrance to the Trinity Chapel was marked by screens. Most of these were of wood, one of them being visible in Carter's sketch of the 13th-century Purbeck marble tomb base when it still rested on the stylobate in St Stephen's chapel [BL Add MS 29,925, fol 128ʳ; Fig 4]. The choir was enclosed by more substantial stone walls [Price 1753, 65], into which episcopal monuments were accommodated at various times. During the 19th-century restoration under Scott's direction, traces of these walls were uncovered behind the choir stalls but have since been obscured.

From 1789 to 1793 Wyatt removed all the surviving screens at the E end, including the altar screen, those in the transepts, and the pulpitum separating the choir from the nave. The choir enclosure, already breached on the south side to accommodate the Radnor pew, was further undermined by the removal of the easternmost bays on N and S sides. Scott's attempts to recreate a medieval interior were largely undone in the 1960s, particularly by the removal of his choir screen and reredos; the choir remains open to view from the crossing, and the 19th-century grille behind the high altar allows an almost uninterrupted vista into the Trinity Chapel (Fig 38).

Of the remaining medieval screens, the stone pulpitum is the most substantial (see pp 175–8). In the W bay of the chancel, on the N and S sides, 14th-century iron grilles forming part of the tombs of Bishops Roger de Martival (d 1330) and Simon de Gandavo (d 1315) form part of the original choir enclosure. Between the eastern crossing and NE transept is a plain stone screen, 3.4 m

54 Iron grille of c 1330 on the de Martival monument (monument 13). The grilles contribute to the functional role of the de Martival and de Gandavo monuments, which form part of the choir enclosure [BB79/6310. B T Batsford]

high, with weathered coping; it is 14th century, with a doorway of *c* 1865. Between the eastern crossing and SE transept is a stone screen, 3.4 m high, with weathered and moulded coping and, on the S side, five niches, largely modern, but retaining 14th-century elements at the base; the doorway is *c* 1865. In the SE transept, to the W of the Bridport tomb, enclosing the vestry, is a screen incorporating 17th-century carved openwork rosewood panels; it was brought from India, the gift of Mrs Morris Fletcher in 1932. Between the N aisle of the chancel and St Catherine's chapel is a stone screen 2.7 m high, pierced by a window of three trefoil-headed lights; it is probably 15th century. The line of this screen is continued in the NE transept, by an oak screen of seven bays; the lower zone is panelled, the upper zone has cinquefoil-headed and ogee-headed lights; one bay has a doorway with a two-centred head; above, is a hollow-chamfered cornice with vine-scroll and brattishing; the screen is mainly 15th century, but rearranged; the cornice is *c* 1865. New screens were made for the S transept *c* 1924, as part of its transformation into a war memorial chapel.

55 15th-century oak screen separating St Catherine's chapel from the choir aisle.
The cornice was added c 1865 [BB73/7508]

56 The Radnor pew, formed in 1779 from the
chantry chapel of Walter Lord Hungerford, made
in 1430 by John Ewley of Bristol [BB74/4670]

The Cathedral retains some remains of the Skidmore screen, principally the cross that surmounted the choir entrance. Other parts have been reused as altar rails at Alderbury church, and the gates from the central choir entrance are now in the Victoria and Albert Museum.

Seating

In the SE transept, there are two plain 17th-century oak benches with two disc finials on each bench-end, perhaps formed from seats formerly in the E part of the nave; pieces of similar benches have been reused as boarding in the second stage of the tower.

In the presbytery, on the S, in the second bay from the E, is a pew formed in 1779 for the use of the earls of Radnor, comprising an 18th-century panelled stone base of three bays enriched with sickles (the badge of Hungerford) and cusped roundels containing shields of arms of Hungerford impaling Haytesbury, Peverell, Berkeley and Hussey, and of Hungerford quartering Haytesbury and Hussey. It had been used as a pew while still in the nave (the indented slabs had originally been set into the floor of the chapel), by the bishop in the early 17th century and subsequently by the bishop and mayor and later by judges and sheriffs during assize court sessions [Fletcher 1936a, 454]. It is reset on stonework of 1779, and to some extent altered, with an iron door and screens of the chantry chapel of Walter, Lord Hungerford, formerly in the nave (monument 52), made in 1430 by John Ewley of Bristol [PRO, SC 6/1119/9; Shortt 1970, 2]. The principal uprights are weathered as in stone buttresses; the plain intermediate uprights pass through moulded iron transoms at two levels, the lower transom enriched with quatrefoils and shields of arms (Hungerford and Haytesbury), the upper transom with quatrefoils. Above, is a moulded cornice of 1779 with shields, similar to the original, enclosing forty-six shields of arms. Charles Frederick's 1735 drawing of the chapel shows that the iron transom with shields was originally above that with quatrefoils, rather than below it, as now. The iron door, now at the centre of the S side, was originally at the W end of the N side and the original brattishing did not enclose shields [BL Add MS 27,349, fol 68]. Inside the pew, the plaster ceiling is painted with heraldry illustrating the descent of both the second earl and his wife from Sir Walter Hungerford, incorporating motifs found in the library at Strawberry Hill (Fig 29). It is furnished with six seats with ogee trefoil-headed oak backs, 19th century.

57   Detail of the heraldic cornice of the Radnor pew of 1779 [BB71/2483]

Stalls

Salisbury Cathedral preserves the earliest complete set of choir furniture in England. A reference in the Close Rolls of Henry III provides a date of *c* 1236 for their construction, for on 18 June in that year a gift of twenty oaks from the forest of Chippenham was made for the making of the stalls [*Cal Close*, 1234–7, 279]. This confirms the testimony of Matthew Paris to the effect that the stalls were provided by Bishop de Bingham (1229–46) [Madden 1869, 260]. They are characterised by carpentry of exceptional quality [Tracy 1987, 5–7]. The Rochester stalls are presumed to have been complete by 1227 when the community took possession of the choir. However, they were more or less completely rebuilt by Scott in the 19th century [Tracy 1987, 4–5].

The 106 13th-century oak stalls are *in situ*, although their foundations have been replaced and the desks and some of the sub-stalls have been renewed. The excep-

tionally large number of seats reflects the large size of the Salisbury Chapter. The four dignitaries were accommodated in slightly larger stalls at the corners of the choir (dean and precentor on the W side, with chancellor and treasurer on the E). By the time the stalls were commissioned, the Chapter consisted of fifty-two canons and four archdeacons and they, together with the four dignitaries, the sub-dean and the succentor, were accommodated in the sixty-two back stalls. In front, forty-four stalls were supplied for the use of the Vicars Choral. The choristers would have been seated on benches in front of the Vicars Choral, but these benches have disappeared.

The decoration of the stalls is of a restrained character. The standards are supported by columns with stiff-leaf foliage capitals and many of the mouldings are enriched with dog-tooth ornament. The stall ends are distinguished by the use of double columns, in some instances with dog-tooth ornament, and a large moulded

58   The south side of the choir stalls of 1236, with poppy heads added in the 1870s and acanthus finials (foreground) of 1671 [BB93/22088]

59   Lion misericord of 1236 [BB74/2727]

quatrefoil. The seat elbows are enriched with foliage bosses, some of which have additional figurative elements and some, notably that on the precentor's stall, have human heads in a naturalistic idiom not unlike the corbel heads in transepts and nave.

All but one of the seats have 13th-century misericords. With one exception they are decorated with stiff-leaf foliage decoration springing from foliage bosses that bear comparison with the vault bosses in the choir aisles. One on the S side is decorated with a lion set between two roses. The carver has split the lion's body to accommodate the wedge shape of the misericord.

The stalls were not originally designed to bear any superstructure; the present canopies are 20th century in date and in some cases the original 13th-century mouldings have been cut away to accommodate them. The stalls were originally backed by the solid wall of the choir enclosure, traces of which were noted by Scott during his restoration of the choir. The inner faces of the walls may have been painted, or decorated with textile hangings, as was the case at Westminster [Binski 1991]. The poppy heads are fine 19th-century additions.

In the 17th century the medieval choir furniture was augmented at Bishop Ward's expense, with Christopher Wren providing some of the designs. Master-Joiner Alexander Fort covenanted for the work in 1671 [Eltringham 1958]. The commission involved the raising of the level of the medieval stalls and their extension into the eastern crossing [Rich Jones 1878, 143 n 1]. New stall backs, a new stall for the dean (paid for by Dr Brideoak, 1667–75) and a new bishop's throne were also commissioned. Some acanthus finials on the lower desk ends survive from this period, together with the dean's oak stall, with panelled front inscribed 'decani 1672' and end finials in the form of hands clasped around oak trees, in a play upon Brideoak's name, now located in the NE transept (Fig 27). In the restoration of the choir of 1777–9 Wren's stall backs were removed and new galleried pews were added behind the prebendal stalls, reached by stairs in the aisles. Less than ten years later,

60   Detail of acanthus finial
by Alexander Fort
[BB74/2732]

61   13th-century oak table
with painted decoration restored
c 1855 by William Burges
[BB69/4395]

Wyatt replaced this scheme with a suite of choir furniture in 'florid gothic style', including new choir screens painted in a dark colour and a suitably splendid bishop's throne (Fig 32). This in turn was removed by Scott.

The present stall canopies were added as a memorial to Bishop Wordsworth (d 1911), but were not installed until 1925.

Tables

In the vestry there is a 17th-century oak communion table with baluster-shaped legs, ogee-moulded rails and stretchers in a Y-configuration, it is now used as a nave altar on occasions.

A circular oak table in the Chapter House is 1.5 m in diameter, with stout chamfered plinth and rail, shafted uprights and framework with cusped ogee-headed arches, formerly painted and gilded. It dates from the late 13th or 14th century. It was altered in the early 19th-century, when its top was removed, although a number of commentators deplored the work [*Gentleman's Magazine* 1833; Smith 1980, 15]. It was repaired and repainted on gesso under the direction of William Burges *c* 1855 [Crook 1981, 294]. In 1730 the table was recorded as being in the N transept [Markham 1984, 22], but by 1801 had been moved into the Chapter House, where it seems to have remained ever since.

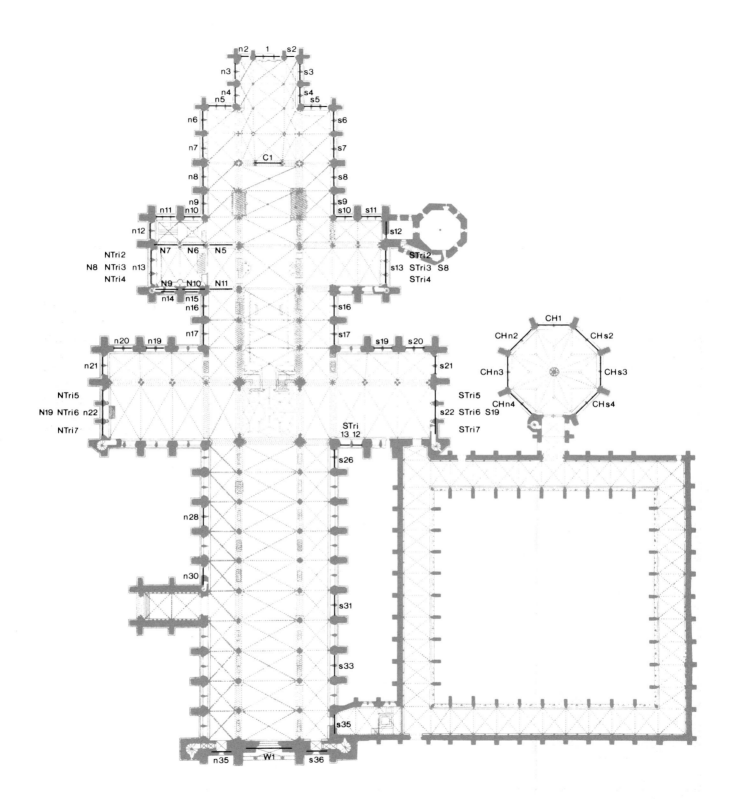

62 Plan of the Cathedral showing the location of stained glass

Glass

Survey

That stained glass once formed an important part of the original décor of the 13th-century Cathedral cannot be doubted. Windows are numerous, large and prominent. Indeed, many historians of the Cathedral repeat the legend that the number of windows correspond to the days of the year [eg Rawlinson 1723, viii]. However, the appearance of the original glazing of the church is now difficult to reconstruct from the greatly disturbed remains, which are now distributed throughout the church. As Charles Winston explained, 'the Inquirer who proceeds to Salisbury must therefore be content with an examination of little less than fragments, and to consume much time in the laborious process of unravelling [a] patchwork made up of glass of different designs and different dates' [Winston 1865, 106]. The impact of both Reformation and Restoration on the medieval glass of Salisbury Cathedral is discussed in greater detail below. The sad fate of so much of Salisbury's medieval glass has often been quoted; Winston, for example, recorded the

fact that during Wyatt's restoration 'whole cartloads of glass, lead and other rubbish were removed from the nave and transepts, and shot into the town ditch'. The glazier William Ranger, Winston's principal informant, had retrieved stained-glass fragments from excavations near the Chapter House [Winston 1865, 106]. Indeed, it has been as a paradigm of neglect and destruction that Salisbury is most often mentioned. Until recent years, and perhaps as a direct consequence of its poor state of preservation, little space has been devoted to it in the standard works on English stained glass, and even less in the standard works on English medieval painting.[3] This neglect belies the importance of Salisbury's stained glass, not just to the history of English glass-painting, but to a better understanding of the European picture. It was Charles Winston, preparing his paper for the Royal Archaeological Institute visit to Salisbury in 1849, who attempted the first scholarly assessment of the 13th-century stained glass of Salisbury Cathedral (published posthumously as Winston 1865). This remains the seminal reference work. In 1930 Canon Fletcher wrote

2 Feet

63   Drawing of the Tree of Jesse, window s33, made 1895 by Clayton and Bell [V&A, Dept of Prints and Drawings, B4a]

a valuable article on the Cathedral's windows that adds little to Winston's account, but provided useful information on the Cathedral's many 19th-century windows [Fletcher 1930a]. More recently the medieval glass has attracted fresh attention [Marks in Alexander and Binski 1987, 140–1; Brown 1992; Marks 1993; 1996], studies that confirm the international importance of the surviving material.

An appreciation of the surviving material is greatly enhanced by the evidence of the considerable body of antiquarian material dating from the 17th to the 19th centuries. 17th-century accounts include that of c 1610 by Nicholas Charles, Lancaster Herald, that of 1644 by Richard Symonds and that of Celia Fiennes c 1682–96.[4] 18th-century sources include the observations of Thomas Gray of 1764 and those of Richard Gough (noted on visits in 1769, 1772 and 1780) [Bodl MS Gough Wilts 3, fol 50[r]].[5] The 19th-century sources are by far the richest, notably the drawings of 1801–2 by John Carter, sketches of c 1820 by C A Buckler, drawings by C E Gwilt of 1836 (based on tracings of 1835 by C Nash), Octavius Hudson's drawings of 1843, Charles Winston's watercolours of 1849, a sketchbook of 1895 by the firm of Clayton and Bell and large-scale watercolours in the Cathedral's own archives dating from the time of Scott's restorations.[6] N J Westlake and L F Day published illustrations based on earlier drawings [Westlake 1881; Day 1897] and Lethaby published some observations [Lethaby 1926] at the time of the reorganisation of the W window glazing by Lowndes & Drury in 1922.

The surviving 13th-century stained glass comprises a small amount of historiated glass attributable to the eastern arm of the church, a greater quantity of painted and unpainted grisaille from the church and a smaller collection of figure panels and grisaille originating in the Chapter House but now located in the church.

The Cathedral church: the historiated glass

The historiated glass attributable to the church consists of parts of a Tree of Jesse, panels depicting the Adoration of the Magi, and the annunciation to Zacharias, all remaining in the Cathedral, to which can be added a panel depicting the martyrdom of St Stephen, fragments of border and part of the Annunciation inscription preserved in Grately parish church near Andover, installed in the church after their removal from the Cathedral in the late 18th century [Winston 1865, 107 n 1]. A case can be made for this figurative glass having originated in the eastern arm of the Cathedral and thus dating from the period c 1220–36. Matthew Paris attributed the glazing, together with the provision of the choir stalls and the lead on the roof of the choir, to the episcopate of Bishop Robert de Bingham

(1229–46), [Madden 1869, 260]. The church was consecrated in 1258 and the entire church, probably inclusive of the Chapter House, was said to be finished in 1266. Recent documentary research has revealed that the choir was probably ready for use c 1236, when timber for the choir stalls was provided [Simpson 1996, 11]. The iconography and style of the glazing allows an even narrower chronology to be proposed for some of the panels.

It is for the eastern arm alone that eye-witness descriptions of figurative glass survive from the period prior to major destruction and reorganisation in the late 18th century. Celia Fiennes remarked that 'the large windows of the church but especially the Qoire are very finely painted and large of the history of the Bible' [Morris 1995, 37]. While Fiennes cannot always be trusted as a reliable witness, Thomas Gray, the poet, has been established as an observant student of Gothic forms [Roberts 1993, 49–68], and when visiting the Cathedral in 1764, he remarked upon the figurative glass in the choir. Richard Gough noted in what is possibly a reference to glass, perhaps in the SE transept, 'there are many rondeaux of history paintings but obscured by moss and age' [Bodl MS Gough Wilts 3, fol 50[r]]. Comparative material is not plentiful in England, but the 13th-century windows of Canterbury and Lincoln Cathedrals [Caviness 1981; Morgan 1983] convey some impression of what a Salisbury window may have looked like, containing narrative scenes within geometric frames, surrounded by lush, densely coloured, conventionalised foliage. Four foliage borders survive and can be associated with the figurative panels. One can be paralleled at Canterbury in glass dating from c 1200 [Caviness 1981, 15 and fig 40]. Neither the Canterbury nor the Lincoln windows in their original arrangement combined historiated scenes with grisaille. At Salisbury, however, there is evidence that at least some of the historiated panels were set into grisaille, for Carter's drawing of the Salisbury annunciation to Zacharias associates it with one of the grisaille designs and one of the borders. The framing shape of the grisaille echoes that of the historiated panel, suggesting that this association was original [BL Add MS 29,939, fol 57[r]]. This grisaille pattern has no cross-hatched ground, unlike the majority of the painted grisaille designs originating in the Cathedral church.

Apart from Matthew Paris's attribution of glazing to the patronage of Bishop de Bingham, there is no specific documentary evidence for the chronology of the Cathedral glazing. It seems unlikely, however, that the Trinity Chapel and retrochoir, whose altars were consecrated by Bishop Richard Poore in 1225, remained unglazed until Bingham's accession. One of the altars dedicated in 1225 was in the chapel of St Stephen and all Martyrs at the E end of the S-choir aisle with a

64   *The Martyrdom of St Stephen, probably made for the east window of St Stephen's chapel, consecrated 1225. Now in St Leonard's Church, Grately, Hampshire [BB96/3932]*

window above the altar (s5). This window would be the most likely location for the panel of the Martyrdom of St Stephen now at Grately, identified by a Lombardic inscription STEPHANUS ORANS EXPIRAT. The narrative medallion is enclosed within a lozenge with foliage sprays at the corners. A stylistic comparison confirms a date of *c* 1225 for this panel; the treatment of drapery, with its fluttering lower hems, can be compared

favourably with the Becket miracle scenes from the Canterbury Trinity Chapel ambulatory of *c* 1220 [Caviness 1981, 163–4]. In common with the Canterbury scenes, the Salisbury panel relies on strong gesture, silhouetted against plain, dark backgrounds. The framing device used at Salisbury is paralleled not at Canterbury, however, but in the Charlemagne window in Chartres Cathedral of *c* 1225.[7]

The most substantial surviving section of historiated glazing is the fragment of a Jesse Tree now in the left-hand light of window s33, but located in the central light of the W window until 1922–4, when it was rearranged in the nave, together with glass from the Chapter House. Carter had seen it in the N transept. It had been moved to the W window by the time Winston saw it in 1849, having been moved there *c* 1819 [Winston 1865, 108]. Despite its heavily corroded state, the basic design of the window is clearly discernible. The figure of Jesse is missing, but two enthroned figures remain, surrounded by a vine inhabited by angels and prophet figures with outstretched hands and upturned foliage sprays from which leaves and small busts emerge. The upper enthroned figure has a crossed nimbus, a book in his left hand and his right hand raised in benediction, identifying him as Christ. The other figure can be identified as female and must therefore represent the Blessed Virgin. Both figures are seated on thrones with high, curved backs. A careful counter-change of background colours, with the enthroned figures set against red and the subsidiary figures displayed against blue, enhances the legibility of the design.

The Tree of Jesse, expressing Christ's genealogy in visual terms, was popularised by Abbot Suger at Saint-Denis in the 1140s [Grodecki 1976, 71–80] and was quickly incorporated into the iconography of the great church, appearing in England at York Minster before 1180 and at Canterbury *c* 1200. Its popularity persisted into the 13th century, with surviving French examples at Soissons, Troyes, Beauvais, Saint-Germain-lès-Corbeil and the Sainte-Chapelle in Paris. After Canterbury the Salisbury Jesse is the most important English example of the first half of the 13th century, although there are smaller examples at Westwell (Kent) and Kidlington (Oxon). An appropriate setting for the Salisbury Jesse, an iconography honouring the Blessed Virgin as well as her son, would have been the Trinity Chapel, the site of the daily mass of the Virgin and in effect a Lady Chapel. The original location of the York Jesse is uncertain, although Archbishop Roger's choir has been proposed [Zarnecki, Holt and Holland 1984, 136]. At Canterbury the Jesse is located in the Corona Chapel to the E of the Trinity Chapel [Caviness 1981, 172–4]. The heavily restored Westwell Jesse fills the E window.

Compositionally the Salisbury Jesse is very different from the earlier York and Canterbury examples, which are closer to the Saint-Denis model, with frontally disposed figures, seated on bench-like thrones, grasping the symmetrical framing vine with both hands. The Salisbury vine is arranged in vesica shapes that enclose the enthroned figures. At neither Canterbury nor York was the vine apparently inhabited by subsidiary figures.

In France the Jesse Trees in the Sainte-Chapelle and Saint-Germain-lès-Corbeil both have subsidiary figures of prophets, but they are enclosed in architectural niches, while the enthroned figures are seated on benches and grasp the vine. The Salisbury Jesse is unusual in having a vine inhabited by both prophets and angels. The thrones provide a strong architectural component to the composition and frame the seated figures. The standing figures in the vine balance lightly and elegantly on the vine stems. Their gesturing arms and forward-leaning postures convey a sense of movement entirely unlike the static *gravitas* of the York and Canterbury windows. In its lightness and grace, the Salisbury Jesse most closely resembles that at Westwell, recently dated *c* 1220 [Marks 1993, 140].

The absence of comparable material in stained glass makes a detailed stylistic analysis difficult, but it would seem that the distinctive features of the Salisbury Jesse Tree may reflect a specifically Salisbury painting tradition. This is suggested by a comparison of the Jesse with the work by a group of Salisbury-based manuscript illuminators led by the so-called 'Sarum Master', dated to the mid century [Hollaender 1943]. This illuminator and his shop produced manuscripts for the nearby nunneries of Amesbury and Wilton [Oxford, All Souls College, MS Lat VI; London, Royal College of Physicians, MS 409] and decorated a Bible by the scribe William of Hales for Thomas de la Wyle, Master of the Salisbury Schools [BL Royal MS I.B. XII]. It has been suggested that the monumental nature of this artist's work, particularly apparent in the Amesbury Psalter and Missal of Henry of Chichester [Manchester, John Rylands Library, MS Lat. 24], reflects the influence of contemporary wall painting and perhaps the original paintings on the choir vault in particular [Morgan 1982, 125; 1988, 87]. That stained glass made for the Cathedral should perhaps also be regarded as a formative influence in this illuminator's style can also be argued. In both glass and manuscript the figures display an elongated elegance and are clothed in drapery with troughed folds and fluttering hems. The figures share a light and dainty posture, with one foot turned at right angles to the picture plane and the other with toe projecting towards the observer. The Jesse Tree on the Beatus page of the Amesbury Psalter [fol 7^r] shares certain compositional characteristics with the Cathedral window; it is richly inhabited, and, although its flanking prophet figures are placed under simple canopies, it is similar to the window in its use of naked demi-figures emerging out of upturned foliage sprays. A comparison of the high-backed thrones in the window with that on which the Virgin sits in the Beatus page of the Missal of Henry of Chichester is also useful.

In its present form, with border, the Jesse Tree is too

65   *Window s33, south-nave aisle. Panels from the 13th-century Jesse Tree, perhaps made for the Trinity Chapel (consecrated 1225), with panels from the Chapter House and later fragments in an arrangement dating from 1922–4. [BB78/1074]*

wide to fit the central light of the Trinity Chapel E wall. It has been associated with the border design from at least the beginning of the 19th century, when part of it was in the nave and was drawn, with border, by John Carter [BL Add MS 29,939, fol 57ʳ]. Winston questioned the authenticity of the arrangement but finally concluded that the borders were original to the window. However, the foliage of the vine itself shows some signs of having been cut down slightly, a fact noted by Lethaby. The panels were subsequently set into the central light of the west window. No final conclusion can be reached as to the original location of this window, although the addition of the borders to a slightly cut-down window could account for the discrepancies in size.

At Saint-Denis, Chartres and the Sainte-Chapelle the Jesse Tree was accompanied by an Infancy and a Passion window. At Canterbury it was accompanied by a typological Passion window. In Beauvais the two lights of the window in the axial chapel unite the Jesse Tree and the Infancy. Of a Passion window no trace survives or was recorded at Salisbury, although there is some evidence for an Infancy window; among the Salisbury fragments

at Grately are traces of the Annunciation to the Virgin, while in window s33 in the nave is a cusped panel depicting the Adoration of the Magi. An alternative location uniting these scenes might have been a window dedicated to the life of the Virgin Mary, a suitable subject for the Lady Chapel. Another historiated panel in window s33, enclosed in an identical frame to the Adoration of the Magi, depicts the annunciation of the birth of St John the Baptist to Zacharias, a very unusual scene, attributable to an extended Infancy cycle, but which might also have originated in the chapel of St John the Baptist in the N transept.

The relatively poor preservation of the Zacharias panel makes stylistic analysis problematic. Comparison with the St Stephen panel does, however, reveal a number of significant differences, notably the different framing device, the absence of any explanatory inscription and the association of the historiated panel with a panel of grisaille which replicates the same framing shapes and has abandoned the cross-hatched grounds that typify so much of the cathedral grisaille but are absent in the Chapter House (see Fig 75). Corrosion has affected the

66   *The Adoration of the Magi, window s33, figures from an early 14th-century Crucifixion and angel medallions from the Chapter House* [BB78/1077]

drapery painting, and, while there are general affinities with the St Stephen panel, the drapery appears to be in a calmer mould, without the fluttering hem noted in connection with the St Stephen scene. These observations tend to support a slightly later date for the Zacharias panel, and by implication the Adoration of the Magi

67   The Annunciation to Zacharias, window s33 (c 1220–40) [BB78/1078]

scene which is related to it in style and frame shape. These panels could therefore be part of the glazing attributed by Matthew Paris to the patronage of Bishop de Bingham. On the evidence of the Carter drawing [BL Add MS 29,939, fol 57[r]], it would seem that these historiated panels were set into grisaille with foliage borders, in an arrangement that resembled the window of *c* 1225–50 at West Horsley (Surrey). It is in the years around the middle of the century that historiated panels begin to be associated with grisaille and foliage borders. The differences in date between these glazing phases may not be very great as the chronology for the eastern arm that can now be proposed brings the Trinity Chapel and retrochoir and the choir and transept chapels closer together in date than was perhaps envisaged by earlier writers.

The Cathedral church: grisaille glass

The collection of grisaille, both painted and unpainted, is one of the most important in Europe and adds very considerably to an understanding of the functional role and stylistic development of this kind of glazing. A precise chronology of it cannot be reconstructed, as it is all now *ex situ* and the original location of most of it cannot be established with any certainty. Some painted grisaille panels (Marks types 3B and 3E[8]) were sketched *in situ* in the W windows of the N transept by John Carter in 1801–2 [BL Add MS 29,939, fol 55[r]] and remained there until at least 1849 [Winston 1865, 108]. Winston saw two of the unpainted grisaille patterns in the E windows of the N-transept clerestory. Four other unpainted designs had recently been removed from unspecified clerestory windows [Winston 1865, 121]. A window in the W wall of the S-transept triforium (STri13) contains an unpainted interlace design, but as the glass has been releaded it is impossible to say whether it is *in situ*.

It seems likely, however, that grisaille was once the principal glazing mode in the choir aisles and nave, and that historiated glass, perhaps in combination with grisaille, was confined to those windows above altars. The evidence for the medieval glazing of aisles and nave is very scanty. References to these windows mention only

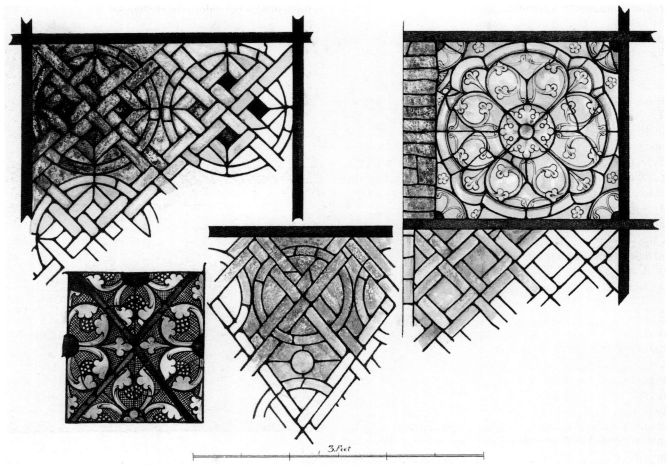

3.Feet

68   Drawing of painted and unpainted grisaille. Clayton and Bell 1895 [V&A, Dept of Prints and Drawings, B4a]

later medieval glazing, which by the 15th century had displaced the 13th-century glass in a number of places [Long 1859, 135].

Of the unpainted grisaille, five designs survive, and Winston recorded a sixth [BL Add MS 35,211, IV, fol 191]. Three of the surviving five, together with the pattern recorded by Winston, employ small amounts of coloured glass, introduced at the cardinal points of the pattern. The surviving panels are now concentrated in the SE transept windows (s13, STri2, STri3, STri4 and S8). This type of glazing was long believed to be confined to churches of the Cistercian order.[9] Recent research into both Cistercian glazing [notably Zakin 1979] and grisaille glazing in other churches has demonstrated that this type of glazing was employed wherever financial expediency or particular circumstances made it appropriate. In parish churches, financial constraints may have been paramount.[10] At Salisbury, York Minster and possibly Lincoln, it was used in a clerestory setting where its strong design was legible from a distance.[11] At Salisbury there may also have been a practical reason for this choice, for the vaults of the choir and eastern transepts were decorated with elaborate paintings that required adequate illumination.

The Salisbury patterns can be compared to continental examples; a variation of the design recorded by Winston (Marks 2D) is found in a Cistercian context at La Bénisons Dieu and Pontigny and in the Benedictine church at Orbais, all panels dated from their architectural context to the late 12th and early 13th centuries. The simple Salisbury interlace (Marks 2E) is also found in the York Minster nave clerestory (c 1180?) and was once found in the Augustinian church of St Jean in Sens (c 1230–50). The Salisbury 'fishscale' (Marks 2C) is paralleled in the clerestory glazing of the Swiss collegiate church of Notre Dame de Valère bei Sitten, together with a design very close to another Salisbury design (Marks 2A), dated to the period c 1209–35 [Beer 1956, 127]. A comparison of the surviving Salisbury grisaille glass with continental examples emphasises the preference of the Salisbury glaziers for angular and geometric patterns in preference to sinuous and foliate motifs.

The largest quantity of surviving grisaille at Salisbury is of the painted variety. Approximately fifteen designs or parts of designs survive; the fragmented nature of some of the panels and the subtle variations on a theme make an exact count difficult. Winston recorded the existence of between twenty and thirty designs. Grisaille glass has long been regarded as the poor relation of full-coloured and historiated glazing. To some extent this is true, for the glass employed was largely manufactured in England and was thus cheaper than the imported coloured glass used in historiated windows.

However, this view belies the complexity and sophistication of grisaille windows, overlooking the consummate skill in the cutting, painting and leading-up of these complex designs. The creation of so many grisaille designs suggests considerable organisational skills within the glazing workshop(s). There is no evidence concerning the number or nature of the glazing teams employed to glaze the Cathedral in the 13th century. Individual workshops were generally small, however. For particularly large commissions, several separate teams could be employed, or the Dean and Chapter could establish a large Cathedral studio for the purpose [Brown and O'Connor 1991, 24]. 15th-century references to glaziers at work in the Cathedral and the presence of a glaziers' shop above the vault of the Trinity Chapel supports the possibility that there was once a Cathedral glazing team, although this could well have been a later medieval initiative, established for maintenance rather than for the original glazing of the building. Each separate design required the preparation of a fresh glazing table for the layout of the design to scale. The complexity and diversity of shapes of glass to be cut ready for the glass-painter and subsequent assembly after firing would have represented a considerable challenge.

69 Painted grisaille of c 1225–58 drawn 1843 by Octavius Hudson. [V&A, Dept of Prints and Drawings, B3a, 4157.25]

70 Window n35. Painted grisaille of c 1225–58, with medallions of c 1260–6 from the Chapter House and arms of Thomas Ap Rice, dated 1569 [BB93/16177]

The grisaille designs contain many elements recognisable in the contemporary tile pavements. One grisaille design in particular (Marks 4A) resembles a tiled pavement, being constructed from a repeated lozenge motif, although it is also close to a grisaille design found at Lincoln [Morgan 1983, grisaille type 15]. Another design (Marks 4D) sets a quatrefoil design against a background of a repeated quarry with a foliage spray similar to a design found at Lincoln [Morgan 1983, grisaille type 2]. It was Winston who was the first to demonstrate that the Salisbury grisaille designs are for the most part of exceptional complexity and sophistication, achieved by the progressive superimposition of one decorative layer on top of, and overlapping with, another [Winston 1865, pl II]. The lead line is of considerable importance in reinforcing the design, and, although the frameworks of the design are essentially of a geometric nature, the cut-lines often follow the sinuous lines of the foliage. All but one

of the grisaille designs made for the church employ cross-hatched backgrounds. Most of the designs also use small amounts of coloured glass to accentuate and highlight the patterns. The evidence for the use of coloured ornamental borders with the grisaille is somewhat ambivalent. Britton indicates a plain glass fillet [Britton 1836, pl 26], while Carter and Hudson suggest an ornamental border [Carter 1845, pl LXXIX, fig R].

That the grisaille was important to the overall aesthetic of the Cathedral cannot be doubted. As a vehicle for the communication of a devotional message, its role was probably confined to those windows above an altar, although the glass was on permanent display, unlike so much else associated with an altar. The introduction of so much grisaille, which even in its present corroded state can still sparkle with a silvery light on a sunny day, can be interpreted not as a cost-cutting economy, but as a conscious decision to provide the building with a particular kind of illumination. A similar choice was made at York in the glazing of the Minster's new transepts in the period c 1240–50.

The Chapter House

The Chapter House escaped the 'improvements' of the late 18th century, although, by the early 19th century, the 13th-century stained glass was in a poor state of repair. Although Turner's watercolour of 1796–7 [RCHME 1993a, frontispiece] showing the Chapter House interior looking east, suggests that it ended the century with much of its grisaille glass intact, its decline thereafter was swift. Buckler's watercolour of 1810, looking W, shows four windows entirely plain glazed, with the exception of the heads of the main lights of the W window and the smaller compartments of some of the smaller tracery openings [RCHME 1993a, pl 47]. Carter's important sketches of 1801–2 and Cattermole's view published in 1820 show the E window in greater detail and confirm the identity and disposition of the shields of arms described in the 17th century by Nicholas Charles, Lancaster Herald (1610), and Richard Symonds (1644), and in the 18th century by Richard Gough.[12] No mention is made of any figurative glass in these accounts, but Winston's research established the disposition of the historiated panels, as he had had an opportunity to gather the testimony of those engaged in the removal of the glass only a few years before [Winston 1865, 111–15]. By the mid 19th century all the glass had been removed and resited, initially in the great W window and W windows of the N- and S-nave aisles. A reglazing of 1922 distributed some of the Chapter House glass in the right-hand light of window s33 in the S-nave aisle. G F Sargent's watercolour of 1852, painted shortly before the major restoration with which Burges was involved, shows the

71   *Window s33. Glass of* c *1260–6 from the Chapter House [BB78/1075]*

Chapter House plain glazed, and with the W window boarded up. In 1861 a completely new glazing scheme by the firm of Ward and Hughes was installed, which in very general terms re-created the effect of the medieval scheme. Two of these windows have since been removed.

The combination of surviving glass and antiquarian evidence makes possible a reconstruction of the 13th-century scheme. The figurative glass was confined to the tracery openings of each window. Each large octofoil contained a medallion with the figure of a bishop and a king under a simple architectural canopy. The single surviving medallion is now in the S-nave aisle (s33). The elongated quatrefoils below contained figures of vested figures of bishops, and possibly kings. Two of these panels containing bishops survive in s33 and Winston records 'a regal personage' in a similarly shaped frame lying in the glaziers' workshop [BL Add MS 35,211, III, no. 186]. This has since disappeared. In the flanking smaller quatrefoils were small medallions containing angels bearing attributes derived from the book of Revelations. These attributes are remarkably similar to those carried by angels in medallions on the vaults

of the eastern transepts and in the spandrels of the pulpitum of *c* 1236. Eight angel medallions survive, displayed in nave windows s33, n35 and s36.

The figure style of the Chapter House bishops and kings represents a larger-scale and more unruffled version of the Sarum illuminator's style. Faces convey a melancholy gentleness, with wide eyes, arched brows and downturned mouths. The posture of the figures, facing forwards, looking straight ahead, allows little variation or characterisation. None the less, the position of the feet, in a pointed-toe stance, is reminiscent of the elegance of the illuminator's style. Figures of Christ and two bishops at East Tytherley in Hampshire appear to be the work of the same glaziers.

The antiquarian accounts of the Chapter House clearly identify the original location of the six surviving shields of arms that are now glazed into the base of the W window and provide evidence of the existence of at least three more. These six shields – England (*gules three leopards passant guardant or*), France (*azure powdered with fleur de lis or*), Provence (*paly gules and or*), Clare (*or three chevrons gules*), Cornwall (*argent a*

72   Window s33. Angel medallions of c *1260–6 from the Chapter House [BB78/10976]*

73 The west window; arms of England ancient c 1260–6, originally in the east window of the Chapter House. Removed c 1819 [BB93/16163]

74 The west window; arms of Cornwall, c 1260–6, from the Chapter House east window [BB93/16173]

lion rampant gules, crowned or within a bezanty border sable) and Bigod (*or a cross gules*) – were recorded by Nicholas Charles, Richard Symonds, Richard Gough and John Carter. Additionally, the arms of England with an azure label of five points were recorded by Charles, Symonds and Gough, those of Warenne (*checky or and azure*) by Gough and Carter and those of Peter of Savoy, earl of Pevensey (*or an eagle gules*) by Charles, Symonds and Gough. Carter also sketched a shield in the north window not recorded elsewhere which apparently bore a 'blue-lyon' rampant on a white ground. This same shield was recorded in 1733 in a window in the library, where it was associated with a prayer for Chancellor Andrew Holes (d 1470) [Bodl MS Gough Misc Antiq 4, fol 24]. The insertion of this shield in the Chapter House may reflect the glazing activity of the 1470s recorded in the Fabric Accounts (see p 94). In the base of the W window is a composite shield with a 16th-century green demon surrounded by a 13th-century bezanty border. Winston speculated that this was all that remained of a differenced shield of Cornwall. Its provenance cannot now be established and it is not recorded by any of the antiquarians mentioned above.

The iconography of the Chapter House glazing scheme thus had a strong commemorative flavour.[13] The identity

of the bishops and kings cannot be established, but Bishops Herman, Osmund, Jocelin, Roger and Richard Poore would all be deserving of commemoration, as would Kings William I and Henry III. A reverence for the figures of the past and particularly the bishops of the See had already found expression in the translation of the bodies of Osmund, Jocelin and Roger from Old Sarum. Every day the obits of the Cathedral's revered dead were read out in the Chapter House. The provision of an elaborate pavement meant that burials beneath its floor were not envisaged; the windows ensured that the departed were present in an alternative form.

The heraldry present in the E window, which may originally have extended to the other windows as well, continues this commemorative theme. Carter's sketch makes their original appearance in the E window clear; they were arranged near the head of each light, set directly into the grisaille [BL Add MS 29,925, fol 81ʳ]. In 1958 Hugh Shortt proposed what remains the most plausible explanation of the significance of the shields, which he identified as representing Henry III, an established benefactor of the Cathedral, together with prominent members of his family and immediate circle [Shortt 1958]. Henry's own arms were accompanied by those of the Lord Edward (his son), Eleanor of Provence (his wife), Richard of Cornwall (the king's brother), King Louis IX (the king's brother-in-law), Peter of Savoy (the queen's uncle), Gilbert de Clare, earl of Gloucester, Roger Bigod, earl of Norfolk and John Warenne, earl of Surrey. Although Queen Eleanor lived until 1291, the other arms suggest a date for the glazing in the 1260s. The king and his brother died in 1272; Roger Bigod died in 1270 and his successors adopted the arms of the marshallcy [Wagner 1967, 116]. Peter of Savoy adopted the arms of Pevensey in 1241 and died in 1268 and at his death his titles passed to Prince Edward.

The arms represented in the shields in the Chapter House at Salisbury were mirrored in the sculpted shields carved on the spandrels of the eastern bays of the nave aisles at Westminster Abbey, carved between 1253 and 1260 [RCHME 1924, 53, 55-6 and pls 102-3]. Seven of the shields found at Salisbury appeared in stone at Westminster (England, France, Provence, Cornwall, Clare, Bigod and Warenne). The Westminster chapter house, completed by 1253 and glazed thereafter, had a glazing scheme very similar to that at Salisbury, with shields of arms set into grisaille [Lethaby 1925, 238].

The Chapter House grisaille now concentrated in windows n9 and s11 can be distinguished from the bulk of the earlier grisaille in the church by its abandonment of the cross-hatched background and the stylised bunches of grapes, although the transition to a lighter grisaille without cross-hatching had begun in the later phases of the glazing of the church. The painted foliage is itself lighter and looser in treatment, although it none the less remains conventionalised. By comparison, the grisaille in the Chapter House of York Minster, glazed c 1285, is already naturalistic. It is clear from both Carter's sketches and Winston's description that the Chapter House grisaille windows had decorative coloured borders (of which three designs can be identified), although the borders are simpler and looser than those associated with the windows of the church.

Three Chapter House grisaille designs remain in the Cathedral. A fourth was recorded *in situ* by Carter, but is now preserved in the form of a single panel in the Pitcairn Collection at Bryn Athyn, USA. In October 1850 Winston saw this panel in the glaziers' shop at Salisbury and identified it as the Chapter House design recorded by Carter [BL Add MS 35,211, III, no 180]. He also noted that 'part of a similar pattern is inserted in the great south transept'. Window s19 retains heavily corroded medieval grisaille, but until the glass is removed from its present location for closer examination, it will be difficult to verify Winston's statement. The panel in Bryn Athyn has been published [Hayward and Cahn 1982, 229-231; Corpus Vitrearum Checklist II, 1987, 136]. The panel was sold by dealer Roy Grosvenor Thomas. Carter's drawings

suggest a further three grisaille motifs and two more border designs, although the designs are shown in outline only [BL Add MS 29,939, fol 82ʳ]. This suggests that each of the seven Chapter House windows was glazed with a different grisaille design. Only two designs were copied by the firm of Ward and Hughes in the 1860s.

The figure style of the Chapter House glass, a consideration of the heraldic evidence and the character of the grisaille – freer and more relaxed than the darker forms in the church, but not yet naturalistic – all point to a date of c 1260-70 for the Chapter House glazing. Recent research on the tiled pavement has suggested a similar date and dendrochronological examination of the roof timbers has also favoured a date confirming the medieval statement that the Cathedral, including the Chapter House, was complete by 1266.

Panels of 13th-century glass attributed to Salisbury are preserved in the Toledo Museum, Ohio and the Victoria and Albert Museum, but, although made up of 13th-century fragments, the pattern into which they have been leaded cannot be substantiated as a Salisbury design. The Toledo and V&A panels were also acquired from dealer Roy Grosvenor Thomas. The V&A catalogue includes a note to the effect that the panel was made up by Grosvenor Thomas from fragments found in boxes in the Cathedral. However, there is nothing to suggest that the designs into which the fragments were leaded resemble an original Salisbury grisaille design. The Toledo panel has been published [Corpus Vitrearum Checklist III, 1989, 218]. Further fragments are leaded into small

75   Chapter House grisaille, drawn in 1843 by Octavius Hudson. [V&A, Dept of Prints and Drawings, B3a, 4157.8]

76   *John Carter's drawings of the Chapter House windows in 1801–2 [BL Add MS 29,939, fol 82ʳ]*

panels now in the stained-glass museum at Ely Cathedral and excavations in the vicinity of the Chapter House have recovered heavily corroded fragments of 13th-century grisaille since leaded into panels and now located in Winchester Cathedral and Boyton and Laverstock parish churches. Their poor condition means that they add little to the understanding of the surviving corpus.

Later medieval glazing

The evidence for later medieval glazing activity in the Cathedral is scanty, although it is clear that the original 13th-century scheme had been compromised by later additions. Almost the only survival from the later Middle Ages is the shield of Henry VII in the W window, said to have been removed from the S aisle of the nave [Fletcher 1930a, 241]. The heraldic character of some of the late medieval windows attracted the attention of Richard Symonds. On the S side of the Trinity Chapel, he recorded the heraldry in a 15th-century window, which included the arms of Popham and Zouche on a banner supported by a greyhound, accompanied by a donor figure [Long 1859, 129–30]. In the N-choir aisle was a window containing heraldry and an inscription to Archdeacon Sydenham [Long 1859, 135]; this was still legible in 1728 [BL Add MS 5,833, fol 145ᵛ]. In the 1640s another window on the N side also contained heraldry (*Gules a fess between four bars gemell argent. Per pale indented sable and argent, a chevron gules fretty or)* [Long 1859, 135]. The stained-glass memorial to Dean Gilbert Kymer (1449–63) has disappeared without a trace [Rich Jones 1881, 317]. Richard Gough, an 18th-century visitor to the Cathedral, recorded a fragment of an impaled shield in the W wall of the SE transept [Bodl MS Gough Wilts 3, fol 50ʳ]. His collections relating to the Cathedral also contain valuable evidence of the 15th-century glazing of the library and lecture room over the cloister [Bodl MS Gough Misc Antiq 4, fols 24–7]. Gough's source was fellow antiquary Smart Lethieullier of Aldersbrook, Essex (1701–60), who communicated the information to him in January 1750 [Bodl MS Gough Antiq 4, fol 37]. Ten windows containing heraldry and the names of canons were described in January 1733 (although the observer noted that all the windows had once been filled with painted glass), and suggest a glazing scheme dating from the time of the building's construction in 1445. It seems likely that this scheme commemorated the benefactors of the project, and, of the six identifiable figures, all were members of the chapter in 1445, with the exception of Bishop John Chaundeler, who died in 1426. Some impression of the scheme may be conveyed by the roughly contemporary scheme surviving in the library of Balliol College, Oxford. The Salisbury Cathedral library glass was probably removed *c* 1820, when it was reported to be neglected and the glass broken [FOSC Report 1953].

The Fabric Accounts offer no evidence of new glazing commissions in the 15th and early 16th centuries, but do record a continuous programme of maintenance and repair to both glass and ferramenta. A tiny number of glaziers' names emerge in this record; John Rolvys in the late 1470s and 1480s and Jasper Glasyer and John Lyne in 1517 and 1518. The repairs of 1479–80, directed by Rolvys, were extensive, affecting the Cathedral church, the library, the belfry, the Chapter House and cloisters, the only firm evidence that the cloisters were glazed. Glazing grooves survive and Burges noted 'some faint traces of painted glass which once filled the tracery of the arcades' [Burges 1859, 5]. As part of the same programme, Thomas Flege was paid for making 200 new glazing keys for 'St Osmund's Chapel', presumably referring to windows in the Trinity Chapel in the vicinity of the new shrine, and payments were made for new glazing bars in the Chapter House.

The impact of the Reformation

The immediate impact of the Reformation on the Cathedral's glazing is difficult to assess. The documentary sources suggest that by the accession of Queen Elizabeth a great deal of damage had been done; in 1558 the Fabric Accounts record that windows on all sides of the church required boarding up, an operation lasting twelve days. A chapel on the N side required 7 metres of new glass. Bishop Jewel (1559–71) took a personal interest in the renewal and repair of the Cathedral's glazing; the programme was a protracted operation. Ferramenta in the Chapter House and at the W end of the church required repair in 1562 and 1570, and in 1562 a case of Normandy glass was acquired. It would seem that during Jewel's episcopacy a Cathedral glazing shop was re-established [Fabric Accounts, June 1570]. In this period the glaziers were engaged on more than just repairs, however, for in September 1567 payments were made 'For making my Lord Bishop's Arms in one of the new windows in the south part of the body of the Church' and Richard Symonds recorded that 'The windowes in the body of the church are new glased at bottome, north side. Written thus in most of the windowes: Joh'is Jewell Epi'i. 1569' [Long 1859, 140]. A Jewel armorial, formerly dated 1562 [Winston 1865, 124] survives in window s36, with the arms of Thomas Ap Rice and the date 1569 in n35. He held the prebendal stall of Gillingham Major from 1555 to 1558. Despite Jewel's encouragement, however, the episcopal visitation of 1574 found that many windows were still broken [Frere 1910c, 367]. The Fabric Accounts chart continuing repairs to glazing in the eastern parts of the church in 1584–5. Work in the Chapter House continued until the 1630s.

77   Window n35, exterior view to show the glazing keys used to fix the stained-glass panels within the medieval ferramenta [BB93/22078]

78   *Window s36. Painted grisaille of* c *1225–58, medallions from the Chapter House of* c *1260–6 and the arms of Bishop Jewel (formerly dated 1562) [BB93/16181]*

The 18th century

Despite the losses of the 16th and 17th centuries, Francis Price recorded the survival of much painted and stained glass into the first half of the 18th century [Price 1774, 28]. The next period of serious iconoclasm was motivated not by religious considerations, but by aesthetic ones. The custodial attitude of earlier centuries prevailed for part of the 18th century, for in 1772 repairs in the S aisle of the nave were approved [Chapter Acts]. In November 1778 the Chapter considered for the first time the proposals for new glass for the E window of the choir clerestory [Chapter Acts]. The window, installed in 1781, depicts Moses and the Brazen Serpent, executed by glass-painter James Pearson after a painting by J H Mortimer, the gift of Jacob, second Earl Radnor. The window was exhibited at the Pantheon in London and attracted much contemporary interest, not least for its method of construction. Pearson's own advertisement of 1790 mentions a window 'executed in Mr Pearson's peculiar manner, the lead and iron being concealed, and the whole appearing as one entire sheet without division' [Knowles 1951-2, 46]. An Italian visitor who saw the Salisbury window on display at the Pantheon prior to its installation in the Cathedral recorded its unusual construction in his diary [de la Ruffinière du Prey 1982, 25]. Pearson's constructional leadlines broadly follow the outlines of the design, considerably enhancing the window's legibility from a distance. He also employed some pot-metal glasses, in addition to vitreous enamels.

In the more drastic plans for the Cathedral's interior that were soon to emerge, medieval stained glass was to be a major casualty. James Wyatt is normally accused of responsibility for this activity, but the oft-quoted letter from glazier John Berry of Harnham to Mr Lloyd of Conduit Street reveals that the destruction of medieval glass had begun before Wyatt's improvements were properly under way;

16 June 1788

Sir. This day I have sent you a Box full of old Staind and Painted Glass as you desired me to due wich I hope will sute your Purpos it his the best that I can get at Present. But I expect to Beat to Peceais a great deale verey sune as it his of nowe use to we and we Due it for the lead if yow want Eney more of the same sorts you may have what thear his, if it will Pay for Taking out, as it his a Deal of Truble to what Beating it to Peceais his. You will send me a line as sune as Posobl for we are goain to move ore glasing shop to a Nother Plase and thin we to save a greatt Deale more of the like sort wich I ham your most Omble Servunt John Berry. [Nightingale 1881, 226-7]

Subsequent stages in the process are charted in the Chapter Acts. In October 1789 the windows behind the Hertford and Gorges monuments were ordered 'stopt up in the inside' and new windows were ordered for the S side of the choir. Further orders for the glazing of thirteen windows in the S and SE parts of the church were placed, although the displaced glass was to be reused elsewhere. Substantial quantities of displaced medieval grisaille remained in store in the glaziers' workshop above the Trinity Chapel vault until 1896. That much medieval glass was destroyed can be inferred from both John Berry's letter and the testimony of Charles Winston's informant, who assured him that medieval glass had been 'shot into the town-ditch' and was used 'to level the ground near the Chapter House' [Winston 1865, 106].[14] John Carter described his own searches in the rubble discarded in the Plumbery: 'Here let the infatuated Antiquary like me, pore out for broken painted glass, funeral trophies. . . and all the 'off-scowerings' of professional improvers.' [Carter 1803, 642-3]. Some medieval glass was rescued – the Grately fragments were alienated at this time, and it is likely that Salisbury glass in museum collections around the world reflect the same process.[15]

To Pearson's clerestory E window was added another enamel-painted window depicting the Resurrection, designed by Sir Joshua Reynolds and executed by Francis Eginton of Birmingham, installed in the central lancets of the E wall of the Trinity Chapel. The side windows were filled with Eginton quarries 'having a dull red rose stained in the midst of each quarry' [Winston 1865, 126]. In 1792 the Chapter ordered that the Resurrection window be protected by an additional window and that the windows on either side, together with those behind the Gorges and Hertford monuments, be 'painted a dark colour with common paint' [Chapter Acts, 23 June 1792], presumably the thick 'reddish-brown ground' noted by Winston. The intention was to suffuse the choir with a 'solemn and dim religious light' [Britton 1836, 60], the 'sober light which befits a place of devotion' [Dodsworth 1814, 179]. This penumbral atmosphere was captured by Turner (Plate 5). Other windows, including the W window, were filled with plain coloured glass arranged in geometric patterns. Carter derided the 'large, ill-adapted, common geometrical divisions, in squares, diamonds, frets, etc, cut out of modern stained glass of plain colours, red, blue and yellow, sold by the pound' [Carter 1803, 1123]. These arrangements have disappeared completely, but presumably resembled the surviving late 18th-century arrangements by William Peckitt in St Martin's church, Stamford [RCHME 1977, 19b-21a].

Changing taste soon overtook the 18th-century glazing scheme. The Resurrection window was criticised for

79   Window s4, memorial to Bishop Thomas Burgess (d 1837). By Clayton and Bell, 1872, in 13th-century medallion style [BB93/22053]

'a theatrical stiffness' and an absence of 'dignity of expression' in the painting of the face [Britton 1801, 57]. Winston examined both 18th-century windows, recognising the merits of design and execution of the Pearson window, but questioning the suitability of the medium and style of the Reynolds Resurrection, which, unlike the Pearson window, used no pot-metal glass and relied exclusively on white glass and vitreous enamel [Winston 1865, 125–9]. In his consideration of these windows, Winston was touching upon the issues at the very heart of the debate underpinning the Gothic revival in stained glass, and, in his call for the use of more authentic materials in the making of stained-glass windows, he alludes to one of his most important personal contributions to the evolution of Victorian stained glass.

The 19th and 20th centuries

The Reynolds window survived until the 1850s. The geometric glass in the W window was removed in the early years of the 19th century. Between 1819 and 1824 the glazier John Beare filled the W window with armorials from the Chapter House, panels from the Jesse Tree and a collection of early 16th-century fragments purchased in London, some of which Winston described as from Normandy and some of which are said to have come from a church near Exeter [Winston 1865, 124]. The new arrangements were described in terms that would have surprised Carter: 'It is very appropriate to the elegant edifice in which it is placed, and the brilliancy of the effect cannot fail to satisfy the lover of ancient glass' [SJ, 7 June 1824]. The arrangement of medieval glass formerly in the E windows of the N- and S-choir aisles probably also dated from this period [Fletcher 1930a, 247].

The tide of restoration and renewal that gathered pace in the Cathedral in the 1850s had a major impact on the glazing. The first Gothic-revival window to be installed in the Cathedral was a five-light memorial to Dean Francis Lear by William Wailes of Newcastle, installed in 1854 to replace the Reynolds Resurrection in the Trinity Chapel. In 1933 its removal was already being contemplated, in favour of a design by Ninian Comper [Fletcher 1930a, 248]. In the event, it survived until the years after the Second World War.

With the exception of the 1861 Ward and Hughes glazing of the Chapter House, the Lear memorial window was to remain an isolated precursor of the Gothic revival in stained glass, for the main period of Victorian glazing dates from the 1870s and 1880s, coinciding with the major restoration of the Cathedral's interior directed by Scott. In this re-creation of the Gothic interior, stained glass played an essential part. If the Cathedral had lost much of its medieval glass, it could at least be filled with new glass in an appropriate medieval style.

Many of the windows pay conscious homage to the surviving 13th-century grisaille, while some, notably in the Chapter House and in the N and S transept (n22 and s22), are deliberate copies of medieval designs. Many of the major Victorian firms are represented at Salisbury, including Clayton and Bell, Ward and Hughes, O'Connor and Company, James Powell and Sons, Burlison and Grylls, and Morris and Company. Clayton and Bell contributed the greatest number of individual windows, although the work of James Powell and Sons has perhaps had the greatest impact, especially in the glazing of the NE transept.

The patronage of the Radnors continued to be important in the Cathedral's glazing history and was probably instrumental in introducing the firm of James Powell and Sons to the Cathedral. Powells had been employed by the fourth earl in 1879, for the E window of Alderbury church [V&A, AAD, 1/5-1977, 240], using a design ('Noli me Tangere') supplied by Henry Holiday. A reredos had also been commissioned [V&A, AAD, 1/5-1977, 264]. A year later the family commissioned Powells to make a window in the Cathedral to commemorate the countess [V&A, AAD, 1/15-1977, 385] with a window in the earl's memory in 1890 [V&A, AAD, 1/9-1977, 219]. The figures for both windows (s8 and S9) were designed and cartooned by Holiday, and are conceived in the monumental, classical style of his maturity, executed in pale 'art colours'. In one respect, however, Holiday found the windows unsatisfactory; the architect, G E Street, insisted that the figures be surrounded by panels of greenish grisaille, which Holiday found 'a perpetual eyesore' [Holiday 1896, 120]. His later Salisbury window (s31) was made in 1891 after the establishment of his own studio and glass-works at 20 Church Row, Hampstead [Cormack 1989, 5], where he was joined by William Glasby, formerly chief glass-painter at Powells. The window, with its rich, deep colour, achieved by using slab glasses of irregular thicknesses, reveals Holiday's increasing preoccupations with the qualities of his materials. The window was chosen by the artist as one of the illustrations for his book *Stained Glass as an Art* [Holiday 1896, fig. 10].

Holiday had succeeded Edward Burne-Jones as chief designer for Powells. In the S-choir aisle (s17) is an important product of Burne-Jones's later activities as a stained-glass designer, executed by Morris and Company, the firm for which he was sole designer from 1874 onwards. As with most Morris and Company windows, it was a collaboration between Burne-Jones, the designer of the figures, William Morris, who designed the distinctive foliage decoration and chose the glass to be used, and the skilled craftsmen and glass-painters who executed the window at the firm's Merton Abbey works.

80   Window s8, memorial to Mary, countess of Radnor, d 1880. Designed by Henry Holiday and made by James Powell and Sons [BB93/22073]

The cartoons were commissioned for the Salisbury window at a cost of £80 [Sewter 1975, 167]. They were subsequently translated into a pair of tapestries in 1894, with the addition of a pomegranate border designed by J H Dearl and both are now in the Victoria and Albert Museum. The design proved popular and later tapestry versions were made for All Saints, Brockhampton, Herefordshire (1902) and Eton College Chapel (1905) [Parry 1996, 290]. The coloured designs are now in the Fitzwilliam Museum in Cambridge. Sadly, the window, depicting the *Angeli Ministrantes* and the *Angeli Laudantes*, is partly obscured by the Mompesson monument and is not seen to best effect.

Another Powells window, in the N-choir aisle (n8), is the product of an interesting collaboration between the firm and an amateur glass-painter, Helen Mathilda, countess of Radnor. The countess first dealt with the firm in July 1898, when she undertook to glaze the chapel at Longford Castle with glass in imitation of the Cathedral's 13th-century grisaille. The firm provided glass-painting lessons and the necessary materials, and fixed the windows upon completion [V&A, AAD, 1/63-1977, 39]. Her next glass-painting endeavour was the more ambitious three-light window in the S transept of Britford church [V&A, AAD, 1/14-1977, 88, 131], made in the winter of 1898. Her greatest undertaking was undoubtedly the Cathedral window, in memory of her husband, the fifth earl, depicting four archangels, four name-saints of the family with armorials on a grisaille ground, begun in November 1900 [V&A, AAD, 1/15-1977, 62]. Despite her own clear description of regular visits to the Powells studio [Radnor 1927, 186–7] and the inscription in the window itself, which identi-fies the Dowager Countess as its creator, subsequent

81   *Window s31, memorial to John Henry and Henrietta Jacob. Installed 1891. Made by Henry Holiday in his Hampstead Studio* [BB93/22061]

descriptions of the window have doubted her personal involvement in its execution [Fletcher 1930a, 247].

Powells's most dramatic scheme at Salisbury was that for the NE transept. With the exception of a single window by the firm of Burlison and Grylls (n11, *c* 1886), all the windows at all levels of the elevation are by Powells, centred on the memorial to Bishop Beecher Webb (1901–7), depicting a vision of the Heavenly Jerusalem (n13), designed by J W Brown [V&A, AAD, 1/18-1977, 244]. The vision fills the main lights of the N wall, with complementary angel figures in the windows above.

Stained glass was chosen as the principal vehicle for the commemoration of the fallen of the First World War. All three windows in the S transept forming the memorial (s19, s20 and s21) were executed by Clayton and Bell. The somewhat uncomfortable juxtaposition of the three windows reflects the circumstances of the memorial's evolution. The original intention had been to make the N-nave aisle the 'Warrior Aisle' and two of the windows were installed there in 1920. The subsequent decision to make St Michael's chapel in the S transept the memorial chapel led to the removal of the glass to windows s20 and s21 in 1924 and the addition of a new window (s19) in that year [Fletcher 1930a, 252]. While s19 and s20 are rather unexciting windows, with a traditional arrangement of saints under canopies, the so-called 'Victory Window' in s21, designed by Reginald Bell, is a more inventive composition, with powerfully drawn figures and strong colour. The window attracted contemporary attention [Drake 1922] and was also singled out for praise in one of the few general survey works to include post-medieval English stained glass [Woodforde 1954, 63].

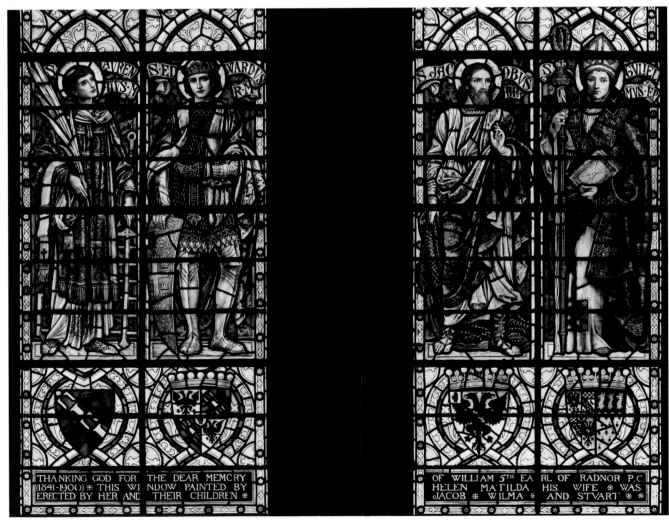

82   Window n8, memorial to William, fifth earl of Radnor (d 1900). Designed and painted by Helen Mathilda, dowager countess, and glazed by James Powell and Sons. Installed in 1902 [BB95/5296]

83 Window n13. Designed by J W Brown for James Powell and Sons. Commissioned in 1908 as a memorial to Dean Allan Beecher Webb (d 1907) [BB95/5302]

The Victory window exemplifies one strand in the English glass-painting tradition of the first half of the 20th century, developing out of the work of those Victorian firms who increasingly favoured late medieval or early Renaissance models as a source of inspiration. The single Burlison and Grylls window in the cathedral (n11), reminiscent of early 16th-century German glass, is another exemplar. This development is also expressed in the work of Christopher Webb. Webb's Salisbury windows (n5, s5 and n28) are characteristically lightly painted and rely on delicate decorative detail and pale colour. Another, more progressive trend is represented by Edward Woore's 1932 memorial window in the S-choir aisle, dedicated to Dean Page Roberts (n7).

84 Window n11, memorial to Isabel Kerr Hamilton (d 1886). By Burlison and Grylls in a late 15th-century/early 16th-century German style [BB95/5300]

85 Window n7, memorial to Dean Page Roberts (d 1920) and his wife. Made in 1932 by Edward Woore [BB93/15953]

*86 St Michael, engraved glass screen made for De Vaux College
by John Hutton. Now installed above the Consistory Court entrance
[BB93/16203]*

Woore was one of the most talented pupils of Christopher Whall, the leading artist of the English Arts and Crafts movement in stained glass [Cormack 1980].

Woore's own mature work was characterised by strong draughtsmanship and a limited but dramatic palette using slab glasses of intense colour contrasting with tinted white slabs.

The Cathedral's Victorian glass came under threat in the 1960s. Two of the Ward and Hughes windows in the Chapter House were removed in 1967 and were destroyed before public outcry put a stop to the work. The W window remains plain-glazed, although the E window was replaced in 1982 with a window by the Cathedral studio.

In 1980 the Cathedral acquired its most recent window, replacing the medieval glass installed in the Trinity Chapel in the post-war years (which in turn replaced the Lear memorial of 1852) with the intensely blue 'Prisoners of Conscience' window by Gabriel and Jacques Loire of Chartres. Broadly abstract in its design, close examination reveals figurative detail expressing the window's theme. Reception of the window has been mixed. While some have praised it for its homage to a French 13th-century scheme, others have criticised this very same colour scheme, questioning its suitability for its English setting [Dunlop 1980; Stephens 1981–2, 73–4]. The Chapter has also acquired a number of pieces of engraved glass. Laurence Whistler's memorial to Rex Whistler, a resident of the Close before his death in the Second World War, is in the form of a prism depicting the Cathedral in all Four Seasons, mounted on a rotating plinth in the NE transept [Booker and Dunlop 1990]. Above the entrance to the Consistory Court from the W walk of the cloister is a glass screen incorporating an engraved figure of a trumpeting angel by New Zealand artist John Hutton, best known for his ethereal W screen for Coventry Cathedral. At the time of writing attention has shifted from creation to conservation.

Inventory

The numbering of windows follows the system of the Corpus Vitrearum Medii Aevi. In the written account and on the plan (Fig 62), arabic numerals have been used in preference to roman. Grisaille types follow those adopted by Marks [1996, figs 3 and 4].

1, n2, s2 The Prisoners of Conscience, by Gabriel and Jacques Loire, fills all five lights in the east wall. Unveiled May 1980. This is the latest of a series of windows in this position. In 1791 all three were reglazed by Francis Eginton of Birmingham. The E window contained a Resurrection after a design by Joshua Reynolds, painted in vitreous enamels. The flanking lancets contained quarry glazing. This was removed in 1854 in favour of a window in memory of Dean Lear by William Wailes. The Lear window was itself removed after the Second World War, replaced by an arrangement of medieval glass formerly in the eastern windows in the N- and S-choir aisles. This has now been installed in window n9.

n3, n4 commemorate George David Boyle, dean 1880–1901. Twenty medallions recount the Acts of the Apostles, by Clayton and Bell, in a 13th-century style, with figure medallions displayed against stylised foliage.

n5 commemorates the poet George Herbert (1593–1632), rector of Bemerton 1630–2. A literal depiction of Herbert's poem 'Love-Joy'.

> As on a window late I cast mine eye
> I saw a vine drop grapes with J and C
> Annealed on every bunch. One standing by
> Ask'd what it meant. I (who am never loth
> To spend my judgement) said, It seem'd to me
> To be the bodie and the letters both
> of *Joy* and *Charitie*; Sir you have not miss'd
> The man reply'd; It figures JESUS CHRIST

Christ the Good Shepherd stands against a vine dropping grapes marked 'J' and 'C'. By Christopher Webb. Signed with his St Christopher maker's-mark and the names of his glass-painters, Frank Alban Pinnock and Thomas Walden. Dated 1953. Partly obscured by the Gorges monument [FOSC 1954, 21]. From *c* 1819 until 1946 this window contained an arrangement of 13th-century Salisbury grisaille and medieval fragments purchased in London [Fletcher 1930a, 247]. In 1946 Christopher Webb removed the glass to the Trinity Chapel and in 1980 it was moved again to its present location in s11 [Spring 1987b, 22].

n6 commemorates the laying of the foundation stone of the new Cathedral on 28 April 1220. Arms of those present or represented at the ceremony: Henry III, Archbishop Stephen Langton, Pope Honorius III, Richard Poore, William Longespee, earl of Salisbury and Ela, countess of Salisbury. Background of 13th-century-style grisaille. In panel 1a is a depiction of the foundation ceremony. Designed and made by the Cathedral Studio. Installed 1989 [FOSC 1989, 24].

n7 commemorates William Page Roberts, dean 1907–20, and his wife, Margaret. Old Testament scenes using slab glass in striking colours and a range of tinted whites: 1a Ruth and Obed with Naomi and Boaz; 2a Ruth and Boaz in the cornfield; 3a Ruth pleads with Naomi; 1b David's charge to Solomon; 2b David and Goliath; 3b David and Saul. Signed by Edward Woore. Made in 1932 [Cormack 1980].

n8 commemorates William, fifth earl of Radnor (1841–1900). Name saints of the family: St Lawrence, St Edward King and Martyr, St James and St William. Seraphim above. At base, arms of Bouverie, Radnor and Radnor quartered with Pleydell and Chaplin. Designed and painted by Helen Mathilda, dowager countess of Radnor. Glazed by James Powell and Sons. Commissioned November 1900, installed May 1902 [V&A, AAD, 1/15-1977, 62].

n9 A two-light window containing 13th-century grisaille, type 3G of *c* 1220–58 in panels 2a and 2b and one design of *c* 1260–6, from the Chapter House, removed from the Trinity Chapel E window in 1980 [Spring 1987b, 12]. Also from the Chapter House, a border design. At the base of the window, in panels 1a and 1b, are two early 16th-century Netherlandish panels: 1a The Baptism of Christ; 1b Abraham receiving the angels. The window now commemorates Charles Myers, canon and treasurer (d 1948) and Robert Quirk, canon and treasurer 1938–49.

n10 commemorates John Watts, rector of Tarrant Gonville (d 1872), and his son, Robert Rowley Watts, sub-dean (d 1911). The Presentation in the Temple and the Baptism of Christ, with angels above. By James Powell and Sons and stylistically related to other Powells glass in the NE transept (see below). Commissioned by Miss Watts in November 1911 [V&A, AAD, 1/20-1977, 49] and installed June 1912 [V&A, AAD, 1/66-1977, 214].

n11 commemorates Isabel Elizabeth Kerr Hamilton (d 1886), wife of Bishop Walter Kerr Hamilton. The Nativity, Crucifixion and Resurrection, surrounded by the Corporal Acts of Mercy. The Archangels Gabriel, Michael and Raphael stand at the top of each light. By Burlison and Grylls in a late 15th-century/early 16th-century German style.

n12 commemorates Morris Miles of Southampton (d 1908), and members of his wife's family. Depicts the visionaries of the Old and New Testament, SS John, Peter, Stephen and Paul and Jacob, Isaiah, Moses and Ezechiel against a luxuriant foliage background. By James Powell and Sons. Designed by James Cotton Powell, perhaps assisted by James Hogan. Installed November 1909 [V&A, AAD, 1/18-1977, 334].

n13 commemorates Allan Beecher Webb (1839–1907), bishop of Bloemfontain 1870–83 and Grahamstown 1883–98 and dean of Salisbury 1901–7. Depicts 'the Paradise of God and the Heavenly Jerusalem' (Rev 1: 8), and is complemented by the angel figures in ruby and blue in the triforium and clerestory windows above and to the E and W of it. Window N8, actually of angel heads, resembles medieval grisaille when viewed from a distance. The window was commissioned from James Powell and Sons in 1908 by the Dean and Chapter [V&A, AAD, 1/65-1977, 285]. It was designed by J W Brown [V&A, AAD, 1/18-1977, 244]. The triforium windows

(NTri2–NTri4) were commissioned at the same time. The clerestory windows which form part of the composition (N5–N9) were commissioned in 1910 [V&A, AAD, 1/36-1977, 170].

n14, n15 were the gift of Miss Louisa Maude Ottaway, in thanks for the weekly service of intercession; n14: the Assumption; n15: the Transfiguration. By James Powell and Sons, 1913 [V&A, AAD, 1/66-1977, 337]. The Powells' cash-book entry for £650 is dated 26 November 1913, and records a transaction with Mrs Webb of Embankment Gardens, Chelsea.

n16 commemorates Catherine (d 1883), wife of Chancellor Robert George Swayne. Illustrates Christ's words to the Apostles, 'Unless ye be as one of these' (Matt 18: 3). Background of 13th-century-style grisaille. By Clayton and Bell.

n17 commemorates Anthony Huxtable, archdeacon of Dorset and prebendary of Torleton (d 1883). The archangels Michael and Gabriel above Gideon's offering; the charge to fight the Midianites and Raphael and Uriel above Isaiah's vision and commission. By Clayton and Bell.

n19 Two lights removed from the S transept in 1924 [Fletcher 1930a, 244]. *Light a* commemorates Canon William MacDonald (d 1862) and depicts the Entombment, the Marys at the tomb and Noli Me Tangere. *Light b* commemorates John Douglas (d 1807), dean of St George's Chapel, Windsor, and bishop of Salisbury 1791–1807, and his son William, precentor and archdeacon of Wiltshire (d 1815), although stylistically it also appears to be *c* 1860. Depicts Christ's charge to Peter, his appearance to Thomas and the Road to Emmaus. Armorials of the See impaling Douglas and Ogatoun, with Garter and motto. Both lights by Clayton and Bell.

n20 Two lights moved from S transept in 1924 [Fletcher 1930a, 243]. *Light a* commemorates Charles Garland Verrinder, head verger (d 1879), depicting Melchizedek and David and an angel with harp. By Clayton and Bell. *Light b* commemorates Andrew Bogle Middleton (d 1879), depicting Christ and the woman of Samaria and Isaiah bringing water to the city. By Ward and Hughes.

n21 Two lights moved from S transept in 1924 [Fletcher 1930a, 243]. *Light a* commemorates Sir George Alfred Arney, Chief Justice of New Zealand (d 1883), depicting Moses receiving the Law, Moses bringing the Law to the people and the Sermon on the Mount. By A O Hemming. *Light b* commemorates Louisa Bowes Read, who died in childbirth in 1883, and her infant son, Sidney Bowes Watson Read. It depicts the dying mother and child and their reception into Heaven. By Ward and Hughes.

n22 commemorates Eleanor, widow of Dean Hamilton. Erected 1895 by her daughter Dame Katherine Hulse. Together with NTri5–NTri7 and N19 above, contains 13th-century-style grisaille, with armorials in the triforium and clerestory; NTri5 Mason, NTri6 Hulse, NTri7 Hamilton, N19 the Cathedral. By A O Hemming.

n28 commemorates the citizens of Salisbury who died in the Second World War. The arms of the See and the city with figures representing every branch of the armed and civil services. On the left, the archangel Gabriel with figures from the three branches of the armed services, with representatives of the Fire Service, Home Guard and Civil Defence; on the right, St George above representatives of the female services. Signed and dated by Christopher Webb, 1949.

n30 commemorates members of the Glider Pilot Regiment who died 1942–5. The Ascension of Elijah and Elisha and the city of Dothan. The badges of the Army Air Corps and the Glider Pilot Regiment appear at the base. Signed and dated 1950 with the compass mark of Harry Stammers.

n35 A two-light window filled with 13th-century grisaille in original 13th-century armatures. 1a–4a grisaille type 3E of *c* 1220–58; 5a angel issuing out of a cloud within medallion. From the Chapter House, *c* 1260–6; 1b–4b grisaille type 3E, *c* 1220–58; 5b angel in medallion, as 5a. A1 quatrefoil containing arms of Thomas Ap Rice, with 3 quarterings and 'THOMAS/ANNO 1569/APRICE'.

s3 commemorates Miss Mary Harley Fisher (d 1871). The Infancy and Ministry of Christ. *Light a* (top to bottom): the Annunciation, the Annunciation to the Shepherds, the Nativity, the Adoration of the Magi, the Presentation in the Temple. *Light b* (top to bottom): the Christ Child in the Temple, the Baptism, the Healing of the Sick, the Sermon on the Mount, the Raising of Lazarus. 13th-century style, on foliage backgrounds. By Clayton and Bell.

s4 commemorates Bishop Thomas Burgess (d 1837). Erected 1872. *Light a* (bottom to top): the wedding at Cana, the Way of the Cross, the Deposition, the Entombment, Christ's charge to Peter. *Light b* (bottom to top): the Betrayal, Mary and Joseph of Arimathea(?), the Crucifixion, the women at the empty tomb, Christ appearing to Thomas. 13th-century style on foliage backgrounds. By Clayton and Bell.

s5 commemorates Clifford Wyndham Holgate, chancellor (d 1903). The central light is almost completely obscured by the Hertford Monument. Outer lights contain angels and armorials related to Holgate and places with which he was associated; Henry III, Winchester College, Holgate, Longespee, Brasenose College, Wordsworth. By Christopher Webb (maker's mark), 1950.

s6, s7 commemorate George Morris of Downton (d 1884). s6: *light a* (top to bottom): the sealing of the sepulchre and St Mary Magdalene telling Saints Peter and John of the empty tomb; *light b* (top to bottom): angel unsealing the sepulchre and SS Peter and John at the empty tomb. Set against 13th-century-style grisaille. s7: *light a* (top to bottom): Mary Magdalene encounters the angels at the sepulchre and Christ displays his wounds to the disciples; *light b* (top to bottom): Christ meeting the Marys at the sepulchre and Christ and the seven candlesticks. Set against 13th-century-style grisaille. By Clayton and Bell.

s8 commemorates Mary, countess of Radnor (d 1880). Erected by her twelve children. Holy women of the Old and New Testament, dressed in classical drapery against pale foliage: the Virgin Mary, Mary the mother of James, Mary of Bethany and Mary Magdalene, above Sarah, Hannah, Ruth and Esther. Designed by Henry Holiday and made by James Powell and Sons [V&A, AAD, 1/5-1977, 385]. The window was installed in 1881 [V&A, AAD, 1/58-1977, 85].

s9 commemorates Jacob, fourth earl of Radnor (d 1891). Holy men of the Old and New Testament: Saints Joseph, James, John the Evangelist and Joseph of Arimathea, above Jacob, Moses, Joshua and Solomon. Pale foliage backgrounds. Also designed by Henry Holiday and made by Powells [V&A, AAD, 1/9-1977, 219].

s10 commemorates men of the Wiltshire Regiment. *Light a*: the Crimea War 1854–55; scenes from the life of Joshua. *Light b*: the Sutlej campaign 1845–6; St Michael, St George and the Centurion Cornelius (Acts 10). By O'Connor and Co.

s11 contains glass installed in the Trinity Chapel in 1946 by Christopher Webb and relocated here in 1980 [Spring 1987*b*, 22]. Composite armorials fill the base panels: 1a Old Sarum, 1b Bishop Ward, 1c Hungerford. The two outer lights contain 13th-century painted grisaille from the Chapter House, *c* 1260–6. The centre light contains a panel of unpainted grisaille of *c* 1225–58, type 2A, and a border design from the Chapter House, *c* 1260–6. There is also a collection of imported medieval panels of various unidentified provenances: 2b two unidentified figures; early 16th century; Netherlandish? 3b partial figure of St Christopher; early 16th century; French or Netherlandish? 4b fragmentary figure of St Augustine; early 16th century Netherlandish or French? 5b composite panel; nimbed figure offers a wafer to a figure in bed (head does not match body); early 16th century; 6b death of the Virgin Mary; early 16th century; French or Netherlandish? 7b Christ in Majesty with cross and orb, flanked by the Virgin and St John; composite, late 16th or early 17th century; 8b lily in a pot in a wreath, motto, 'Salve Sancta Parens'; by Christopher Webb, 1946. Beneath are two 15th-century quarries with 'Ihesus' and 'Maria'.

s12 commemorates Mary Wharton (d 1876). Martha greeting Christ and the Raising of Lazarus. By Clayton and Bell.

s13 A large collection of 13th-century grisaille formerly stored in the roof above the Trinity Chapel until 1896. Gathered by Canon Gordon. Installed at the expense of Mrs Hamilton and arranged by A O Hemming. Described by light (left to right) and from bottom to top of light. *Light a*: painted grisaille type E, *c* 1220–58; unpainted grisaille type 2A; painted grisaille type 3D and 3G, *c* 1220–58; painted grisaille type 3F, *c* 1220–58; painted grisaille type 3E, *c* 1220–58; painted grisaille types 3H and 3C, *c* 1220–58; painted grisaille type 3E, *c* 1220–58. *Light b*: unpainted grisaille type 2E, *c* 1220–58; unpainted grisaille type 2E and painted grisaille type 4A, *c* 1220–58; painted grisaille type 4A, *c* 1220–58; painted grisaille type 4B, *c* 1220–58; painted grisaille type 3D, *c* 1220–58; painted grisaille type 3C, *c* 1220–58; painted grisaille type 3A, *c* 1220–58; painted grisaille type 3G, *c* 1220–58. *Light c*: painted grisaille type 4E, *c* 1220–58; painted grisaille type 4F, *c* 1220–58; painted grisaille type 3E *c* 1220–58; painted grisaille type 3A, *c* 1220–58.

STri2 *Light a*: unpainted grisaille type 2A, *c* 1220–58 and a lattice of fragments. *Light b*: unpainted grisaille types 2A and 2C, *c* 1220–58.

STri3 *Light a*: unpainted grisaille type 2A, *c* 1220–58; unpainted grisaille type 2E, *c* 1220–58 and fragments. *Light b*: painted grisaille type 4E and unpainted grisaille type 2A, *c* 1220–58.

STri4 *Light a*: unpainted grisaille types 2A and 2E, *c* 1220–58, with fragments. *Light b*: unpainted grisaille type 2A, *c* 1220–58 and fragments.

S8 Four lights containing 13th-century grisaille. *Light a*: fragments of painted and unpainted grisaille, including types 2E and 2C, *c* 1220–58. *Light b*: fragments and unpainted grisaille type 2A, *c* 1220–58. *Light c*: fragments and unpainted grisaille types 2A and 2E, *c* 1220–58. *Light d*: fragments and unpainted grisaille type 2A and painted grisaille type 4A(?), *c* 1220–58.

s16 commemorates Leopold George Duncan Albert, duke of Albany (younger son of Queen Victoria) (d 1884). Jacob's dream and the sealing of the Servants of God and St John recording what he witnessed, from the Book of Revelation (7: 4). By Clayton and Bell.

s17 commemorates Captain George Eyre Townsend, RA (d 1879). Two of a planned six lights, depicting the Orders of Angels. These are the Ministering and Praising Angels (*Angeli Ministrantes* and *Angeli Laudantes*), in rich greens, blues and rubies, with some gold-pink. Figures designed by Sir Edward Burne-Jones, foliage in lower half of window designed by William Morris. Executed by Morris & Co [Sewter 1975, 167].

s19, s20 commemorate the men of the diocese who died in the First World War. Figures and armorials. s19 depicts David and Jonathan and Peter and Paul above Bishops Bingham and Poore and St Alban and King Alfred. s20 depicts Saints Luke and Dorcas and Saints Stephen and James the Greater; above Saints Andrew and George and Saints Patrick and David. By Clayton and Bell. Installed 1924, when glass now in windows n19 to n21 was relocated in N transept [Fletcher 1930*a*, 252].

s21 A two-light 'Victory Window', depicting the Crucifixion and Christ in Majesty. Designed by Reginald Bell, executed by Clayton and Bell, 1920.

s22 commemorates Dean Hamilton (d 1880). Like the matching window in the N transept, it should be read with the glass in the triforium and clerestory above (STri5–STri7 and S19). 19th-century grisaille in imitation of medieval grisaille in the SE transept (s13); S19 contains some very heavily corroded grisaille from the Chapter House. By James Bell (Bell and Beckham), directed by G E Street.

STri12 commemorates Elizabeth Jane Vaux. Installed 1911. St Nicholas by James Powell and sons [V&A, AAD, 1/66-1977, 214].

STri13 Unpainted 13th-century grisaille (type 3, *c* 1225–58), possibly *in situ*, albeit releaded.

s26 commemorates Dr William Martin Coates (d 1886). The healing of the Centurion's servant, the healing of the widow of Nain's son, the healing of the woman with an issue of blood and the healing of Jairus's daughter. Intervening panels of 13th-century-style foliage. By Clayton and Bell.

s31 commemorates John Henry Jacob and Henrietta, his wife. Inscription dated 1890. Christ blessing the children. Designed by Henry Holiday and made in his Hampstead Studio, supervised by William Glasby, formerly chief glass-painter at Powells [Hadley and Hadley 1991, 53]. Installed 1891 [Hadley and Hadley 61].

s33 contains an important collection of medieval glass, some from the Chapter House and some from the Cathedral church. In 1819 much of this glass was in the W window, but was moved and rearranged here in 1922-4 by Lowndes and Drury, in memory of Canon Gordon. The two lights preserve two 13th-century foliage border types, type 4H of c 1225-58 and one of c 1260-6 from the Chapter House. *Light a* contains the remains of a 13th-century Tree of Jesse, c 1225. Oval vine stems enclose the enthroned figure of Christ in Benediction, flanked by censing angels, and the enthroned Virgin Mary flanked by prophets. The two vesica shapes are separated by two demi figures emerging from foliage. The Jesse Tree may have originated in the Trinity Chapel. *Light b* contains figurative glass from both church and Chapter House. At the apex is a cusped medallion containing the annunciation to Zacharias in the Temple (c 1225-40). Beneath is a large medallion containing a bishop and a king beneath a canopy from the Chapter House (c 1260-6). Below is a medallion containing an angel in benediction emerging from clouds, two bishops in elongated cusped lozenges and a further three angels in medallions (c 1260-6), all from the Chapter House. Below, to the left, a fragmented figure dressed in ruby glass, with arm raised holding a sword(?) – part of the martyrdom of a saint (?); to the right, two fragmented kneeling figures, all early 13th century. Below is a further cusped medallion containing the Adoration of the Magi (c 1225-40) flanked by early 14th-century figures of the sorrowing Virgin and St John, probably from a Crucifixion. At the lower corners of the light are two more angel medallions from the Chapter House, one censing and one holding a crown. At the base of the panel is a partial unit of grisaille type 4D, c 1225-58.

s35 commemorates John Charles Brown Angell (d 1879), and Sophia Patterson Angell (d 1874). Manoah and Hannah. By James Powell and Sons. Installed in 1911 [V&A, AAD, 1/66-1977, 137].

s36 two lights containing 13th-century grisaille type 3B, c 1225-58. At the apex of each light is a medallion containing an angel, formerly in the Chapter House, c 1260-6. In the tracery quatrefoil, a 16th-century armorial of Bishop Jewel within a wreath (formerly dated 1562) and 'IOANNES IEWELL/ANNO .../EPISCOP SAR'.

C1 The E window of the choir clerestory is the only choir clerestory window now containing stained glass. Moses and the Brazen serpent, designed by J H Mortimer, painted in enamels on a mixture of clear and pot-metal glass by James Pearson. The gift of Jacob, second earl of Radnor, whose arms once appeared at the apex of the window (removed 1874). The glass is supported on a shaped iron armature [FOSC 1979, 22-4]. The shaped iron frames were characteristic of Pearson's windows. Surviving examples include the St Peter window (formerly the E window) in the N triforium of Ely Cathedral (c 1770); the Agony in the Garden in St Botolph's, Aldersgate, in the City of London (1788) and the portrait of George III from Windsor Castle, on loan to the Stained Glass Museum at Ely (1793).

W1 contains an arrangement of medieval glass, much of it of foreign origin, first assembled in 1819 by the Cathedral glazier

John Beare. Rearranged and releaded 1924 by Lowndes and Drury. The four figures under canopies, two with scrolls in French, are probably from a single French source, possibly Rouen or Dijon [Fletcher 1930a, 242]. Other panels are said to be from in or near Exeter [Winston 1865, 124]. 1a The arms of Clare, c 1260-6; from the Chapter House; composite shield with bezanty border; field made up of fragments, including demon. 2a St Barbara under a canopy; 16th century; French? 3a Composite medallion of reclining figures; 16th century; French or Netherlandish? 4a St Anthony (?), praying before the Cross; early 16th century; French? 5a Unidentified figure and fragments within a medallion; 16th century. 6a Composite figure and St Peter; 16th century; French? 1b Arms of Provence and arms of England ancient; both c 1260-6, from the Chapter House. 2b An arrangement of five cusped tracery panels set against background of 13th-century foliage; two scenes from the legend of the finding of the True Cross, the Crucifixion and two angels with Passion instruments; all early 16th century; said to be French [Winston 1865, 124]. 3b Enthroned Archbishop in benediction; putti at his feet; 16th century, continental. 4b medallion with St Peter vested as a pope; 14th century, French or English. 5b Composite Crucifixion with the Virgin and St John and two unidentified flanking figures; 16th century. 6b Christ in Majesty in a mandorla, supported by apostles(?); 16th century, Netherlandish? 7b Arms of England within a garter; dated 1506. 1c Arms of Richard, earl of Cornwall, and Roger Bigod, earl of Norfolk; c 1260-6, from the Chapter House. 2c St Catherine; companion figure to 2a. 3c Medallion of the Betrayal of Christ; 16th century, French or Netherlandish. 4c St Anthony; companion figure to 4a. 5c Medallion with one figure leading another (the damned led by a demon?); 13th century, English. 6c Composite figure of a bishop in benediction; 16th century. The two outer lights are framed with sections of border from the Chapter House, c 1260-6, while the central light is framed in border type 4H of c 1220-58.

The Chapter House

After the removal of the remaining medieval glass in c 1819, (see windows s33, s36 and n35), the windows of the Chapter House were all filled with a scheme of grisaille glazing by Ward and Hughes, installed in 1861. The new windows emulated the medieval grisaille patterns and original arrangement; each one contains foliage grisaille in the main lights, with a figurative medallion of a bishop and king in the main tracery octfoil, and bishops in the elongated lozenges below. The lower quatrefoils contain smaller medallions with angels emerging from clouds. The scheme is a remarkably harmonious and sympathetic one, preserving the aesthetic effect intended by the medieval designer of the Chapter House glazing.

In 1967 two of these windows (the E and W) were removed. The outcry was sufficient to stop further removal and a general programme of repair was instituted instead. The window over the entrance has remained plain-glazed, but the E window was filled in 1982 by the Cathedral glaziers, and now commemorates the National Farmers' Union and, in broad terms, reproduces the pattern of the Ward and Hughes window it replaces.

Monuments, Floor Slabs, Coffins and Brasses and Indents

Survey

Salisbury Cathedral is not, perhaps, most renowned for its funerary monuments, although it is possessed of a large number. Their quality is variable and their condition often poor. This is particularly true of those medieval monuments disturbed and repositioned by Wyatt in the 18th century. Indeed, Wyatt's decision to remove most of the monuments from the E end to the nave, where they were repositioned in orderly lines under the arcade, has exacerbated the problems of identification and assessment of the original patterns of burial in the medieval Cathedral. Some monuments were actually destroyed as a result of the 'improvements'; the rebuilt monument variously attributed to Bishops Poore and de Bingham (10) was effectively demolished in the 18th century, only the original coffin lid and effigy being preserved. The tomb chest of Bishop Beauchamp and the tombs of his parents and brother, formerly in the Beauchamp chantry chapel, were lost. The canopies over the tombs of Sir John Cheney and Sir Robert Hungerford were also lost, and their tomb chests are now made up of second-hand fragments. It was the cavalier treatment of the monuments that excited some of the fiercest criticism of Wyatt [Milner 1798; Carter 1803]. Wyatt was not, however, solely responsible for the disturbance of medieval monuments. Some interference in the original disposition of medieval monuments can be attributed to late medieval activity. The construction of the Hungerford and Beauchamp chantry chapels on either side of the Trinity Chapel, with their entrances in its N and S walls, caused other monuments, notably that of Sir John Montacute formerly against the N wall of the Trinity Chapel (57), to be moved. Those slabs now presumed to represent Bishops Roger and Osmund had already been moved from the Trinity Chapel into the S aisle of the nave by the time Leland visited the Cathedral in 1542 [Toulmin Smith 1964, 265; Chandler 1993, xxvii], only to be moved into their present location in the north aisle, perhaps c 1676–7 when seating was introduced in the nave [Wordsworth 1915, 46–50]. Visiting the Cathedral in 1644, Captain Symonds remarked upon the paucity of floor slabs and brasses, most of which had been robbed [Long 1859, 140]. The monument of the so-called 'Boy-Bishop' (62) in the nave had also been disturbed [Price 1774, 65]. Further disturbance occurred as a result of the repaving of the choir in 1684, when those memorials in the chancel pavement were resited in the NE transept. In the 1770s the iron enclosure of the Hungerford chantry in the N-nave aisle was dismantled and moved to the choir (see p 73), leaving the slabs and indents to be raised by Wyatt onto a chest of second-hand materials. Further losses of floor slabs were sustained as a result of Wyatt's policy of cutting them up to repave the Cathedral, and a number of ledger stones, some with indents for brasses, were obscured when medieval monuments were resited on top of them in the nave arcade [Spring 1979]. Turner's evocative watercolour of the Chapter House and vestibule prior to its restoration in the 1850s shows a number of carved stones set into the vestibule pavement [RCHME 1993a, frontispiece]. These were presumably removed when the vestibule floor was renewed.

Attempts to reconstruct the original disposition of the Cathedral's medieval monuments are aided by the existence of a number of 18th-century plans of the interior, pre-dating Wyatt's work, and marking the position of the most important monuments. The best known is that published in 1796 by Richard Gough in his seminal work *Sepulchral Monuments in Great Britain*, although comparison of this plan with the original drawing in the Bodleian Library [Gough 1796, II, pt 2, pl xxxix; cf Fig 15] reveals that the engraver made a number of mistakes in preparing a version for publication, principally the transposition of the monuments in the transepts. Gough acquired the original 'among some papers of Mr Vertue'. In 1740, on a visit to Salisbury, Vertue was shown a new plan of the Cathedral commissioned by Bishop Sherlock, probably made under the direction of Price [Walpole Society 1937–8, 129]. Also of considerable importance is the 'Ichnographical Plan of the Cathedral Church of Salisbury' (Fig 14) preserved in the British Library [BL King's Top Coll XLIII, fol 39], dating from the period after 1696 and before 1745. This plan may be Bishop Sherlock's original. How it came into the possession of King George III is not known. It was

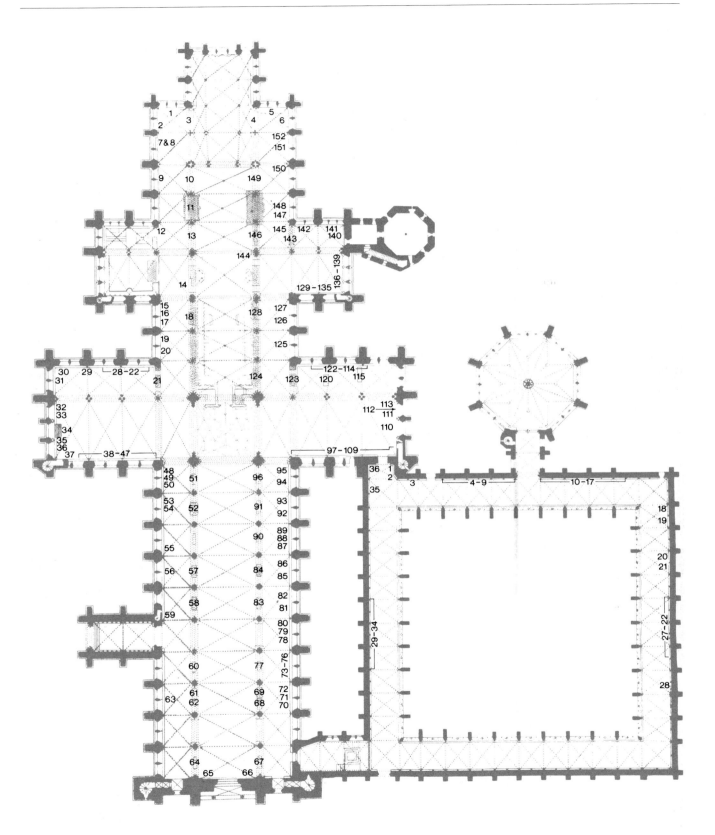

87   Plan showing the location of the monuments

presented to the British Library in 1828. To this roll-call can be added the plan of 1735 by Charles Frederick in another British Library manuscript [BL Add MS 27,349, fols 44ᵛ–45ʳ], although the plan is inaccurate in places and this manuscript is more useful for its drawings of individual monuments. The plans, while assisting in the siting of monuments within the Cathedral, all share a number of incorrect attributions, and a number of monuments are marked but not identified. Also of considerable importance are the pre-Wyatt drawings of the monuments themselves. Without doubt the most important collection is that of John Carter, made in the 1780s, some commissioned by Richard Gough [BL Add MSS 29,925, 29,928, 29,939]. Those made in 1734 by Charles Frederick are also useful [BL Add MS 27,349], albeit less scholarly than Carter's, although they include some details not recorded by Carter. Thomas Trotter's drawings made c 1798 for Sir Richard Colt Hoare are valuable for their record of surviving polychromy [Devizes Museum, album 1, 0322].

Salisbury is fortunate in having documentary evidence for the earliest burials in the new Cathedral; William de Waude, dean and chronicler of the new undertaking, records that on 14 June 1226, the feast of the Trinity to which the easternmost chapel was dedicated, the bodies of Bishops Osmund, Roger and Jocelin were translated from the old cathedral to the new [Rich Jones 1884, 55], together with the stone slabs which covered their coffins. It may be assumed that they were installed initially in either the Trinity Chapel or retrochoir, the only part of the structure complete at that time. This translation was motivated by a desire to preserve historical continuity between the old building and the new and to maintain a tangible link with those renowned and prestigious figures prominent in the history of the See and the benefaction of the fabric. Above all, it reveals the Chapter's clear intention to seek the canonisation of Osmund, whose shrine would be a focal point of devotion in the eastern arm. Peter Kidson has suggested that the Trinity Chapel was originally conceived as a memorial chapel for St Osmund [Kidson 1993, 56]. In the treasurer's inventory of 1222 reference is already made to 'Sancti Osmundi', whose chasuble and staff are included in the list of venerable relics [Rich Jones 1884, 131], and in 1226 William de Waude speaks of 'Blessed Osmund'. In 1228 the Dean and Chapter began to gather testimony in support of the formal process.

The Cathedral preserves three tomb slabs traditionally associated with these early translations (4, 68, and 69), together with a tomb base of polished Purbeck (90).

88 Purbeck marble tomb base of St Osmund, c 1226 (?) (monument 90) [BB71/2657]

Several writers have attempted to attribute these monuments to each of the three translated bishops, with varying degrees of success [Gough 1770; Raby 1948; Shortt 1971; Stroud 1984, 1993], although the evidence remains ambivalent, complicated by their removal from their original positions in the Trinity Chapel and retrochoir. It is possible that some rethinking of Osmund's commemoration in the new Cathedral may have followed the unfruitful attempts to secure his canonisation in the 13th century. Some reorganisation certainly occurred at the time of Osmund's eventual canonisation in January 1457, when an appropriately splendid shrine was constructed and Osmund's body was moved to a new timber coffin. In 1542 Leland saw both relief slabs (68 and 69) in the N aisle of the nave [Toulmin Smith 1964, 265]; they were subsequently moved to their present position in the S aisle. Further relocations accompanied Wyatt's 'improvements', when the Purbeck feretory (90) was moved from its position on the stylobate of the SE chapel to its present position under the S-nave arcade.

There can be little doubt as to the original function of the 13th-century Purbeck feretory (90), which marked Osmund's first burial place in the new Cathedral. Leland is quite unequivocal in describing the Purbeck tomb base as 'S Osmund's first tumbe... while the shrine was a makyng' [Toulmin Smith 1964, 264]. Its form is very close to Becket's first tomb in the crypt at Canterbury Cathedral, depicted in so many of the miracle scenes in the stained glass, and which was itself superseded by the construction of the shrine to which Becket was translated in 1220. The involvement of Elias of Dereham at both cathedrals suggests that this similarity is probably no coincidence. The original location of the Salisbury feretory is unclear. It may be questioned whether its position on the stylobate of the SE chapel, where Leland saw it and Carter drew it, and where it remained until 1789, was the position for which it was originally made (see Fig 4). That it was in a position that admitted pilgrims is suggested by its form, with three oval holes in the long sides. The testimony gathered as part of the canonisation process sheds light on the use to which these openings were put; in the late 14th century one John Bemyster was cured by placing his head and hands in openings within the tomb [Malden 1901, 57–8]. The commission of 1228 was able to find plenty of evidence for miracles at the tomb, the earliest taking place in the

89   Detail of inscription on edge of monument 69, attributed to St Osmund (d 1099) [BB75/5840]

old Cathedral. It is clear from the description of the cures that the tomb, in both old and new cathedrals, was accessible to the faithful. The evidence gathered by the commission of 1424 reveals that nearly all the miracles described had happened at the tomb, or as a result of a visit to it, a pattern very similar to the Canterbury experience, although, of the later Salisbury miracles, rather fewer were associated with the tomb itself. By the time the second commission was gathering testimony in 1424, a far smaller proportion of miracles was taking place there. The location of a saint's tomb or shrine behind the high altar is well attested (eg St Swithun's at Winchester and St William's last shrine at York), and this seems to be one possibility for the feretory (90) at Salisbury, although its form makes it unlikely that it was directly against the western face of the choir screen; the presence of holes on both sides suggests a location with sufficient space to admit the devout to both long sides.

The construction of the new shrine in 1457, necessitated the translation of St Osmund to a far more accessible location, probably in the retrochoir (an experience paralleled by the translation of Swithun at Winchester). This may always have been intended as the focus of the cult. In the early 13th century it could not have been foreseen that the canonisation would be so long deferred.

Which of the two tomb slabs traditionally linked with Osmund's name can be safely associated with the tomb base and the first burial in the new Cathedral has been a matter of debate [Raby 1948; Shortt 1971; Stroud 1984, 1993]. The date ANNO MXCIX (the year of Osmund's death) cut into monument (4) (Fig 23) cannot be regarded as conclusive proof, for in 1644 Symonds described it as 'lately written' [Long 1859, 130]. Monument (69), with its relatively high-relief effigy (Fig 3), is unlikely, on stylistic grounds, to date from c 1099, the year of Osmund's death, although hexameter epitaphs similar in style to that which runs round its edge were found on ledgers of the late 11th century excavated at Old Sarum [RCHME 1980, 21]. It has been suggested that Bishop Roger (1102–1139) may have embellished Osmund's tomb at Old Sarum, commissioning a new coffin lid but preserving an epitaph recorded on an earlier slab, even before its translation to the new Cathedral [Stroud 1984]. The verse epitaph, referring to the high birth of the man commemorated, could however, equally refer to Bishop Jocelin (d 1184). A recent reconsideration of the meaning of the ambiguous Latin inscription has now made a convincing case for the attribution of the slab to Osmund [Stroud 1993]. Furthermore, it would have fitted quite comfortably on top of the Purbeck base (90), which is pierced with holes (foramina) in its long sides. The base with carved effigy on top would have served as

90   Monument 68, attributed to Bishop Roger (d 1139) [BB73/ 7071]

a 'tomb-shrine' of the type formerly venerated in the crypt of Canterbury (St Thomas Becket) and at Winchester (St Swithun). Unfortunately Leland attaches no name to the effigial slab, which by the 16th century was located in the S-nave aisle [Toulmin Smith 1964, 265]. The second slab to bear an effigy, in low relief with a head restored perhaps in the 14th century (68), bears no identifying inscription, but the richness of its decoration, and a stylistic affinity with that of Abbot Gilbert at Westminster (d 1121) and Bishop Nigel at Ely (d 1169), support an attribution to Bishop Roger (d 1139). By the time of Leland's visit, it too had been moved to the nave aisle [Toulmin Smith 1964, 265]. The canonisation of Osmund in 1457 gave new impetus to his cult, and the accommodation of the new shrine may well have been the reason for the removal of Bishop Roger's slab to a position of lesser prominence in the Cathedral.

The first completely new burial at the E end was that of William Longespee, earl of Salisbury (d 1226), who had been present at the laying of the foundation stones in 1220. He was afforded the sort of position normally reserved for a founder, his monument (96) having originally been placed on the stylobate between the Trinity Chapel and the NE chapel. The Longespee tomb is of exceptional quality. Considerable traces of pigment survive on the wooden chest, which was once richly gessoed to receive paint and gilding. This is particularly noticeable on the N side, which was no doubt afforded some protection by the screen dividing the Trinity Chapel from the chapel of St Peter and the Apostles against which it once stood. The effigy, of Tournai marble, was also painted. Symonds recorded the tinctures on the shield, which bears the charges in high relief [Long 1859, 130]. The figure lies in calm repose, with the shield half drawn across the body. The right hand lies on the thigh. The unruffled drapery lies in regular folds, with a touch of naturalism created by the way in which some has fallen over the edge of the foliate fillet on the right-hand side. Close stylistic affinities with the standing knights on the W front of Wells Cathedral (c 1225–50) have long been recognised [eg Stone 1955, 115].

The honour accorded to Longespee was enhanced by the fact that in its early centuries the Cathedral had very few secular monuments of any note, the only other notable 13th-century memorial (61) being that sometimes attributed to William's son, also William (d 1250). In comparison to the effigy of his father, that of the younger William, if it is he, is of inferior quality. A certain liveliness is afforded by the action of drawing the sword from its scabbard, but the figure is poorly proportioned and less carefully carved. Any heraldic detail must have been painted, for there are no carved charges on the shield; the 18th-century plans offer no identification for this monument.

91   Monument 96, William Longespee (d 1226) [BB77/10052]

1   Polychrome on the pulpitum, c *1236 [BB93/16209]*

These Arms in the corresponding Niches
on the opposite side of the Monument.

ÆGIDIUS DE BRIDEPORT,

X.ᵗʰ Bishop of SARUM.

2   The tomb of Bishop Medford (d 1407), drawn c 1798 by Thomas Trotter, who recorded traces of the medieval paintings,
now lost [Library of WANHS]

Dr THOMAS BENNET,

Precentor of the Cathedral of SARUM.

3　The tomb of Thomas Bennett (d 1554), drawn by Thomas Trotter, c 1798, before the removal of the paintings on the rear of the canopy
[Library of WANHS]

4   *The interior of the Chapter House, 1852, by G F Sargent [Salisbury and South Wiltshire Museum]*

5 The choir looking east, 1796, by J M W Turner [Salisbury and South Wiltshire Museum]

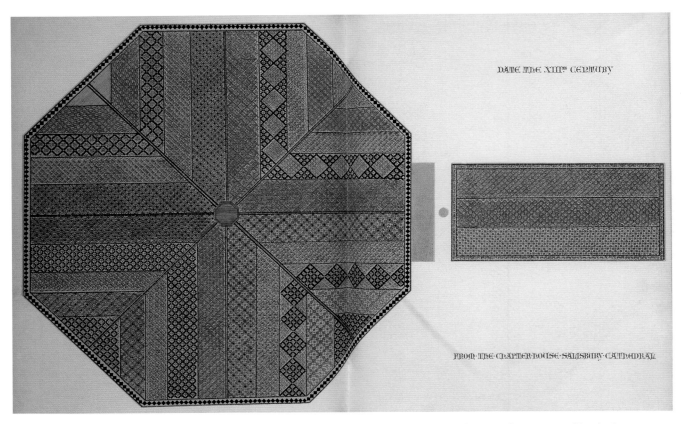

DATE THE XIIIᵗ CENTURY

FROM·THE·CHAPTER·HOUSE·SALISBURY·CATHEDRAL

6   Watercolour of the Chapter House pavement in Specimens of Tiled Pavements *by Henry Shaw, 1858 [Society of Antiquaries of London]*

7   *The Hertford monument [BB71/2609]*

THEY·CALLED·HIS·NAME OBED·HE·IS·THE·FATHER OF·JESSE·THE FATHER·OF·DAVID

To the Glory of GOD and in loving memory of WILLIAM PAGE ROBERTS, Dean of

8   *The Page Roberts memorial window (1932) by Edward Woore [BB93/6221]*

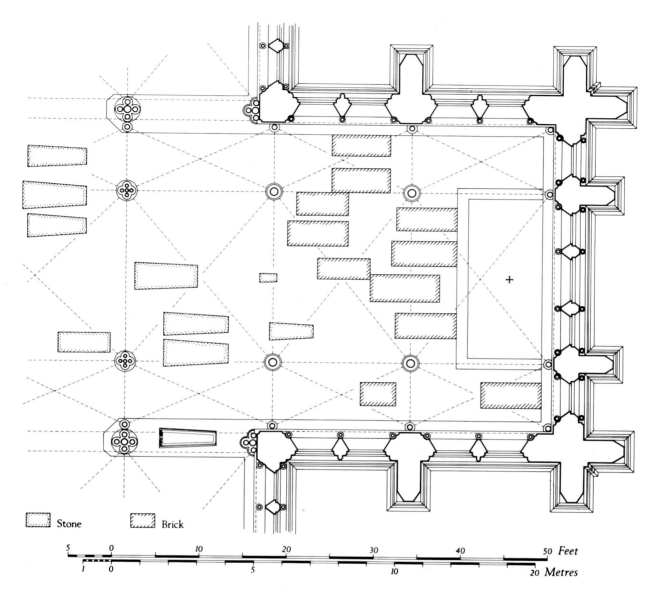

Stone   Brick

5 0   10   20   30   40   50 Feet
1 0   5   10   20 Metres

92   Plan showing the position of graves found under the pavement of the Trinity Chapel in 1962

The Trinity Chapel was also the burial place of Bishops de Wickhampton (d 1284) and de Braunstone (d 1288). The early sources state that de Wickhampton and de Braunstone were buried on the S side of the Trinity Chapel [Malden 1912, 345]. Leland, on the other hand, describes them as being either side of Bishop Nicholas Longespee (d 1297), who was buried beneath a slab with a brass at the entrance of the Trinity Chapel [Toulmin Smith 1964, 264], a little to the W of St Osmund's shrine. They are shown in this position on the plan of 1735 and this location is also suggested by Symonds's reference to flat stones 'of some of the

bishops' in the Lady Chapel [Long 1859, 140]. Bishop Scammel (d 1286) may also have been buried in the Trinity Chapel [Malden 1912, 345]. Gough records the discovery of several episcopal burials, one of them Longespee's, during the repaving of the Trinity Chapel under Wyatt's direction [Gough 1796, ccxxxi]. Any memorials in the body of the Chapel and retrochoir must have been flat, like Bishop Longespee's, in order not to impede the passage of processions.

For any prelate with plans for a more ambitious memorial, the Trinity Chapel offered limited opportunity, and episcopal burials soon moved outside its confines.

*93   Monument 10, attributed to Bishop de Bingham
(d 1246) [BB71/2297]*

At the NE corner of the choir in an aedicule entirely reconstructed by Scott, stands the monument (10) variously ascribed to Bishop Poore (d 1237, at Durham) and Bishop de Bingham (d 1246). Scott, loyal to the early tradition, maintained that it was Poore's monument that he had restored [Stamp 1995, 307–8], and Malden also supported the idea that the monument (10) was Salisbury's tribute to Bishop Poore. Leland's testimony as to the inscription on a tablet in the Trinity Chapel (now lost) confirms that Poore was buried in neither Salisbury nor Durham (to which he was translated in 1229), but at Tarrant Crawford in Dorset [Toulmin Smith 1964, 262–3]. It has, however, been plausibly suggested, by Canon Rich Jones among others, that the monument commemorates not Bishop Poore, but Bishop de Bingham, known to have been buried on the N of the high altar [Malden 1912, 344]. Bingham is credited by Matthew Paris with having furnished the choir [Madden 1869, 260], providing the stalls and glass. This position would certainly be appropriate to the man who had seen the choir through to completion. It is perhaps interesting to note that the drapery style of the effigy can be usefully compared to the linear treatment of drapery in the Paris Apocalypse [BN Nat MS Fr 403], attributed to the illuminator known as the Sarum Master, and datable to *c* 1245–50. The small figure of an angel holding a sun and moon in the aedicule above the effigy's head echoes a motif found on the pulpitum, on the choir transept vaults, and in the stained glass of the Chapter House. The angel itself is vested in fully broad-fold drapery, a feature unlikely before 1250.

Bishop de Bridport (d 1262) chose a location on the junction of the ambulatory and the SE transept, with a monument (143) creating a screen into the chapel of St Mary Magdalene. Architecturally and iconographically, it is one of the most sophisticated and ambitious in the Cathedral, modelled in part on the earlier Poore/Bingham monument (10), but also recalling the miniature architecture of shrines [Roberts 1983]. This character is perpetuated by the unusual depiction of biographical scenes in the spandrels of the gables on both the N and S elevations, in scenes using the 'vertical' perspectives found in the reliefs in the Chapter House arcade.

Of the other 13th-century bishops, Walter de la Wyle (d 1271), founder of the Collegiate church of St Edmund, was originally buried in the chapel of St Edmund in the N transept, but has since been relocated in the S-nave arcade. His much defaced effigy (91) now lies on top of a tomb chest made up of later fragments. William de la Corner (d 1291) was buried even further from the E end, in the eastern end of the nave [Malden 1912, 345], between the morning altar and the altar of the Holy Ghost. The monument of the so-called 'Boy Bishop' (62)

94   South elevation of monument 143, of Bishop de Bridport (d 1262) [BB74/4640]

may actually be that of de la Corner, for the monument was once located further E and was protected by an iron grille [Price 1774, 65; Bodl MS Gough Maps, vol. 32, fol 48]. De la Corner's three 14th-century successors preferred the choir, and Simon de Gandavo (d 1315) (146) and Roger de Martival (d 1330) (13) are commemorated by monuments which combined the mason's, metal-worker's and brassmaker's skills [Tatton-Brown 1995a]. The grilles (Fig 54) on both tombs are early examples of the cold-worked geometric forms adopted by English smiths in imitation of carpenters' work [Alexander and Binski 1987, 175]. Their closely similar designs and choir-screen function suggest that they were planned contemporaneously. The de Martival monument (Fig 12),

95   Monument 146, of Bishop Simon de Gandavo (d 1315). [BB93/15918]

in particular, represents a streamlined version of the 'micro-architecture' phase of English tomb design, encompassing the Crouchback tomb at Westminster, the

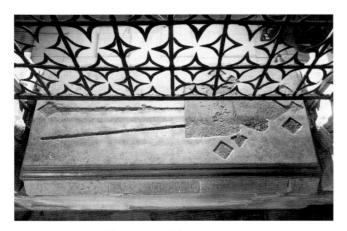

96 Detail of brass indent and iron grille of the de Martival monument (13) of c 1330 [BB77/10049]

bishop's throne at Exeter, the tomb of Edward II at Gloucester and the tombs of the Despensers at Tewkesbury. The effigy has been replaced by a brass (lost), creating a structure closer to an altar with reredos than a tomb chest.

With its wealth of Purbeck marble, it is hardly surprising that brasses, so closely associated with the Purbeck marblers, made an early appearance as part of funerary monuments at Salisbury. The earliest was probably that of Bishop Longespee (d 1297), with its prominent textual strip recorded by Leland [Toulmin Smith 1964, 264], and was typical of this earliest phase of English medieval brasses, to which the lost brasses of de Martival and de Gandavo also belonged. The brass had replaced the effigy, but the monument was personalised through the incised demi-figure and the inscription strip. The apogee of this trend at Salisbury is to be found on the de Wyville brass (Fig 121), in which the brass is the most pretentious and decorative aspect of the memorial, with a long inscription setting the image in a historical context, stressing the bishop's worldly achievements.

97   *Monument 123, of Bishop Medford (d 1407), once richly coloured (see Plate 2) [BB71/2346]*

Remarkably few of the Cathedral's subsequent 14th and early 15th-century bishops are commemorated in the Cathedral, many having left Salisbury for other appointments. Of those that were in possession of the See at the time of their death, one, Robert de Hallum, died while attending the Council of Constance in 1417 and was buried in the Cathedral there, where he was commemorated by a brass [Malden 1912, 347–8]. Of those buried at Salisbury, the most impressive display was perhaps that of Richard Medford (d 1407). His monument in the S transept (123) is a substantial screen tomb, with alabaster tomb chest and effigy. The panelled canopy is covered with heraldic devices and armorial bearings recalling his career in the royal service with niches and pedestals for statuary (lost), while to the E the flat panelling was decorated with painted imagery (Fig 97 and Plate 2). Vestigial traces of paint are plentiful. Bishop John Chaundeler (d 1426) was buried in the nave, and, although his tomb was seen by Leland [Toulmin Smith 1964, 265], no trace of it has survived.

The canonisation of St Osmund in 1457 and the construction of the shrine in the Trinity Chapel was to be the catalyst for a renewed spate of tomb-building at the E end, led by Bishop Richard Beauchamp (d 1481), during whose episcopate the long-delayed canonisation was achieved. In his will, made in 1461, Beauchamp mentions a chapel 'newly built', probably a reference to the two-storey structure built against the eastern face of the choir screen. Leland describes this as 'a riche tumbe and a chapel over it' [Toulmin Smith 1964, 264], the lower storey of which was eventually to be the resting place of Bishop John Blythe (d 1499), beneficiary of Beauchamp's decision to build a more ambitious monument to himself, a chantry chapel added externally to the S side of the Trinity Chapel. Bishop Blythe's tomb chest and battered effigy are now enclosed in this first Beauchamp monument, now relocated in the N transept (34). Its wooden first storey was removed in the late 18th century [BL Add MS 29,925, fol 120ʳ]. The Beauchamp chantry chapel (Fig 18) housed the tombs of the bishop, his parents and his brother, Lord St Amand. From Schnebbelie's drawing of the interior it would appear

98   Chantry chapel of Bishop Audley (d 1524). The bishop was buried beneath the floor of the chapel (monument 11) and its southern elevation incorporated an Easter sepulchre [BB71/3286]

99   Vault of the Audley chantry. Internally the chapel still bears considerable traces of medieval pigment [BB71/2324]

that all of these monuments were architectural rather than sculptural in character, with panelled sides and canopies filled with heraldic shields. Beauchamp's tomb chest was originally surmounted with a brass with shield and inscription, although by the 17th century this had disappeared with the other brasses [Long 1859, 132]. The Beauchamp chantry complemented the slightly earlier one on the N side of the Trinity Chapel, constructed by Margaret (Botreaux), the widow of Robert, Lord Hungerford.

The last of the major pre-Reformation episcopal monuments was that of Edmund Audley (d 1524), a chantry chapel on the N side of the choir (11), to the W of the Bingham monument. The chapel was dedicated to the Assumption of the Virgin Mary (as was the nearby high altar), the subject of a sculpted reredos above its altar, with an altar and Easter sepulchre set into the S side; the bishop himself was buried beneath the chapel's floor [Shortt 1973, 8]. Audley had already built a chantry for himself while bishop of Hereford [RCHME 1931, 103–4]. In the upper storey of the chapel is a vault boss depicting the Assumption of the Virgin Mary, suggesting that his devotion to this subject pre-dated his arrival in

Salisbury. Externally, the Salisbury chapel is richly decorated with Audley's initials and his heraldry, together with IHS and Maria monograms. The chapel was once brightly coloured, externally and internally, making it a conspicuous target for Reformation iconoclasts.

Of the senior members of the Chapter, surprisingly few have left substantial memorials behind them, and all are late in date. Dean Gilbert Kymer (d 1463) obtained permission to build a chantry at the altar of the Relics and it is likely that the panelled screen tomb and chest separating the chapel of St John from the N-choir aisle (21) is his. This rather plain monument, very similar to Bishop Medford's monument on the S side, was once adorned with brasses, including on the surfaces of the blank shields along the sides of the tomb chest. There was also an inscription strip. Treasurer Henry Sutton (1495–1505) subsequently left money for two entrecloses between the chapel and the choir aisle and the tomb chest has the seatings for metal grilles.

The only other identifiable clerical monuments date from the early decades of the 16th century. The earliest, that of Chancellor William Wilton (d 1523), comprises a short quatrefoil-panelled tomb chest with heraldic

100   *Monument 6, of William Wilton (d 1523), decorated with the punning device for Wilton's name [BB78/1019]*

shields topped with a Purbeck slab, surmounted by a recessed canopy decorated with panelled tracery, with a niche for imagery (lost) on the eastern jamb, creating a combination of wall monument and altar (6). The monument is extremely close to a group of early 16th-century monuments surviving in London and environs [Cherry 1984], for five of which there is documentary evidence of a combined funerary and Easter-sepulchre function. The Wilton monument is, however, in the wrong position to have served this function, standing to the S rather than the N of the altar in St Stephen's chapel. The London examples appear to have had brasses either on the slab on the tomb chest or on the wall of the surmounting recess; there is no evidence for either here, and any imagery that may have adorned the tracery of the recess, together with the sculpture from the eastern jamb of the canopy, has disappeared.

Salisbury preserves two monuments from the period of the Marian restoration of Roman Catholic orthodoxy. The monument of Precentor and Chancellor Thomas Bennett (d 1558) combines tomb chest and recess, with the tomb chest supporting a cadaver effigy (14). Bennett appears to have been a man of flexible principles, for he had aquiesced in the religious changes of the Reformation and yet remained in office during Mary's reign. The iconography of his monument, executed during his lifetime, reflected standard late medieval forms. In the eastern jamb of the canopy was a sculpted Crucifixion (now defaced), while painted on the reredos was the image of the kneeling Bennett in life, dressed in academic robes. The painting survived into the late 18th century to be recorded by Schnebbelie [1791] and Thomas Trotter (Plate 3). Of almost identical date and form to Bennett's monument was John Capon's (d 1557) (128), also executed during his lifetime (it bore the date 1555), which originally occupied a similar recess in an almost equivalent position in the S-choir aisle. Drawings of the tomb chest and recess prior to its dismantling show no effigy, as on the Bennett chest, but the wall of the recess was apparently decorated with the bishop's mitre and staff, although in what medium is not clear [BL Add MS 27,349, fol 64]. Another, and probably earlier cadaver effigy (18) is traditionally attributed to Archdeacon Sydenham (d 1524), although the tomb chest on which it presumably rested has now disappeared. Sydenham's image in life was apparently depicted in glass in the window opposite, where Symonds recorded his bidding scroll and heraldry [Long 1859, 135]. The loss of so much stained glass has effectively removed all evidence of an important alternative vehicle of commemoration.

The evidence for the kind of memorials favoured by the less exalted members of the Chapter is very limited.

Many were no doubt commemorated by ledger stones and floor slabs (probably with brasses), a class of monument that has fared badly at Salisbury. Restoration work in the nave in 1979 uncovered a number of medieval burials set into the stylobate of the nave, one of which was identifiable as that of a 14th century priest [Spring 1979, 11]. The nave seems to have been favoured by a number of later medieval Cathedral clergy. John Machon's 15th-century Act book [Malden 1904] records the positions of a number of these burials, several described as being under a marble slab. Only Andrew Holes (d 1470), chancellor of the Cathedral, requested burial elsewhere inside the church, in the chapel of St Mary Magdalene in the SE transept. Many more Cathedral clergy were buried in the graveyards to the W and N. In front of the image of the Virgin on the W front seems to have been particularly popular. The Cathedral churchyard was to be another casualty of Wyatt's improvements.

Very few notable secular monuments augmented those of the Longespees during the earliest centuries of the new Cathedral's history. Only in the late 14th century was William Longespee joined in the Trinity Chapel by another knight, John Montacute, earl of Salisbury (d 1389). His armoured effigy (57), once richly painted and gilded, rests on a tomb chest decorated with shallow niches and pedestals (empty). By the 18th century Montacute had been positioned on the stylobate to the east of William Longespee. In repositioning the monument in the nave, Wyatt had to make up the northern face of the chest with second-hand materials, suggesting that it had once been against a wall. The most likely explanation is that the monument originated on the N wall of the Trinity Chapel from where it was moved c 1460 to accommodate the door into the Hungerford chantry.

The other major secular memorials were those to the Hungerfords. Walter (d 1449) was buried together with his wife Catherine (Peverell) in a cage-like chapel in the N aisle of the nave, in a chantry established during his lifetime, dedicated to the Annunciation of the Virgin Mary [Nicolas 1826, 257; Fletcher 1936a; Shortt 1970]. Walter and Catherine were commemorated by large brasses set into slabs that were originally set into the nave pavement. They were later joined there by their grandson, Robert, Lord Moleyns and Hungerford (d 1464), also marked by a brass (lost). The chantry was served by two chaplains and the structure survived until 1778, when it was dismantled and reconstructed in the choir, where it was made into a pew for the Radnors (see p 73).

Walter's son, Robert (d 1459), was commemorated in a far more splendid fashion [Fletcher 1936b; Shortt 1970]. In his will Robert requested burial at the altar of St Osmund, attracted E by the saint's new shrine. At a

101 Alabaster effigy of Robert Hungerford (d 1459), formerly located in the chantry chapel added to the northeast of the Trinity Chapel. Moved in 1789 to its present location in the south-nave aisle (monument 84) [BB74/4693]

102 Detail of Robert Hungerford's effigy [BB93/15949]

103 Alabaster effigy of Sir John Cheney (d 1509) (monument 51). Until 1789 the effigy lay on top of an elaborate canopied chest (see Fig 104) at the west end of Bishop Beauchamp's chantry chapel [BB75/3645]

cost of £497, his widow, Margaret Botreaux, had a new chapel built for her husband and herself, decorated with a series of paintings that greatly impressed Symonds in 1644 and were still remarkable enough in their dilapidated state to be recorded in 1789 by Jacob Schnebbelie (Figs 16 and 17). It was provided with ornaments and vestments valued at a further £200, and was served by two chaplains [Jackson 1869]. It was, according to an inscription recorded by Symonds, consecrated in the 1460s; the already partially defaced inscription included the words '... A.D. M.CCCCLX... mensis Octobri' die xiiij°' [Long 1859, 131]. Robert's alabaster effigy, resting on a tomb chest made up of architectural fragments, now lies in the S-nave arcade (84). It was originally located in a recess in the south-eastern bay of the chapel, beneath a canopy decorated with heraldry. This did not survive the demolition of the chapel. Margaret (d 1477) lay in the centre of the chapel in a tomb chest surmounted by a slab with a brass that had been lost by the time Symonds visited it. The chest was drawn by Frederick in 1735 [BL Add MS 27,349, fol 66], but had been dismantled by the time Schnebbelie drew the chapel's interior; the open grave can be seen and slabs with panelled tracery lie in stacks against the walls. Her monument remains unidentified and has also been presumed lost. Robert's effigy,

resting on a tomb chest made up by Wyatt, but perhaps including material from the original chest, is dressed in Milanese-inspired armour described by Symonds as resembling a 'lobstar' [Long 1859, 131]. It is finely detailed and still retains considerable traces of paint. Margaret was a literate and capable woman possessed of considerable business acumen. Her father-in-law, Walter, bequeathed to her his 'best Legend of the Lives of the Saints in French, and covered in red cloth' [Nicolas 1826, 257], and it is tempting to speculate the degree to which the chapel's decorative scheme reflected Margaret's own devotional interests. Her own will, made in 1476, was far longer than her husband's, and was concerned almost exclusively with arrangements for the disposition of her very considerable landed property [Nicolas 1826, 310].

The other notable alabaster effigy is that of Sir John Cheney (d 1509), formerly in the SW corner of the Beauchamp chantry chapel, but moved to the N-nave aisle in the 18th century (51). The effigy on its tomb chest was originally positioned beneath a canopy, with space at the E end to admit the officiating priest. The quatrefoil-panelled tomb chest had already become heavily defaced by the time John Carter drew it in 1781 [BL Add MS 29,925, fol 130^r].

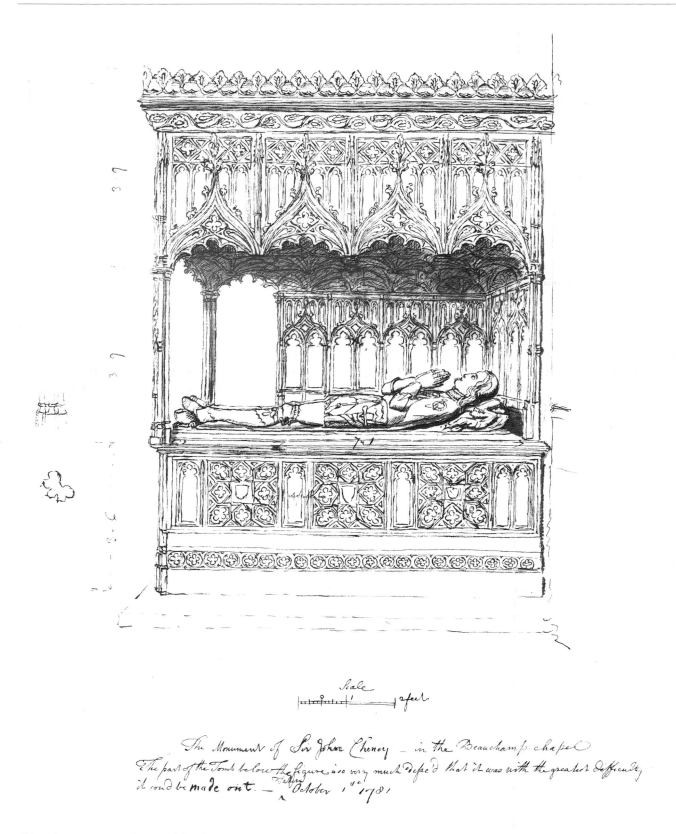

Scale |ı·ı·ı·ı·ı·ı·ı| 2 feet

The Monument of Sir John Cheney — in the Beauchamp chapel
The part of the Tomb below the figure is so very much defac'd that it was with the greatest Difficulty
it coud be made out. — October 1st 1781.

104   John Carter's 1781 drawing of the Cheney monument [BL Add MS 29,925, fol 130ʳ]

Thomas Bennett's monument (14), although post-Reformation in date, is entirely medieval in sentiment and was to be the last medieval monument of any distinction. The uncertainties of the Reformation do not seem to have encouraged the commissioning of funerary monuments; the abolition of chantries and the defacing of objectionable imagery, probably including Bishop Audley's relatively new chapel, no doubt increased feelings of apprehension and further undermined confidence. Energetic Bishop Jewel (d 1571) and his successor Edmund Gheast were both buried in the choir, the former with a simple floor slab and the latter with a modest brass, removed, together with de Wyville's brass, during the repaving of the choir in 1684. Jewel, responsible for the restoration of the fabric and, to a certain extent, the prestige of the Cathedral, was also commemorated in the extensively repaired windows. Symonds saw his initials in quarries in the windows of the nave [Long 1859, 140], and his arms can still be seen in window s36 (Fig 78). The impoverished Bishop John Coldwell (d 1596) was also buried in the choir, apparently in Bishop de Wyville's grave, and the location of Bishop Cotton's burial (d 1615) is unknown [Malden 1912, 349].

The resurgence of interest in substantial funerary monuments in the 17th century was led not by the Cathedral's bishops, so prominent in its medieval endowment, but by members of the Chapter and, above all, by prominent members of its secular congregation, reflecting the post-Reformation rehabilitation of the Cathedral church in the life of the city after a period of decline and neglect. Many of those commemorated in the Cathedral in the 17th century opted for simple tablets with a preponderance of heraldry and genealogical information. The simplicity of these tablets was no doubt partly a reflection of the limited resources of the donors, but was perhaps also prompted by a desire to avoid controversial subject matter in a period in which the post-Reformation iconography of the smaller monument had yet to mature. The Cathedral became an increasingly important location for secular and dynastic display, and patrons were quick to exploit those prominent locations made newly accessible by the removal of altars from the chapels at the E end; the Gorges and Hertford monuments (1 and 5) dominate the chapels of St Peter and St Stephen, for example. A number of these new monuments reveal that Salisbury patrons were aware of the latest continental-influenced styles current in London and disseminated to the provinces as a result of the cosmopolitan connections of wealthy patrons [A White 1992]. Westminster Abbey was the monument of particular importance, described as 'a powerhouse of ideas', in this period [A White 1989]. Several Salisbury monuments reveal a debt to Westminster models.

Of particular importance in this context is the Hertford monument (5) erected c 1625, commemorating Edward Seymour, earl of Hertford (d 1621), his wife Catherine Grey (d 1563) and their sons, Edward, Viscount Beauchamp (d 1612) and Thomas Seymour (d 1600). The earl had already commissioned monuments at Westminster Abbey, to his first wife Frances Seymour and to his mother, the duchess of Somerset. The latter is very close in style, albeit smaller in scale, to the monument at Salisbury, which has recently been identified as one of the most important works of William Wright of Charing Cross [A White 1994, 67]. The monument typifies the 'monumental skyscraper' of the early 17th century, effigies beneath a coffered vault, with a classical canopy of towering height decorated with paint and coloured stone. In depicting the sons of the earl and countess kneeling in filial duty, as if alive, at the head and feet of their parents, the monument has conveyed a curiously altered version of events. In reality, both sons had predeceased their father, and yet for posterity the generations are restored to their more natural and logical order.

The Gorges monument (1), occupying the altar location in the chapel of St Peter, commemorates Thomas Gorges (d 1610) and his wife, Helena Schnachenberg, and was erected by their son c 1635. It was formerly attributed to Epiphanius Evesham [Esdaile 1942, 53–62], but has more recently been attributed to an unidentified but prolific workshop, responsible for a number of monuments in the Cathedral (including the Mompesson monument (125)), together with a group of monuments in Dorset and Wiltshire. The geographical spread of the works suggests that the workshop was based in Salisbury.[16]

The 17th-century monuments also offer glimpses of the post-Reformation life of the Close, and Chapter clergy are more frequently represented in the surviving monuments, a reflection, perhaps, of the enforcement of more regular residence among the canons from the time of Bishop Jewel onwards [VCH III, 187–9]. A new element in funerary commemoration in the Cathedral is the appearance of the devout laywoman and an entirely new element in the social fabric of the chapter, the clerical wife. One of the earliest 17th-century monuments (93) is that on the S wall of the nave to Elihonor Sadler, a resident of the Close, and the epitome of a stern and devout Christian gentlewoman. Elihonor kneels at a prie-dieu with hands joined in prayer, inside a classically conceived niche with Corinthian columns and entablature. She is depicted in life rather than in death, representing the useful and active Christian life. Elihonor's monument is also a reminder of the westwards shift in the devotional emphasis of the post-Reformation cathedral.

105   *Monument 5, of Edward Seymour, earl of Hertford (d 1621) and his family, probably the work of William Wright [BB77/10058]*

106   The Hertford monument: figure of Thomas Seymour [BB71/2590]

107   *The Mompesson monument (125) in the south-choir aisle. The monument was originally located on the north wall, where its recumbent figures would have been correctly orientated [BB71/2599]*

108   Monument 93, of Elihonor Sadler, who died in 1622 and was commemorated close by the seat she regularly occupied in the nave [BB71/2361]

109   Bishop Davenant's monument (127) of c 1641 [BB71/2360]

Bishop Jewel had introduced a preaching rota, and fixed seating for the use of those listening to the sermon delivered from the nave pulpit was provided. At her own request, Elihonor's monument was erected close to the pew she had occupied for fifty years.

The more modest wall tablets commemorating Mary Barnston, wife of canon residentiary John Barnston (d 1625) (145), and Margaret Tounson, widow of Bishop Tounson (d 1634) (81) are reminders of the new feminine presence in the Chapter's very midst. The post-Reformation Chapter was encouraged to participate more fully in the life of the city, and the addition of a wife to the domestic circle of a resident canon no doubt contributed to the achievement of this end. The nave seating mentioned on Elihonor Sadler's monument was intended primarily for the use of the mayor and corporation and their wives, but Chapter wives also participated in the resultant disputes concerning precedence, a factor contributing to the removal of the pews at Archbishop Laud's insistence in 1635 [*Wilts N&Q* I, (1893), 23]. Despite the Chapter's efforts to integrate the Cathedral into the life of the city, however, civic dignitaries are conspicuous in their absence among those commemorated here.

The 17th-century Chapter counted several significant scholars in its ranks, and a number of the monuments reflect their scholarly and academic preoccupations. Price records the brass formerly on the N wall of the choir, which recounted at length the career of the theologian and linguistic scholar Dean John Gordon (d 1619), an early benefactor of the Cathedral library [Price 1774, 81]. Bishop John Davenant's monument (d 1641), (127) charts his illustrious achievements as Doctor of Divinity, while Bishop Seth Ward's memorial (d 1689) (132) is decorated with a selection of scientific instruments, and Canon John Priaulx's monument (d 1674) (85) stresses his educational qualifications and his thorough knowledge of languages, arts and sciences.

Very little serves as a reminder of the Civil War and Commonwealth, a troubled period in the Cathedral's history. The most evocative monument, presumably erected after the Restoration, is that of Sir Henry Hyde of Hele (d 1650), executed for his royalist allegiance, who 'finished life kissing the axe... to suffer the envied martyrdom of Charles I' (92). In the absence of a Cathedral administration, Sir Henry's brothers took an active interest in the care of the Cathedral fabric, to such an extent that the first post-Restoration bishop, Seth Ward, found the fabric in surprisingly good repair. Their involvement is recorded on the monument (101) of Sir Robert (d 1665), one of the 'Preservers of the Cathedral and Spire' from the Roundheads, and is implied in the Latin epitaph on the brass of his brother, Bishop Alexander (d 1667). Indeed, the S-nave aisle and S transept

is dominated by memorials to the Hyde family, with three of the twelve sons of Sir Lawrence (d 1641) and Lady Catherine (d 1661) (both commemorated by floor slabs, see p 157) and their grand-daughter Elizabeth (89) all buried in close proximity.

On almost all of the post-Restoration monuments, the depiction of a likeness of the person commemorated, a standard element in medieval tomb iconography and one which persisted into the Elizabethan and Jacobean period, has largely given way to a prominent text panel, bearing what in some cases amounts to a *curriculum vitae*. Notable exceptions are the monuments of Bishop Ward (132), with a bust at its apex, and that of Robert Hyde (101), Chief Justice of England. His black-and-white marble monument with white marble portrait bust is copied from the almost identical monument in Westminster Abbey to the judge Sir Thomas Richardson (d 1635) by Hubert le Sueur, a conscious emulation of a type of monument apparently favoured by a number of men prominent in the legal profession and attributed to Joshua Marshall [A White 1989, 31–40]. The use of coloured pigments on memorials, an essential characteristic of all medieval monuments and one which continues in the decoration of effigies in the early 17th century, also declined, with a greater reliance on varied and contrasting coloured stones, increasingly of foreign origin. The Purbeck marble and alabaster so commonly used for medieval tombs gave way to more exotic marbles.

After the wealth and variety of the 17th century, Salisbury Cathedral's 18th-century monumental heritage is rather disappointing. A large number of 18th-century monuments survive, but relatively few are of great distinction. The great majority are wall tablets, classically conceived, most with some sort of heraldic bearing, employing a range of coloured stones. Figurative sculpture of any kind is almost wholly absent, confined to the occasional sorrowing cherub (D'Aubigny Turbeville, d 1696 (65); Samuel Rolleston, d 1766 (148)). The notable exception is on the impressive monument to Thomas Wyndham, Baron Wyndham of Finglass (d 1745), by Michael Rysbrack (66), with its classically draped, sorrowing female figure. Once again, it is Westminster Abbey that provides a comparison for a Salisbury monument, for Thomas Wyndham's memorial is a version of an earlier design by Rysbrack, for the monument to Nicholas Rowe.

The commemorative portrait, an element retained on the more ambitious Elizabethan and Jacobean monuments, was largely banished in favour of the allegorical figure; a sorrowing contemplative figure of Moral Philosophy on Bacon's memorial (44) to James Harris (d 1780), while Literature, Justice, Benevolence and Science adorn Flaxman's monuments to Walter (d 1807)

110 *Monument 101, of Robert Hyde, d 1665, recorder of Salisbury, Chief Justice of Common Pleas and benefactor of the Cathedral [BB74/4643]*

111   *Michael Rysbrack's monument (66) to Baron Wyndham of Finglass (d 1745) [BB71/2372]*

112 Detail of the heraldic cushion on monument 66 [BB73/2376]

Below: *114 The classical urn was chosen to embellish the monument to Bishop John Hume (d 1782) (monument 112) [BB73/5796]*

(31) and William Long (d 1818) (29). A sorrowing Muse uncovering an image of the Good Samaritan is the main element of his monument to William Benson Earle (d 1796) on the western wall (39). Even the classical urn is used sparingly (Bishop John Hume, d 1782 (112); Dean Rowney Noel DD, d 1786 (130)), although Thomas Trotter's album reveals that several have been removed. There is relatively little evidence of the individual or personal involvement of the person commemorated in the design of the monuments, and few reflect their personality or interests, although a number identify the person responsible for their erection. An exception to this is the grey marble memorial (134) to Dean John Clark (d 1757), distinguished mathematician and brother of Samuel Clark the metaphysician, which is appropriately decorated with mathematical instruments and records his close friendship with Sir Isaac Newton.

The closing years of the 18th century and the early decades of the 19th century witnessed the installation of a small group of monuments in the Romantic mould, all located in the NW transept, including Flaxman's monuments to the Longs and William Benson Earle. The most impressive is undoubtedly Francis Chantrey's large monument to James Harris, first earl of Malmesbury (d 1820) (42), with its life-size reclining figure, representing the earl

113   John Bacon's monument to James Harris (d 1780) (monument 44) with allegorical figure of Moral Philosophy
[BB93/15933]

115   *Sir Richard Colt Hoare (d 1818), historian of Wiltshire, by R C Lucas (monument 33) [BB71/2375]*

116   John Carline's 15th-century-style monument to Edward and Rachel Poore (monument 110), made in 1817, was one of the earliest manifestations of the Gothic revival in the Cathedral [BB71/2432]

clasping a book and gesturing with outstretched arm, executed in 1823. Although the monument is dominated by a portrait figure, the image is entirely unlike the medieval tomb chest with effigy, for the earl is depicted in life, the epitome of the confident, graceful, accomplished aristocrat. R C Lucas's seated figure of Sir Richard Colt Hoare (d 1818) (33) is a late manifestation of this type, dating from 1841.

Even this group of monuments with their strong classical flavour have eclectic Gothic elements within them. Chantrey's Harris monument (42) employs a shallow Gothic 'canopy' behind the figure, with panelled tracery flanking the long epitaph. By the mid century the Gothic style prevailed almost completely, at Salisbury as elsewhere. Of particular interest is the monument on the S wall of the S transept (110) to Edward Poore (d 1780) and

his wife Rachel (d 1771). This canopied table tomb in 15th-century-style, executed in 1817 by John Carline of Shrewsbury, is one of the earliest fully fledged Gothic Revival monuments in the Cathedral and was recognised as an important work by contemporary observers, one of whom described it as 'perhaps one of the most perfect specimens of Florid Gothic in the Kingdom' [quoted in Gunnis 1980, 80]. In fact, the majority of 'florid Gothic' works in the cathedral are the work of William Osmond (1791–1875), appointed mason to the Cathedral c 1818. One of his earliest works in the Cathedral (c 1822), a wall tablet to Sarah Hayter (38), is in a classical style, but his subsequent work is in a Gothic idiom; 15th century in the case of Bishop Fisher's table tomb (115) and Anna Eliza Slade's wall monument (119), moving to a hybrid 13th-century style for his later work, typified by his monument

117   William Osmond's 1828 monument to Bishop Fisher (monument 115) imitating a 15th-century table tomb [BB93/16196]

118   George Gilbert Scott restored the monument he believed to be a cenotaph to Bishop Poore from John Carter's drawings recording its appearance before its destruction in 1789. Only the coffin lid with effigy is 13th century. Monument 10 is here attributed to Bishop de Bingham (d 1246) [BB71/3290]

to Henry Hatcher (d 1846) (50). Osmond's monuments in the Cathedral are numerous but not very distinguished, despite his close friendship with the brilliant A W N Pugin, who derided Osmond's prolific wall memorials, describing them as 'blisters' [Gunnis 1980, 285].

The most impressive and artistically distinguished Gothic Revival monuments are all associated with the major restorations and refurbishments of the Cathedral undertaken in the second half of the century. The most important works commemorate those bishops most closely involved in this, reflecting the revival of episcopal initiative in the care of the fabric. On the S side of the choir, matching the restored Poore/Bingham monument in which Scott took such pride, and closely reflecting its form, was his memorial, unveiled in March 1881 [Wheeler 1901, 4], to Bishop Walter Kerr Hamilton (d 1869) (149), in whose memory the restoration of the choir was undertaken. On the S wall of the S-choir aisle

is the tomb recess and effigy of Bishop George Moberly (d 1885) (151), designed by Sir Arthur Blomfield, unveiled in July 1888 [Wheeler 1901, 26]. The installation in 1914 of the effigy and tomb chest of Bishop John Wordsworth (d 1911) (3) brought to an end the great tradition of large episcopal monuments; subsequent memorials, to Bishop Ridgeway (d 1921) and Bishop St Clair Donaldson (d 1936), both by A G Wyon, have been of a more modest nature (114 and 9).

As the Cathedral has become crowded with free-standing and wall-mounted monuments, other forms of memorial have appealed to the bereaved families of the Cathedral's churchmen. This, coupled with a desire to make a more utilitarian contribution to the life of the Cathedral, focused attention on alternative forms of commemoration. The Skidmore choir screen commissioned by Scott to replace Wyatt's screen, was a memorial to Dean Lear (d 1850), for example. The cloisters and

119   Scott's design for the monument to Bishop Walter Kerr Hamilton (d 1869) (monument 149) unveiled in 1881, closely reflected the de Bingham monument opposite [BB93/16194]

Chapter House were restored in memory of Bishop Edward Denison (d 1854), and he and Dean Allan Beecher Webb (d 1907) were both remembered in stained glass, although Bishop Denison's window was subsequently replaced. Indeed, the decision to fill the windows of the Cathedral with new stained glass provided an attractive alternative to the monument in the 19th and early 20th centuries.

One new class of monument is worthy of consideration in a discussion of the contribution of the 19th and 20th centuries – the War Memorial. Two world wars and other less celebrated conflicts have left their mark on the Cathedral interior. A new element in funerary commemoration is the regimental memorial, commemorating both officers and enlisted men, and often paid for by subscription. This reflects the improving status of the ordinary soldier in the course of the 19th century and the increasing importance of the county regiments, to

which the local community had a strong loyalty. The dead of the Wiltshire Regiment are remembered in the glass of the SE transept in memory of the Sutlej campaign (1845–6) and the Crimean War (1854–5), and on the fine copper and enamel wall monument in the N-nave aisle (56), commemorating the casualties of the South African war (1900–3). The terrible toll of the First World War is recorded in a number of memorials to individuals, all the sons of prominent county families (eg 32, 59 and 111), while the generality of the Wiltshire dead was commemorated in the eastern aisle of the S transept, which was transformed into a memorial chapel, with two windows installed in 1924 (s19 and s20), presided over by the dramatic 'Victory Window' of 1920 (s21). The dead of the Second World War are also commemorated in glass, in the N-nave aisle (windows n28 and n30). The second half of the 20th century has yet to contribute any monuments on an equivalent scale.

120   *Monument to the fallen of the South African war in the north-nave aisle (monument 56). Enamel on copper with art nouveau overtones [BB93/15930]*

Inventory

Monuments in the Cathedral

Chapel of St Peter and the Apostles

(1) On E wall, canopied table tomb with effigies of Sir Thomas Gorges (d 1610) and his wife, Helena (Schnachenberg, Dowager Marchioness of Northampton), erected by his son, 1635; impressive monument of Bath stone [Fletcher 1932, 16–34]. Canopy, supported by fluted pilasters and twisted Corinthian columns, surmounted by obelisks, polyhedra and figures representing the Virtues. Interior of the canopy decorated with cherub heads and seven oval reliefs described as representing the *dona Spiritus Sancti*, including the sacrifice of Cain and Abel, Judgment of Solomon, Samson slaying the Philistines, and Joseph interpreting Pharaoh's dream. Shields of arms of Gorges, quarterly of six, in several places, impaling Schnachenberg quarterly of eight. S side, arms of Parr, marquess of Northampton, quarterly of twelve, impaling Schnachenberg quarterly of eight.

(2) On N wall, beaten brass wall tablet to Jane Morris Weighall (d 1906), by Omar Ramsden and Alwynn Carr. Very similar to monument (152) on N side of choir.

The Trinity Chapel

(3) on N stylobate, recumbent white marble effigy of Bishop Wordsworth (d 1911) on black marble tomb chest. Signed and dated George Frampton, 1914.

(4) Reset on S stylobate, tapering coffin lid of black Tournai marble, with chamfered sides and plain top with incised margins. Probably 11th or 12th century, brought from Old Sarum [RCHME 1980, 20]. Traditionally associated with St Osmund, it bears the inscription ANNO MXCIX (the year of Osmund's death), added in 16th or 17th century. In 1644 Symonds described the inscription as 'lately written' [Long 1859, 130]. The 18th-century plans show this coffin lid at the centre of the Trinity Chapel, in which position it would have covered a small stone receptacle 0.6 m x 0.3 m, discovered there (empty) in 1962. The position was consistent with the possible location of St Osmund's shrine from *c* 1457. The coffin lid may have been associated with the burial of Osmund in 1226, or it may have been placed in this position during the Marian period in an attempt to rehabilitate the shrine [Stroud 1984, 50–4]. In 1789 Wyatt placed the coffin lid in the third bay from the E of the N-nave arcade. Scott moved it to its present location.

Chapel of St Stephen and the Martyrs

(5) Occupying whole of E wall and obscuring much of the E window of the S aisle, tall wall monument with flanking obelisks. Recumbent effigies on marble tomb chests of Edward Seymour, earl of Hertford (son of Protector Somerset) (d 1621), and his wife, Lady Catherine Grey (d 1563) [see Fletcher 1927, 153], flanked by kneeling figures of their sons Edward and Thomas. Probably erected *c* 1625. Of variegated marbles, central compartment with coffered ceiling containing Latin inscription and heraldic display, including Seymour quarterly of fourteen impaling Grey quarterly of sixteen. Upper levels decorated with obelisks, allegorical female figures, surmounted by heraldic achievements with supporters [see Fletcher 1927 and *Wiltshire Gazette*, 29 July 1926]. Attributed to William Wright of London [A White 1994, 67].

(6) Against S wall, William Wilton (d 1523), chancellor of the Cathedral from 1506. Stone altar tomb with panelled sides and moulded Purbeck top; above, recessed reredos with six coupled trefoil-headed panels and, on E, canopied niche for image (lost); above reredos, canopy with moulded entablature inscribed *Fiat Voluntas Dei* and with three shields charged; E, badge of Henry VIII and Catherine of Aragon, half rose and half pomegranate; centre, the See (defaced) impaling Audley; W, a cross between four birds with an engrailed border (unidentified). Shields in cusped and sub-cusped quatrefoil panels on three faces of tomb chest charged (E to W): 'W'; 'WIL' (below a cap); *Fiat Voluntas Dei*; a tun below a cap; a cross.

Ambulatory

N wall

(7) 15th-century tomb recess with richly moulded four-centred head and continuous jamb ending in small shaft bases; in recess, contemporary tomb slab with ogee and hollow-chamfered edges, top hidden by coffin lid (8). Tomb opened in 1910 to disclose headless skeleton, but no evidence of episcopal burial [Malden 1912, 340–1].

(8) Reset in recess of monument (7), Purbeck coffin lid with ogee-moulded sides, top with plain embossed cross, probably 13th century. Some slight evidence of dowel holes to receive a brass on N arms of cross. The 13th-century coffin lid had been positioned in this 15th-century recess by Wyatt's time and there is no record of its former position. In the past it has been assigned to Bishop Roger (d 1139) and to Bishop Roger de Martival. Modern ascription to Bishop Longespee is certainly mistaken. Until 1789 Longespee's monument was in the pavement at the entrance to the Trinity Chapel; it consisted of two exceptionally large floor slabs with indents for heraldry [Price 1774, 73; Gough 1796, II, pt 1, pl CCCXXIX]. George Vertue noted the overall size of the floor slabs as 17 ft x 7½ ft (5.3 m x 2.3 m) [Walpole Society 1937–8, 129].

North-chancel aisle (proceeding E to W)

(9) In first bay, on wall, relief portrait in bronze of Bishop St Clair Donaldson (d 1936), surmounted by broken pediment with impaled arms of the See and Donaldson. Signed by A G Wyon.

(10) Opposite, reset in first bay of arcade, early 13th-century carved Purbeck coffin lid with effigy of bishop in trefoil-headed niche flanked by pinnacled buttresses and surmounted by tympanum containing angel holding sun and moon; traditionally taken to be a cenotaph in honour of Bishop Richard Poore, founder of the present cathedral [Dodsworth 1814, 212]. Bishop de Bingham (d 1246), responsible for the completion and beautification of the choir, and known to have been buried on the N side of the choir [Malden 1912, 343], and is the more

likely candidate for this position, traditionally reserved for a founder. Monument now in 19th-century aedicule designed by Scott in the Early English style, the original having been destroyed in 1789 during Wyatt's enlargement of the chancel, when the effigy and remains of the tomb were moved to St Catherine's chapel. See Britton [1836, pl XIII]. The original aedicule is depicted as the frontispiece of Milner [1798], taken from the drawing by John Carter made for Gough in 1781, at which time its vault had been taken down and the cavity filled with a 'common deal case or box' [BL Add MS 29,925, fol 119^r]. From 1789 to c 1865 the coffin was placed on a table tomb in St Catherine's chapel. The discovery in 1789 of a burial under the monument, albeit apparently not an episcopal one, cast doubt on the cenotaph theory, and it was first suggested that this might be the tomb of Bishop de Bingham [Rich Jones 1879, 50, 88]. Scott took an 'especial' interest in its restoration [Stamp 1995, 307–8] and used Carter's drawing as the basis for his reconstruction.

(11) Arcade, second bay, tomb and chantry chapel of Bishop Edmund Audley (1502–24), erected in his lifetime. Externally on the N the chapel is of two bays defined by pinnacled shaft-buttresses with concave sides and embattled caps; between pinnacles, mitred shields (for charges see below) on rich cornices with vine-scroll friezes and traceried brattishing. Each bay has a window of four transomed trefoil-headed lights with vertical tracery in roll-moulded four-centred outer head under casement-moulded square surround. Two W divisions of W window partly occupied by doorway with four-centred head under shield spandrels. S elevation generally similar, but windows without mullions and tracery; E bay contains Easter sepulchre under elaborate double canopy. Inside, two bays of fan-vaulting with heraldic bosses: E, See impaling Audley surrounded by wreath of pomegranates and roses (for Henry VIII and Catherine of Aragon); W, Audley, *a fret*. E wall with canopied niches and, at centre, defaced stone panel depicting the Assumption. Elsewhere, numerous shields charged with the Audley *frets*, the See impaling Audley, IHS, Maria, E.A. in knot, E.S. in knot, St George (Audley was chancellor of the Order of the Garter), and bee rebus. Audley was buried beneath the floor [Shortt 1973, 8]. As bishop of Hereford, Audley had already built a magnificent chantry in that cathedral [RCHME 1931, 103–4].

(12) Third bay, on wall, James Tuchet, Lord Castlehaven, (d 1769). Marble tablet in pedimented surround with cartouche showing blank shield with supporters, coronet and crest.

(13) Opposite, tomb formerly assigned to Bishop de Bingham, now ascribed to Bishop Roger de Martival (d 1330). Attribution to Bingham was generally accepted until 1916, although the 18th-century plans had erroneously transposed this and the opposite monument (146). In 1916 it was suggested [Hope 1916, 184–90] that this monument belonged to de Martival, known to have been buried on the N side of the presbytery [Malden 1912, 346]. Large rectangular Purbeck slab with rebated and hollow-chamfered edges and indents for brasses *(qv)*. Spanning slab and forming barrier between chancel and aisle (see also 146), 14th-century stone canopy comprising cinquefoil ogee arch with moulded and fretted

cusping outlined by ball-enrichment and with ogee label with sleeping-angel crockets and large foliate finial. Cusped iron grille closing archway is original. To E and W of arch, small detached buttresses and coupled openings with gabled heads are filled with fretted tracery and flanked by standards with crocketed pinnacles. Over weather capping, traceried pinnacle composed of miniature windows with crocketed gables, small flying buttresses with gabled finials and large terminal finial. Tomb opened in 1900 disclosing undisturbed episcopal burial [Malden 1912, 343]. The architectural ornament closely resembles that of the 14th-century tower.

North-east transept
(14) Beneath NE crossing, Thomas Bennett, 1554 [*VCH* III, 186]. Bennett died in 1558. Recess flanked by clustered Purbeck wall shafts supporting cornice inscribed *Misericordias Domini in aeternum cantabo*, AD 1554; within recess, panelled tomb chest with seven shields, end shields inscribed 'Thomas Bennet, Anno Domini 1554', other 'TB' and 'DL'; on chest, cadaver effigy resting on rolled rush mat and open shroud. Rear of wall of recess now blank but formerly painted with representation of Bennett in robes of LL.D, kneeling before the Crucifix in relief (now defaced) on the E jamb [Schnebbelie 1791].

North-choir aisle (proceeding E to W)
(15) On wall, John Lowe (d 1631), bencher of Middle Temple, small marble tablet.

(16) Edward Paroissien Eddrup, (d 1905). White marble tablet with grey marble surround.

(17) Robert George Swayne (d 1901). Alabaster and white marble wall tablet.

(18) On stylobate opposite, cadaver effigy similar to that of (14), but more coarsely carved without tomb chest. Assigned by Symonds to Archdeacon Sydenham (d 1524) [Long 1859, 135]. Symonds's identification appears to have rested on the inscription and heraldry which he saw in the window opposite, which survived into the 18th century [BL Lansdowne MS 968, fol 11^v (1702); BL Add MS 5833, fol 145 (1728)]. Sydenham was chaplain to Henry VIII, warden of De Vaux College and archdeacon of Sarum.

(19) Second bay, on wall, Douglas Macleane (d 1925). White marble wall tablet surrounded by gilded alabaster.

(20) Thomas Kingsbury (d 1899). White marble tablet with grey surround. Similar to (16).

(21) Third bay, on stylobate between chapel of St John and north-choir aisle, handsome canopied table tomb sometime ascribed to Bishop Woodville, but more probably of Dean Gilbert Kymer (d 1463) [Malden 1912, 348; Wordsworth 1914, 562]. Woodville held the See for only two years and died at Beaulieu in 1484. The close resemblance between this tomb chest and that which stood formerly at the centre of the N chapel of St Thomas's church [RCHME 1980, lvii, 30], suggests that the monuments are from the same workshop and date from the middle of the 15th century. Kymer willed to be buried

in the 'south wall' of the cathedral [Rich Jones 1881, 317]. Comprises Purbeck marble tomb chest with panelled sides, each quatrefoil enclosing stone shield with dowel holes for lost brasses; top with moulded edge and indent for brass inscription strip; above, Purbeck marble canopy with moulded cinquefoil four-centred arch outlined by hollow chamfers with spaced bosses; E and W responds with cinquefoil-headed stone panelling; spandrels with quatrefoils enclosing shields, formerly with brasses; soffit of canopy with cinquefoil-headed stone panels. Monument has seatings for an iron grille which divided St John's chapel from the aisle. They were probably installed under the will of Henry Sutton, treasurer 1495–1505, who left 20 marks for two 'entrecloses' between the end of the choir and its chapels [Wordsworth 1914, 566]. The tomb was opened in 1983. Burial had been disturbed in 1876.[17]

Chapel of St John the Baptist
East wall (proceeding S to N)
(22) White marble wall monument with broken pediment. Obscured by organ.

(23) Anne Seyner (d ?). Stone wall monument surmounted by urn.

(24) Anna Maria Sturges (d 1803). Similar to (23).

(25) Louisa Brodie (d 1816).

Chapel of St Edmund of Abingdon
East wall
(26) Lettice Cotton (d 1798). White, grey, and black marble wall monument with damaged pediment.

(27) Revd Edward Moore (d 1812) and Mary Moore (d 1822). White inscription tablet with black gable.

(28) Sarah Evans (d 1804) and James Evans (d 1825). White marble tablet.

(29) Between chapels of St Edmund and St Thomas, William Long (d 1818), large monument with flanking marble figures of Learning and Charity in Gothic framework, by John Flaxman.

Chapel of St Thomas
(30) On E wall, W G Maton (d 1835), stone monument in Tudor style by Osmond.

(31) On N wall, Walter Long (d 1807), marble tablet with flanking figures in Gothic architectural framework, portrait medallion and pendant shield of arms of Long. Said to be by Flaxman [Britton 1801, 182].

North transept
North wall (proceeding E to W)
(32) White marble tablet with broken pediment and armorial with motto, to Captain Sir Edward Hamilton Westrom Hulse, d 1915 at Neuve Chapelle.

(33) Sir Richard Colt Hoare, Bart (d 1818), historian of Wiltshire. Seated marble statue by R C Lucas, 1841.

(34) Bishop John Blythe (d 1499), at centre of wall, reset c 1789, concealing rear arch of St Thomas's doorway, stone tomb chest with defaced effigy enclosed in arcaded structure with stone windows surmounted by carved cornice and brattishing; chest with quatrefoil-panelled sides and ends, each panel enclosing blank shield; interior of structure with vaulted ceiling (with traces of medieval pigment) and with blind arcade on N side; eastern bay of blind arcade contains small blocked doorway with four-centred head. The 18th-century plans (Figs 14 and 15), show Blythe's monument in the retrochoir. According to Leland, 'Bishop Beauchamp made a rich tumbe and a chapel over it at the W end of our Lady Chapelle, but... John Blith... was buried under it' [Toulmin Smith 1964, 264]. This two-storey structure was originally set against the E face of the screen behind the high altar. Price described Blythe's tomb as 'under an arch with a closet over it' [Price 1753, 83]. In 1781 John Carter recorded that 'a canopy of wood work has lately been taken way' and showed the structure without the cornice and brattishing [BL Add MS 29,925, fol 120r].

(35) Wall tablet commemorating four Clerks of the Peace, James Swayne 1753–1827, Robert Swayne 1778–1865, William Clark Merriman 1805–1877 and Robert William Merriman 1836–1924.

(36) Sergeant Major John Michael Peniston (d 1858). Gothic canopy with tiled niches. Pendant quatrefoil with initials in central niche. Inscribed brass (by Waller) beneath. By Osmond.

West wall (proceeding N to S)
(37) General George Michell (d 1846). Oval medallion in 13th-century style by Osmond.

(38) Sarah Hayter (d 1822). Arms of Hayter on sarcophagus-shaped tablet by Osmond.

(39) At window level, William Benson Earle (d 1796), tablet with figure of the Muse unveiling a representation of the Good Samaritan. By John Flaxman.

(40) Below, Revd Edmund Benson (d 1835) and Anne (Hunt) (d 1826). Large stone wall monument with painted armorials, in Tudor style by Osmond.

(41) Bust on plinth with inscription, to Richard Jefferies (d 1887). By Margaret Thomas, 1892.

(42) James Harris, first earl of Malmesbury (d 1820). Inscribed plinth with arms of Harris, supporting life-size marble figure of reclining man with book. By Francis Chantrey, 1823.

(43) George Lawrence (d 1861). Inscribed tablet surmounted by kneeling figure of sorrowing woman in classical drapery, leaning on urn. By T Gaffin.

(44) At window level, James Harris (d 1780), inscription tablet surmounted by bas-relief of seated female with medallion portrait. By John Bacon.

(45) Below, Sir James Erasmus Philipps (d 1912), and his wife, Mary Margaret (d 1913). Inscribed classical tablet with foliage ornament on blue and gold mosaic backgrounds and armorial. Flanking niches with coloured marble columns and figures of St David and St Boniface. Erected 1915.

(46) Large pedimented white marble tablet commemorating members of the Harris family, from James Harris (d 1679) to Louisa Margaret Harris (d 1826).

(47) Frederick Webb (d 1846) and his son Augustus Frederick Cavendish Webb, d 1854 of wounds received at Balaclava. Ogee-headed Gothic canopy with armorial in gable. By Osmond.

North-nave aisle (proceeding E to W)

(48) Wall, first bay, James Wickens (d 1827) and Anne, his wife (d 1850). White marble scroll surmounted by pediment and urn on black marble base.

(49) John Stephens (d 1780) and Mary (Bull), his wife (d 1779). White marble tablet with pyramidal pediment and black marble details, bearing long biographical inscription [*Wiltshire Gazette*, 11 Nov 1927].

(50) Henry Hatcher (d 1846), '[historian] of this cathedral and adjoining city. . .'. Stone monument by Osmond in Gothic architectural surround. The epitaph reveals Hatcher to have been the author of the historical part of Dodsworth [1814].

(51) Opposite, reset *c* 1789 on stylobate, Sir John Cheney (d 1509), alabaster effigy formerly on canopied table tomb at SW corner of Beauchamp chapel. Cheney, a supporter of Henry VII, was Bishop Beauchamp's executor [Dodsworth 1814, 199–201; Benson and Hatcher 1843, 543]. Present tomb chest made up of fragments apparently from other monuments. The original tomb chest and canopy, drawn in 1781 by John Carter [BL Add MS 29,925, fol 130^r], was destroyed when the chapel was demolished. Tomb opened in 1973 to reveal 18th-century box containing bones as described by Dodsworth [Dodsworth 1814, 201; Spring 1979, 11]. Below, in stylobate, medieval stone coffin with tapering Purbeck lid, opened in 1973 and found to contain skeleton and pewter chalice [Spring 1979, 11].

(52) Arcade, second bay, Walter, Lord Hungerford (d 1449), and his first wife, Catherine (Peverell). Table tomb constructed 1779 on site of former chantry chapel with fragments taken partly from panelled stone base of chapel and partly from elsewhere, topped by two cut-down Purbeck floor slabs with indents for brasses [Spring 1979, 12]. The chantry chapel, dedicated to the Annunciation, had been licensed in 1429 [Fletcher 1936a, 452]. Iron grilles surrounding the chapel reset in 1779 on S side of the chancel to form family pew for the earls of Radnor (see p 73) [Gough 1796, II, pt 2 159–65; Fletcher 1936a 447–56].

(53) Opposite, on wall, white marble monument with grey marble frame and bronze portrait relief, to Lt-Gen Sir George Montague Harper (d 1922).

(54) White marble tablet with armorial within Purbeck frame, to Horatio, third Earl Nelson (d 1913).

(55) Third bay, on wall, memorial to those who died in the railway accident at Salisbury on 1 July 1906. Pedimented tablet in coloured marble with flanking figures of angels supporting shields.

(56) Fourth bay, on wall, memorial in copper with brass insets, relief medallion, and red and blue enamel detailing, to the Wiltshire dead of the South African War, 1900–3.

(57) Opposite, reset on stylobate *c* 1789, John Montacute, earl of Salisbury (d 1389) [Dodsworth 1814, 196–7]. Panelled tomb chest and effigy in armour, all in sandstone, formerly on stylobate between Trinity Chapel and Chapel of St Peter and Apostles, to E of William Longespee the Elder. See the two 18th-century plans (Figs 14 and 15). The stylobate of the NE chapel is unlikely to have been the original position. As it has no N side (made up of second-hand fragments by Wyatt), the tomb chest probably stood against a N wall and it may be conjectured that it was in the middle bay of the Trinity Chapel. If so, the tomb was probably moved westwards to the adjoining stylobate to make way for the doorway to the Hungerford chantry, *c* 1460. E end of chest with shield of arms of Montacute in a border; S side with four shields: (i) uncharged, (ii) Montacute quartering Monthermer, (iii) Montacute impaling uncharged, (iv) Montacute impaling Monthermer; W end, Isle of Man quartering Montacute [Dorling 1903a, 46–8]; N side composed of reused 15th-century fragments from 'canopies of the Hungerford monument' [Carter 1803, 1022]. Jupon of effigy formerly painted with arms, now blank [Long 1859, 130]. Remainder of effigy and tomb has traces of painting and gilding [Spring 1979, 13].

(58) Arcade, fifth bay, resting on stylobate. Purbeck table tomb, probably second half of the 15th century, with quatrefoil-panelled sides, each quatrefoil with blank shield with dowel holes for brasses (lost); top with dowel holes for lost inscription strip, and defaced indent for brass.

(59) On wall opposite, white marble portrait relief of the soldier-poet E W Tennant (d 1916). Signed A G W (Arthur George Walker RA).

(60) Arcade, seventh bay, resting on stylobate. Late medieval Purbeck table tomb with flat sides, each long side having three plain shields (formerly with brasses) in cusped roundels; between roundels, indents for three scroll-shaped inscription plates; flat top with moulded edges. Possibly *in situ*; both 18th-century plans show a monument in this position. The 'Ichnographical Plan' in the British Library (Fig 14) calls it *episcopus puerorum*, obviously in error.

(61) Arcade, eighth bay, resting on stylobate, 13th-century Purbeck effigy of man in mail armour with shields and sword, legs crossed, said to represent William Longespee (d 1250) [Dodsworth 1814, 192–5; Planche 1859, 115–30], son of the earl of Salisbury of the same name (see 96). The 18th-century plans offer no identification. The British Library plan describes it as 'a Knight Templar unknown'. The younger Longespee's death on Crusade is recorded, with lively illustration, by Matthew Paris in the *Chronica Majora*, but no mention is made of his burial at Salisbury. The effigy was probably set in its present location *c* 1860 [FOSC 1973]. On temporary removal in 1973, six coins of the reign of Charles I were found beneath it, but no burial. Its original position is unknown.

(62) Immediately W, small late 13th-century or early 14th-century effigy in Bath stone representing a bishop with mitre and crosier in canopied niche, 1.1 m long; formerly further E, under seating, but moved to present position c 1676–7 [Price 1774, 65]. Since the recovery of this monument in the 17th century it has provoked a great deal of discussion centred on the improbable theory that it represents a 'chorister bishop' [eg Rawlinson 1723, 70–83; Planche 1859, 121–4]. It was originally protected by an iron grille [Price 1774, 65; Walpole Society 1937–8, 129]. A more likely candidate for commemoration is Bishop William de la Corner, who is known to have been buried in the E part of the nave [Malden 1912, 345–6].

(63) On wall opposite, large inscribed white marble tablet with black frame, to William Coles (d 1789), Jane (Walter) Coles (d 1801), Jane Medlycott, their daughter (d 1824), and her daughter Jane Paget Ainslie (d 1839).

(64) In westernmost bay of arcade, resting on stylobate, 13th-century tapering Purbeck coffin lid with roll-moulded and double-chamfered edges, top retaining traces of a cross in relief.

Nave
West wall
(65) N of W doorway, D'Aubigny Turbeville (d 1696) and his wife Anne (Ford) (d 1694). Upright tablet of slate or Purbeck marble, with moulded stone base and stone cornice supporting cartouche of arms of Turbeville impaling Ford, with putti, and vase finial.

(66) S of W doorway, Thomas, Baron Wyndham of Finglass (d 1745), grey and white marble monument, seated grieving woman, holding staff and harp, with arms of Wyndham. Signed 'Mich[l]. Rysbrack'. For inscription, see *Wiltshire Gazette*, 22 Apr 1926.

South-nave aisle (proceeding W to E)
(67) Arcade, first bay, resting on stylobate. Plain tapering Purbeck coffin and lid with chamfered and roll-moulded edges, probably 13th century. When opened in 1973 a skeleton was found inside [Spring 1979, 5].

(68) Arcade, third bay, reset on stylobate, late 12th-century Purbeck coffin lid, possibly of Bishop Roger (d 1139), with effigy lying in trefoil-headed recess and surrounded by frieze of vine-scroll ornament [Raby 1948; Shortt 1971; Stroud 1984]. Head and mitre restored, perhaps 14th century.

(69) Immediately E, 12th-century Purbeck coffin lid, with effigy of bishop in mitre and chasuble. Verses inscribed on chasuble and along edges of coffin lid. In 1226 it was one of those moved to the new Cathedral. Has been variously attributed to Bishop Jocelin de Bohun (d 1184) [Shortt 1971] and Osmund [Raby 1948]. The most recent examination confirms its attribution to Osmund [Stroud 1993]. It is shown in its present position on the 18th-century plans (Figs 14 and 15), but Leland saw it and the adjacent monument (68) in the N-nave aisle: '*In Bor. Insula navis Eccl. Sepulchra duorum Episcoporum veteris, ut autumant, Sarum. Inscriptio aterius sepulchri: Adfer opem, devenies in idem*' [Toulmin Smith

1964, 265]. They were probably moved to their present location c 1676–7, when seating was introduced into the nave [Wordsworth 1915, 46–50]. In 1226, however, when both were presumably transferred from Old Sarum, they must have been placed in the only completed part of the Cathedral, at the E end. (68) may have been moved out of the Trinity Chapel at the time of the construction of St Osmund's shrine.

(70) On wall opposite, Henry Richard William Farrer (d 1933). Simple stone tablet.

(71) Robert Graves Blackburne Farrer of the Malay Civil Service (d 1928). White marble with flanking palm trees.

(72) William Fawcett (d 1887) and Mary, his wife (d 1889). White marble tablet with fluted pilasters.

(73) Fourth bay, on wall, Henry Fawcett (d 1884). Identical design to (71).

(74) Below, Sarah Maria Fawcett (d 1923). As (71) and (72).

(75) Memorial to Alexander Ballantyne MD, erected by his brothers, John and James, 1783. Wall monument with large white marble sarcophagus on grey marble slab decorated with crossed palm leaves (damaged).

(76) Revd William Brown (d 1784).

(77) Opposite, resting on stylobate, anonymous 15th- or 16th-century Purbeck marble tomb chest with moulded top and panelled sides, with quatrefoils enclosing blank shields; perhaps *in situ*. When opened in 1972 an unidentifiable burial was found in the stylobate below [Spring 1979, 6–7].

(78) Fifth bay, on wall, tablet to Henry Hele MD, white marble with variegated frame surmounted by palm branch and wreath.

(79) Simple stone tablet (modern), Richard Brassey Hole (d 1849).

(80) Below, stone tablet, Bertram Charles Parsons (d 1968).

(81) Sixth bay, on wall, Margaret Tounson (d 1634), slate tablet in painted stone surround with broken pediment enclosing oval cartouche of arms with Tounson impaling Davenant quartering Stanton.

(82) Edward Davenant (d 1639), plain marble tablet with cornice surmounted by arms of Davenant quartering Stanton.

(83) Opposite, reset on stylobate in 1789, stone tomb chest with quatrefoil panels surrounding blank shields and with plain top formed from *mensa* of medieval altar; chest used in 1789 to enclose bones of Bishop Richard Beauchamp (d 1481), whose tomb chest was destroyed during demolition of Beauchamp chantry chapel. Dodsworth [1814, 195] says that the chest came 'from the aisle at the N end of the principal transept', but it is not shown on either 18th-century plan.

(84) Arcade, seventh bay, resting on stylobate, rich alabaster effigy, Robert, Lord Hungerford, (d 1459), brought in 1789 from recess in N wall of Trinity Chapel and set on a tomb chest composed of reused Purbeck marble slabs with 15th-century panelled decoration, perhaps from original tomb chest. A

number of closely similar effigies have been identified [Stone 1955, 131]. Effigy dressed in Milanese-inspired armour, meticulously detailed. Considerable traces of pigment remain. Monument temporarily dismantled in 1974 revealing wooden box of 1789 marked 'bones removed out of the wall of the . . . Hungerford chapel and of St Mary's chapel'. The effigy on top of its canopied tomb chest, set into the recess in the wall between the chantry chapel and the Trinity Chapel, can be seen in Charles Frederick's drawing of 1734 [BL Add MS 27,349, fol 67], and in John Carter's more accurate drawing of 1781 [BL Add MS 29,925, fol 127ʳ], although by this time the opening had been blocked with boards and the northern face of the tomb chest had been badly damaged. Parts of the original monument may be incorporated in (57); others were built by Wyatt into a monument to Bishop Poore in the NE transept [Carter 1803, 1022]. Underneath on stylobate, antecedent Purbeck floor slab with indents (see pp 158–9).

(85) On wall opposite, Canon John Priaulx (d 1674), slate tablet in stone surround with scrolls with a cornice surmounted by cartouche of arms Priaulx impaling ?Ely.

(86) Mrs Mary (Mervin) Cooke (d 1642), slate tablet in stone surround surmounted by arms of Cooke and Mervin.

(87) Eighth bay, on wall, Joseph Gribble (d 1767), black slate tablet with white marble surround.

(88) Archdeacon Henry Stebbing (d 1763), plain marble tablet with cartouche of arms.

(89) Elizabeth, daughter of Bishop Hyde, classical marble tablet, with lozenge of arms of Hyde.

(90) Opposite, resting on stylobate, formerly positioned on the stylobate between Trinity Chapel and St Stephen's Chapel, where it was seen by Leland (c 1540) [Toulmin Smith 1964, 264] and Symonds c 1644 [Long 1859, 130]. Before 1789, when it was removed to the nave, this monument was identified as that of Lord Stourton, perhaps having been appropriated by someone of that name after the dismantling of Osmund's shrine in 1539. In 1542, when Leland visited the Cathedral, the tomb base was still associated with Osmund [Toulmin Smith 1964, 264]. Reset in this position in 1789. 13th-century tomb base of polished Purbeck marble with roll-moulded base with projections for shafts, plain sides with three rounded apertures in each long side, and flat top with roll-moulded edges and leaf-shaped projections for shaft heads. Part of the tomb of St Osmund erected over his body on translation to the Cathedral in 1226. In 1974, when the monument was temporarily dismantled, no grave was found in the stylobate below [Spring 1979, 9].

(91) Arcade, ninth bay, reset on stylobate in 1789, Purbeck effigy of Bishop Walter de la Wyle (d 1270), representing mitred figure lying in canopied niche, much defaced. Carter records that the effigy was formerly in the 'centre chapel in the North transept' [Carter 1803, 1021], ie St Edmund's chapel, on the S side of which a tomb is shown in the 18th-century plans. Leland confirms that Bishop de la Wyle was buried 'ad altare S. Edmundi' [Toulmin Smith 1964, 266]. Tomb chest, largely of 1789, includes slabs of Purbeck marble

with panelled enrichment, probably from tombs and canopies formerly in the Beauchamp chapel [Gough 1796, II, pt 1]. Carter, however, maintained that the tomb was 'made up of the havocked upper parts of the Hungerford monument' [Carter 1803, 1021]. Opened in 1973 to reveal boxes inscribed 'bones from W end of Beauchamp chapel'. Lead coffin beneath contained burial, coins and remains of hawk [Spring 1979, 9–10].

(92) On wall opposite, Sir Henry Hyde (d 1650), black-and-white marble tablet in architectural framework with Ionic columns surmounted by shield of arms of Hyde quartering Norbury and Sibelis.

(93) Elihonor Sadler (d 1622), painted stone wall monument with shield of arms of Sadler and Powell, both impaling St Barbe. Within niche with coffered vault, female figure in profile kneeling at a prie-dieu.

(94) Tenth bay, on wall (formerly in the N transept), Margaret Ashley (d 1679), rococo marble cartouche, surmounted by shield of arms of Ashley quartering Huttoft, impaling Harris. Attributed to Jasper Latham.[18]

(95) Monument with fluted pilasters, broken pediment with armorial, commemorating Bishop Gilbert Burnet (d 1715). Erected 1960 by an American descendant.

(96) Opposite, reset on stylobate in 1789, painted oak tomb chest and painted Tournai marble military effigy of William Longespee, earl of Salisbury (d 1226); mail hauberk and coif, with surcoat; shield charged *azure six lioncels or, three, two, one*, in relief [Long 1859, 130] lying on slightly tapering bed with foliate border; chest with arcaded sides retaining painted, silvered and gilded decoration above earlier colouring [Dodsworth 1814, 201–4]. William Longespee, son of Henry II by Rosamund de Clifford, became earl of Salisbury by right of his wife, Ela d'Evreux, countess of Salisbury. Both William and Ela were present in 1220 at the laying of the foundation stone of the new Cathedral. In the 18th-century plans (Figs 14 and 15), this monument shares the stylobate between the Trinity Chapel and the NE chapel with that of John de Montacute (57); originally it probably stood in the middle of the same bay, but was moved W to make room for the Montacute tomb c 1460. The columns on the S were renewed in 1907.

South transept

West wall (proceeding N to S)

(97) At window level, Milo Sandys (d 1632), slate tablet in moulded stone frame with cornice.

(98) Below, Revd John Selwyn, master of Wigston's Hospital, Leicester (d 1823). White marble tablet draped with foliage, shield of arms below, on black slab.

(99) White marble sarcophagus, with long biographical text on black slab, to Thomas Rennell (d 1824). Said to be by Flaxman [*Wiltshire Gazette*, 26 May 1926].

(100) Charles Ekins of the Bengal Cavalry (d 1849). By Osmond.

(101) Sir Robert Hyde, recorder of Salisbury and Chief Justice of Common Pleas (d 1665); large monument of black-and-white marble with inscription panels, bust and small cartouche of arms of Hyde impaling Barber. By Besnier [Pevsner and Metcalf 1985, 282].

(102) Immediately above, Robert Hay, 17th-century Purbeck tablet in marble surround with broken pediment containing shield of arms of Hay.

(103) Further S, Bishop John Thomas (d 1766), marble tablet with swag, inscriptions and painted shield of arms, of the See impaling Thomas, with Garter and mitre.

(104) Alabaster tablet to John Henry Jacob (d 1905).

(105) S of the doorway to the Plumbery yard, Ursula and Katherine Sadleir, 1641, small black marble tablet with moulded marble frame.

(106) Thomas Henry Hume, treasurer (d 1834), marble tablet in Gothic stone surround with four-centred head, pinnacles, niches, etc, in 15th-century style, by Hopper, London.

(107) Above, Charles Langford (d 1635), painted inscription tablet in moulded segmental-headed surround with spirally fluted cheek-pieces; the arms of Langford quartering Rogers.

(108) S of the cloister doorway, General A L Layard, (d 1823), white marble tablet on slate base.

(109) On S wall, in SW corner, Willoughby Vere Bertie, (d 1812 at 1 year old), and his father, Willoughby Bertie, lost at sea 1810. White marble sarcophagus with sickle and rose, on black slate tablet, by Osmond.

(110) At centre of wall, Edward Poore (d 1780), and his wife Rachel (Mullens) (d 1771). Canopied table tomb in 15th-century style, with heraldry of Poore, by J Carline of Shrewsbury to a design by Revd Hugh Owen [Gunnis 1980, 80], 1817. The tomb is enclosed by iron railings with heraldic pennants [Benson and Hatcher 1843, 582].

(111) Immediately E, Lt-Col Roger Alvin Poore. Killed at Passchendaele, 1917. Marble tablet on slate base.

(112) Bishop John Hume (d 1782), and his wife, Lady Mary (Hay) (d 1805). White marble tablet surmounted by urn and gartered monogram. By T King of Bath.

(113) Stone tablet with chequered fillet, Mark Saurin Poore (d 1931).

Chapel of St Michael

(114) On E wall, Bishop Frederick Edward Ridgeway (d 1921). Stone with bronze half-length portrait relief. By A G Wyon 1924.

Chapel of St Lawrence

(115) Bishop John Fisher (d 1825), canopied table tomb in 15th-century style surmounted by a cushion, the Bible and a crozier. By Osmond [SJ, 24 Nov 1828]. Canopy a later addition.

East wall (proceeding S to N)

(116) James Bennett (d 1859). Gothic gable enclosing white cross on diaper ground. By Osmond.

(117) Elizabeth Douce (d 1810). White marble sarcophagus with inverted torches.

(118) Lt William Fisher of the Bengal Lancers (d 1845). Erected by his brother officers. Elaborate quatrefoil within a medallion. By Osmond.

(119) Anna Eliza (Dawson) Slade (d 1819). Large wall monument in 15th-century style, by Osmond.

Chapel of St Margaret

(120) John Henry Jacob (d 1862). Coffin with armorials and foliate cross, enclosed within arcaded tomb chest with mosaic decoration and inlaid brass on top and inscription strip around base. Designed by G E Street.

East wall

(121) John Douglas (d 1834), marble tablet by Osmond.

(122) William Douglas (d 1819), marble tablet by Osmond.

South-choir aisle (proceeding W to E)

(123) On stylobate between chapel of St Margaret and S-choir aisle, canopied table tomb of Bishop Richard Medford (d 1407), secretary and confidant of Richard II, comprising elegantly arcaded alabaster tomb chest with moulded Purbeck marble top on which lies alabaster effigy of the bishop with greyhounds at his feet; above, Chilmark stone canopy with panelled sides and soffit, four-centred N and S arches outlined by casement mouldings containing friezes of birds carrying scrolls on which are painted black-letter inscriptions honor, deo et glorie; spandrels of arches with carved shield of arms: N, the See and Medford; S, England (after 1405) and Edward the Confessor. Considerable traces of painting and gilding remain. Opened 1982, revealing disturbed burial, but no artefacts found. The tomb had been broken into during the interment of Mary Hurst in 1665 [Spring 1987a, 137].

(124) Opposite, on the stylobate, obscured by the organ console, Purbeck marble floor slab (3.2 m x 1.1 m), largely defaced, but retaining traces of indent and a few letters of a marginal inscription, perhaps medieval, also mortices for protective iron railings [WAM xxxv (1908), 347–50; Bodl MS Gough Maps, vol 32, fol 52].

(125) Now against the S wall, but formerly on the N side (hence figures incorrectly orientated), Sir Richard Mompesson (d 1627), and his wife Katherine (Pagington). The monument was moved from the N side in 1877 to accommodate the new organ. Inferior imitation of the Hertford monument (5). Of painted stone, repainted in 1964, with effigies on tomb chest between Corinthian columns which flank arched recess; above, large central cartouche of arms of Mompesson with four other coats impaling Pagington with three other coats; same heraldry below. Also oblong inscription panel (blank) in strapwork surround; obelisks, painted to simulate marble, flank the monument.

(126) Third bay, on wall, monument, of coloured marble, to Dean George David Boyle (d 1901).

(127) Bishop John Davenant (d 1641), large marble wall monument, with biographical inscription in Latin [see *Wiltshire Gazette*, 10 June 1926], in classical architectural framework surmounted by cartouche of arms of the See impaling Davenant. Gough's engraved plan [Gough 1796, II, pt 1 pl XXXIX] mistakenly shows this monument on the W wall of the S transept. The original drawing (Fig 15), which the engraver was supposed to copy, shows Davenant's monument in its present position. Attributed to Joshua Marshall.[19]

(128) Opposite, on stylobate, remains of monument of Bishop John Capon or Salcote (d 1557). Panelled stone tomb chest with quatrefoils enclosing shields inscribed 'J.C. and E.S., 1555' (sic); chest resembles that of Thomas Bennet (14) and formerly occupied a similar recess. The recess is shown in Charles Frederick's drawing of 1734 [BL Add MS 27,349, fol 64] and in the Gough collection [Bodl MS Gough Maps, vol 32, fol 48ᵛ].

South-east transept

West wall (proceeding N to S)

(129) Commemorating William Chillingworth (d 1643/4), erected 1836 by Canon William Lisle Bowles. By Osmond.

(130) Rowney Noel (d 1786), dean. Marble tablet with urn and arms of Noel quartering two other coats, impaling Boothby quartering Skrymsher.

(131) Commemorating Richard Hooker (d 1600). Erected 1836 by Canon W L Bowles. By Osmond.

(132) Bishop Seth Ward (d 1689), large marble wall tablet, with long biographical inscription [*Wiltshire Gazette*, 8 July 1926] positioned between trophy of scientific instruments at the base and a cartouche of arms of the See impaling Ward within a Garter supported by putti heads at the top; over all, bust of Bishop Ward, mitred.

(133) Below, Canon Seth Ward (d 1690), Bishop Ward's nephew. Oval cartouche with shield and inscription [*Wiltshire Gazette*, 8 July 1926].

(134) Further S, John Clark (d 1757), dean. Large tablet on plinth surmounted by broken pediment and gable decorated with mathematical instruments. Inscription recording friendship with Newton [*Wiltshire Gazette*, 15 July 1926].

(135) Above, small white marble wall tablet commemorating John Jacob, MD, his wife Mary (Clark) and her sister, Frances, daughters of Dean Clark.

South wall (proceeding W to E)

(136) Grecian sarcophagus of John Henry Jacob (d 1828).

(137) Bishop Thomas Burgess (d 1837), large canopied table tomb in 15th-century style. By Osmond.

(138) Mary Ann Moberly (d 1890). White marble relief in art nouveau style with angel with trumpet. Signed E M Rope.

(139) Susanna Carpenter (d 1919). Oval tablet with gilded wreath.

Chapel of St Nicholas

(140) On S wall, E of the door into the treasury, Edith Emily Moberly (d 1901), relief with choristers and lily.

(141) On E wall, Matthew Marsh (d 1840). Canopied niche in 14th-century style. By Osmond.

Chapel of St Mary Magdalene

(142) On E Wall, to the poet W L Bowles (d 1850). Florid Gothic tablet by Osmond (unsigned) [*Builder*, IX (1851), 173].

South chancel aisle (proceeding W to E)

(143) First bay, on stylobate between chapel of St Mary Magdalene and chancel aisle, tomb of Bishop Giles de Bridport (d 1262), during whose episcopacy the Cathedral was consecrated. Monument comprises rich stone and Purbeck aedicule having arcade N and S sides, each of two bays with moulded and enriched two-centred arches of two separated orders rising from Purbeck shafts with moulded capitals and bases. On N side inner order of each bay is wholly of polished Purbeck, having coupled trefoil-headed arches and quatrefoil tracery. Outer order of stone with multiple roll-mouldings and label under moulded and enriched gable with leaf crockets, beast-stops at base, foliate apex. Flanking the bays, Purbeck shafts support moulded Purbeck cornices at eaves of weather stone roof with elaborate foliate finials. On S side details are similar to those described, but inner order has stone tracery and flanking shafts have no finials. E end of the roof has crocketed gable and foliate apex finial. Spandrels on N and S sides contain sculptured bas-reliefs recording events in Bishop Giles's life [Dodsworth 1814, 215–16; Roberts 1983]. Inside aedicule, resting on stylobate, plain tapering Purbeck coffin covered by coffin lid with roll-moulded edges and with effigy of the bishop lying under cinquefoil niche head with gable surmounted by crenellated buildings and flanked by angels.

(144) Within E crossing on S wall, slate tablet carved with achievement of the earls of Pembroke within a Garter, erected 1963 and repeating inscription formerly on 19th-century brass plate in paving. Commemorates various members of the Herbert family between 1600 and 1732.

(145) On wall dividing chancel aisle from chapel of St Mary Magdalene, Mary Barnston (d 1625), small Purbeck tablet in painted stone. Cartouche with eared surround containing painted shields of Barnston and Manning [Dorling 1895, 171]; also epitaph of her husband, Canon Barnston (d 1645) [*VCH* III. 190]. Until 1789 the tablet and hatchment were in the Trinity Chapel, on the N side [Price 1753, 72; Dorling 1894, 314–16]. Of the crest that surmounted the tablet, only the wreath remains.

(146) Opposite, on stylobate, Purbeck marble tomb slab ascribed to Bishop Simon de Gandavo (d 1315), with indent. Above early 14th-century combined canopy and grille similar to that of Bishop de Martival (13), but without cusping, side-openings or pinnacle; ball-flower enrichment on responds. Ogee arch has foliate enrichment, crocketed label and large foliate finial. Together with (13), served as part of the original choir enclosure.

(147) Second bay, on wall, simple tablet with inscription and shield of arms, to Jacob Pleydell Bouverie, 6th earl of Radnor (d 1930).

(148) Samuel Rolleston, archdeacon of Sarum (d 1766), and James Rolleston MD (d 1771); marble tablet with architectural surround and cartouche of arms.

(149) In easternmost bay, on stylobate, Bishop Walter Kerr Hamilton (d 1869). Tomb chest and effigy, designed by Sir George Gilbert Scott, with white marble effigy worked by the Hon the Revd P B Bouverie, 1881 [Wheeler 1901, 4].

(150) On wall opposite, Susan Esther Wordsworth, wife of Bishop Wordsworth (d 1894). Copper inscription plate, moulded marble frame and floral mosaic ground.

Ambulatory
South wall

(151) Bishop George Moberly (d 1885). Canopied recess containing coffin lid with effigy, angel supporters, and quatrefoil reliefs with episodes from the bishop's life. Designed by Sir Arthur Blomfield and executed by Thomas Nicholls (unveiled 1888) [Wheeler 1901, 26].

(152) Beaten bronze wall tablet to Clifford Wyndham Holgate (d 1903), with arms of the Virgin and Child and Holgate.

Monuments in the cloisters

Many of the wall monuments in the cloisters are heavily corroded and weathered but are worthy of study for the concentration of work by Osmond. His workshop clearly offered the client an established set of models to choose from, and several of the cloister monument types are also found inside the church. The N walk (second and third bays) contains a collection of the wooden crosses that marked the first graves of the fallen on the First World War battlefields. These crosses were brought home by the bereaved families and at one time were planted in the cloister garth.

South of door from south transept into east walk

1. William Osmond (d 1875) and his wife and children. White marble.

2. Jane Louise Chapeau (d 1867). Identical to (116) above. By Osmond.

East walk
Bay 1

3. Richard Guy? 184? Tudor Style. By Osmond. Heavily weathered.

Bay 3

4. William Posthumous Chapeau (d 1833), Louise Haydon Chicheley (d 1848), Francis William John Chicheley (d 1831) and Louisa Elizabeth. By Osmond.

5. Beneath (4), marble tablet to Henry Stevens (d 1867), Francis Margaret (d 1879) and Henry Chicheley Chapeau, (d 1877).

6. William Wadham Young (d 1862). By Osmond.

Bay 4

7. Mary Gilbert (d 1854) and husband, Thomas Webb Gilbert (d 1867). By Osmond?

Bay 5

9. John Luxford (d 1813) and his son John Bellamy Bowes Luxford. White marble sarcophagus on grey slate.

Bay 7

10. Caroline, wife of John Luxford (d 1800). White marble tablet set into stone surround and surmounted by an urn.

11. Of Anne and Henrietta Wenyeve. Stone with wreathed urn, oval inscription tablet missing. By Regnart, London.

Bay 8

12. Henrietta Sophia Jacob. Illegible date. Oval Gothic frame by Osmond.

13. Frederick Fawson Lee (d 1899). White marble in stone surround.

Bay 9

14. George Lewes Benson (d 1862) and Sarah his wife (d 1857). By Osmond.

15. Sarah Anne Benson (d 1836). Eight-pointed star enclosing quatrefoil containing inscription. By Osmond.

Bay 10

16. Harry Archer Mount (d 1790). Oval inscribed stone.

17. Below (16), William Young (d 1881). Inscribed lozenge.

South walk
Bay 2

18. Wadham Wyndham (d 1835) and Jane, his wife (d 1856). By Osmond.

19. Israel Vanderplank (d 1797). Plain white marble oval tablet.

Bay 4

20. John Edward Young (d 1832). Classical white marble tablet on slate base. By Osmond.

21. William Arney (d 1824), wife Maria (d 1845) and two sons. Sarcophagus with draped urn. By Osmond.

Bay 6

22. John Ekins (d 1808) and Harriet (d 1827). Pink marble inscribed tomb chest in profile, surmounted by moulded top with fluted urn in white marble.

23. Arthur Thomas Corfe (d 1868) and Frances (d 1847). Inscription on slate tablet inserted into earlier Osmond Gothic surround.

24. Beneath 23, to Arthur Corfe Anael? (d 1866). By Osmond.

Bay 7

25. Christopher Clarke (d 1835). By Osmond.

26. Elizabeth Eyre (d 1850). By Osmond.

Bay 8

27. Daniel Eyre (d 1836). By Osmond.

Bay 9

28. Henry Finley (d 1870) and Caroline Elizabeth, his wife, (d 1863).

North walk

Bay 2 and 3

Wooden crosses from First World War graves.

Bay 4

29. John Greenly (d 1862), Mary, his wife (d 1866) and four grandchildren (d 1855).

30. David Charles Read, Charlotte, his wife (no date) and Raphael W Read, their son (d 1886). By Osmond.

Bay 5

31. Sarah Ann Louisa Middleton (d 1872) and Andrew Bogle Middleton (d 1879). By Osmond.

32. Amy Withams (d 185?). Heavily weathered Osmond Gothic oval.

Bay 6

33. Richard Wilson (d 1839), Jane, his wife (d 1875) and two grandchildren. By Osmond.

34. Revd C H Hodgson (d 1856), Elizabeth Margaret (d 1853) and Revd George Mortimer Hodgson (d 1846).

Bay 11

35. Edward Steward (d 1930). Stone tablet.

Bay 12

36. Immediately N of door into S transept, of William Osmond, 1890.

Coffins in the cloisters

Also in the S walk of the cloisters there is a Purbeck coffin, probably 12th-century, brought from Old Sarum in 1912. There is an adjacent, medieval stone coffin with a shaped interior, and also a coffin lid of unknown origin with floriate cross, partly planed and recarved with a merchant mark and 'SB' in a shield.

Floor slabs

The list includes every floor slab on which a funerary inscription could be recognised. They are generally listed from E to W, with northern ones listed before southern ones. Matter in square brackets, now illegible, is taken from earlier lists, principally the *Wiltshire Gazette*, 22 April 1926, and subsequent issues.

In N aisle of presbytery: William Eyre, 1665; Mary Penelope Cradocke, 1729; John Bampton, 1751 (Bampton imp. Eyre);

black-letter, illegible; earl of Castlehaven, 1769; Morgan Keane, 1758 (Keene imp. Roberts); Grace Keane, 1737 (as last).

In S aisle of presbytery: Eliz. Garrard, 1680 (Garrard imp. Gardiner); Edw. Garrard, 1712 (Garrard imp. *i* Gardiner, *ii* Bennett); Florence Garrard, 1705 (Garrard imp. Bennett); Ann Priaulx, 1702; Susanna Maria Collins, 1673 (Collins imp. Bateman); John Priaulx, 1674; Thos Barford, 1701 (Barford imp. unidentified); Eliz Hawkins, 1701; C Rolleston, 1784; Dorothy Gardener, 1679; Frances Gardner, 1681; Francis Griesdale, 1789; Susanne Light, 1710; Mary Stanley, 1733; Mary Stanley, 1681; Eliz. Willmot, 1712; Thomas Willmot, 1723; Samuel Rolleston, 1766; Mary Cox, 1767; James Rolleston, 1771; Charlotte Rolleston, 1828.

In NE transept: Jane Swanton, 1689; Francis Swanton, 1683; William Swanton, 1681 (Swanton, obliterated, imp. unidentified); Francis Swanton, 1721 (Swanton imp. obliterated); Eliz. Swanton, 1733; Philadelphia Pyle, 1714 (lozenge, Pyle); Thos. Whyte, 1588; Jane South, 1719 (lozenge, South); Eliz. Urry, 1724 (lozenge, Urry with inescutcheon, Goddard); [Wingfield Brockwell, 1727 (Brockwell?)]; Elizabeth Brockwell, 1738; Rawlins Hillman, 1741 (Hillman? imp. Brockhill); Thos. Lambert, 1683; John Lambert, 1689; Thos. Lambert, 1688; [Dionys Lambert, 1683 (obliterated)]; [Rich. Clayton, 1676]; indent; Thos. Lambert, 1694 (Lambert quartering Dunch, imp. in chief Bennett, in base Hearst); indent; Bp. Jewell, brass of 1886 (Jewell); brass of Bp. Wyville, 1375; brass of Bp. Gheast, 1577; John Gordon, dean, 1619; Sarah Woodward, 1697; Susan Hill, 1741; Ann Burch, 1731; Edw. Hardwick, 1706 (Hardwick); Susana Kenton, 1709 (Kenton imp. unidentified); Herbert Kenton, 1709 (Kenton).

In SE transept: Hugh Wynn, 1741; M.G., 1739; John Jacob, 1789 and others; Francis Eyre, 1738 (Eyre quartering Lucy, imp. Hyde); Anne Eyre, 1734 (as last); Alexander Dawson, 1720 (Dawson imp. unidentified); Isaac Walton, 1719; Bp. Seth Ward, 1689 (the See imp. Ward with Garter and mitre); Edw. Young, 1705 (Young); Mary Kelsey, 1717 (lozenge, Kelsey imp. ?Chamberlayne); M.C., 1738; Dionys Seymour, 1730 (lozenge, Seymour imp. Davenant); obliterated; Bp. Thos. Burgess, 1837 (mitre); Wm. Hawkins, 1748 (Hawkins imp. Merewether); Jane Hawkins, 1728 (lozenge, Hawkins); Thos. Wyatt, 1725; Anne Hawkins, 1728; Seth Ward, 1690 (Ward imp. unidentified); Joseph Kelsey, 1710 (arms oblit.); [Margaret Gardiner, 1671]; Thos. Gardiner, 1685; R.N., d.d., 1786; Anne Hody, 1744; slab with border indent. In *St Mary's chapel:* Emily Jacob, 1829; John Henry Jacob, 1828; Edward Jacob, 1812; Charlotte Jacob, 1811.

In N aisle of choir: Sarah Gilbert, 1770; Roland Dennis, 1755; Robt. Gilbert, 1776; Edward Strong, 1756; Wm. Holmes, 1669; Rebecca Holmes, 1670; Thomas Dennis, 1795 and Elizabeth (Bennett) his wife, 1810; T.D.; Prudence Hedges, 1743; [... Hedges, 1763]; Humph. Henchman, 1779; [Jane Henchman, 1726, Thomas Henchman, 1746]; Humph. Henchman, 1779; [Frances Whitwell, 1692 (lozenge, Whitwell imp. unidentified)]; Daniel Whitby, 1725 (Whitby imp. Swanton); Dulcibella Whitwell, 1667; [Maria Whitby, 1724 (lozenge, Whitby)]; [Thomas Henchman, 1704]; [Francis Henchman, 1708]; Charles Henchman, 1707; Henry

Hedges, surgeon, 1689; [Frances Hedges, 1738?]; Dulsabella Swanton, 1678.

In S aisle of choir: indent for priest with canopy?; Mary Strachan, 1825 (see p 158); Magdalene Bowles, 1844; Wm. Lisle Bowles, 1850; [Joseph Bird, 1806]; Eliz. Mompesson, 1751; Sarah Cooper, 1769; Barbara Mompesson, 1676 (Mompesson imp. Waterer); [Sir Thomas Mompesson, 1701]; Charles Mompesson, 1714 (Mompesson imp. Longueville); Barbara Sharpe, 1722 (Sharpe imp. Mompesson); [Katherine Mompesson, 1724]; Henry Mompesson, 1731 (Mompesson); Philip Goldsworthy, 1801; Charles Martyn, 1724 (Martyn imp. in chief Baber, in base Davenant, with inescutcheon obliterated); Rebecca Hooper, 1755; (obliterated); Matthew Marsh, 1840; Rowland Davenant, 1737 (Davenant).

In N transept: Gabriel Ashley, 1703 (Ashley); James Harris, 1731 (Harris imp. quarterly Ashley and Cooper); Eliz. Harris, 1743 (lozenge, as last); George Harris, 1789; Eliz. Harris, 1781; Lydia Brewer, 1675; James Harris, 1780; Robt. Chapman, 1732 (Chapman with crest); Thomas Harris, 1785; Anne Dear, 1720; Eliz. Bird, 1690; Cath. Harris, 1796; Sarah Hayter, 1822; Joseph Albert, 1729; [Eliz. Charman, 1728 (lozenge, obliterated)]; John Osborne, 1821; Thomas Lawes, 1640; Gen. George Michell, 1846; Francis Ashley, 1684; Anne Ashley, 1684; James Harris, 1679 (Harris imp. Townson); Frances Wyndham, 1773 (Wyndham with inescutcheon, Place); Wadham Wyndham, 1783 (as last); Geo. Wyndham, 1746 (Wyndham with inescutcheon, Ashley); Cath. Wyndham, 1752 (lozenge, as last); Cath. Wyndham, 1766 (lozenge, Wyndham); Barbara Wyndham, 1777 (as last); Geo. Wyndham, 1777 (Wyndham); Robt. Benson, 1844; Anna Maria Benson, 1844; Edmund Benson, 1835; Anne Hunt Benson, 1826; Anne Charman, 1755 (lozenge, obliterated); [Rich. Kent, 1759]; [Eliz. Harris, 1749]; Anne Swanton, 1714 (obliterated imp. Hill?); Gabriel Ashley, 1702 (Ashley imp. ?Hill); Harriet Fitzharris, 1815 (Viscount's coronet); Earl of Malmesbury, 1820; Louisa Margaret Harris, 1826; Francis Benson, 1848; Edward Davies, 1843; Wm. Henry Davies, 1842; Eleanor Davies, 1831; Joan Kingdon, 1824; Rich. Peers Adams, 1816; Hannah Dove, 1794; [Gertrude Harris, 1708]; Dorothea Harris, 1672 (Harris imp. Cary); [Thomas Harris, 1678 (Harris imp. Cary)]; Margaret Ashley, 1679 (Ashley imp. Harris); Joan Harris, 1733 (Harris imp. Wyndham); Mary Sandford, 1781 (obliterated imp. unidentified); Charles William Wapshare, 1784; Mary Wapshare, 1811; Geo. Greenup, 1837; Joseph Corfe, 1820; Mary Corfe, 1826; Thomas Dove, 1767; Mary Dove, 1789; [Mary Dove, 1751].

In St Thomas's chapel: Mary Moore, 1822; Francis Pary, 1662, also F. Parry, 1837; Edward Moore, 1812; Eliz. Davies, 1811; Walter Long, 1807 (Long); [Frances Catherine Nassau, 1805]. *In St Edmund's chapel:* Mary Anne Evans, 1847; Lettice Cotton, 1798; Jas. Evans, 1823; Lettice Long, 1840 (lozenge, Long, inescutcheon obliterated); Wm. Long, 1818 (Long, inescutcheon obliterated); Sarah Evans, 1804. *In St. John's chapel:* Mary Anne King, 1844; Mary Ivie, 1808; Sarah Vaughan, 1829; ... 1808; Louisa wife of William ... 1816.

In S transept: William Dodwell, 1785; Susannah Taylor, 1783; Arthur Dodwell, 1815; Anne Hume, 1847; Elinor Thornbrough

Sadler, 1840; Frances Vaughan (Vaughan imp. Daniel); Fredk. Vaughan, 1662 (Vaughan imp. Daniel); [Anne Seymour, 1666]; Dulcibella Courte, 1673 (lozenge, Courte); Mary Evans, 1737; Frances Hawles, 1709; [Thomas Henchman, 1746]; John Thomas, 1766; John Taylor, 1772; J.H., d.d., 1782; A.H., 1757; Lady Mary Hume, 1805; [Anne Long, 1749]; S.G., 1737; E.B., 1789; Maria Coker, 1718 (lozenge, Coker); [Catherine Holt, 1672]; John Holt, 1669 (Holt); Edw. Hearst, 1767 (Hearst imp. Knachbull); Dorothea Talman, 1741; John Talman, 1763; E.T.; Eliz. Dodwell, 1770; C.J.H., 1773; E.H., 1770; H.H., 1782; N.H., 1777; Thomas Henry Hume, 1834; Martha Ridding, 1773; Baptista Sager, 1749; Mary Sager, 1742; W.S., 1729; J.S., 1742; M.A.H., 1736; William Hearst, 1725 (Hearst); Mary Hearst, 1762 (lozenge, Hearst); William Hearst, 1723 (Hearst); Roger Pinckney, 1730; [Anna Pinkney, 1733]; [Eliz. Kent, 1715] (lozenge, Kent, almost obliterated); [Jane Hopson, 1729]; Ruth Lambert, 1669.

In St Margaret's chapel: Robert Hearst, 1660 (Hearst with label); Sarah Hearst, 1713 (lozenge, Hearst imp. Holt?); Edward Hearst, 1707 (Hearst imp. *i* unidentified *ii* Bathurst); William Hearst, 1668 (Hearst imp. in chief Barker, in base Hearst); William Hearst, 1702 (Hearst imp. in chief Hyde, in base Holt?); Margaret Hearst, 1667 (Hearst imp. Hyde); Alice Hearst, 1738 (Hearst imp. Knachbull); Mrs. Nisbet Douglas, 1819; Flora Macdonald, 1826; Frances MacDonald, 1838; Mary Hearst, 1665 (Hearst imp. Barker). *In St Lawrence's chapel:* Hannah Goodall, 1797; Lady Louisa Bludworth (Bludworth quartering unidentified imp. Bertie); [Anna Cary, 1776 (lozenge, Cary)]; Eliz. Cary, 1761 (lozenge, Cary); Eliza Allnutt, 1810; Christian Kerrich, 1827; Anna Eliza Slade, 1819; Katherine Hill, 1806; Cath. Hill, 1819. *In St. Michael's chapel:* Ellen Benson, 1823; Mary Ann Wenyeve, 1799; Walter Kerrich, 1803; Frances Ch. Benson, 1842; Lt. William Benson, 1823; Jane Price, 1814.

In crossing: John Selwyn, 1823; Bridget Selwyn, 1823; [Susanna Thompson, 1760]; Edward Thompson, 1746; Joan Harris (Harris imp. Wyndham).

In nave: Kath. Harvey, 1674/5 (lozenge, Harvey imp. unidentified); Thomas Lord Wyndham, 1745; James Everard Arundel, 1756; Frances Blackborow, 1716 (Blackborow imp. Davy); James Blackborow, 1732 (as last); D'Aubigny Turbeville, 1696 (Turbeville); Anne Turbeville, 1694 (Turbeville imp. Ford); Edward Harvey, 1674 (Harvey); Thos. Mullens, 1715; Rachel Mullens, 1726; Geo. Mullens, 1738 (Mullens imp. Bingham); Sir Edw. Poore, 1838, Sir Richard Poore, 1930; obliterated; obliterated; Hannah Waterman, 1750; [Rich. Page?, 1540]; Dorothea Poore, 1744; [Dorothea Mullens, 1729]; Chas. Mullens, 1730; Wm. Mullens, 1731; Mary Butler, 1667; Rachel Poore, 1771; Edward Poore, 1780; Anthony Walkley, 1717; Samuel Jecock, 1704; F.W., 1782; John Hele, 1723; Cornelia Hele, 1723; [Stephen Morris, 1709]; John Moore, 1799; Cath. Hawes, 1807; Rich. Trickey, 1802; Eliz. White, 1776; Rich. Hele, 1756 (Hele imp. Collier); Amy Hele, 1753; John Meyer, 1795; illegible; Nath. Tucker, 1672; Margt. Comfort, 1702; Jane Hele, 1785; Jenevera Sympson, 1805; Seymour Powell, 1763; Francis Sambrooke, 1660; John Sambrooke, 1670; Susanna Tate, 1722 (lozenge, in chief Sacheverell, in base Tate, imp. unidentified); [Barbara London, 1661]; Eliz. Clungeon, 1665; [Eliz.

Sambrooke, 1706]; Lucy Rothwell, 1760; (obliterated); Margt. Hindley, 1689; Jane Phipps, 1768 (Phipps quartering Hele imp. Hill); James Lewis, 1844; Peter Bourgoin, 1730 (Bourgoin imp. unidentified); Cath. Powney, 1760; Henry Hele, 1778 (Hele, imp. Rolfe quartering Halsey); Jane Hele, 1769 (as last); Edw. Rudge, 1790; G.J. Robinson, 1788 (Robinson); Edw. Fisher, 1818; Sarah Fisher, 1832; Money Fisher, 1837; John Beare, 1837; Kenneth Mackenzie, 1824; Robt. Cutts Barton, 1827; Eliz. Shiel, 1821; Eliz. Charlotte Shiel, 1824; Fredk. Webb, 1846.

In N aisle: Jane Medlycott, 1824; Jane Paget Ainslie, 1839; George Fowles, 1744; Jane Coles, 1801; Willm. Coles, 1789; Dorothy Coles, 1700; Dolly Coles, 1705; Wm. Coles, 1750 (obliterated); Dorothy Coles, 1745 (obliterated); Jonathan Coles, 1740 (obliterated); Wm. Coles, 1673 (Coles imp. obliterated); [Margaret Wastell, 1682]; James Duke, 1679; Mary Duke; Richard Sharpe, 1682 (Sharpe); Rich. Drake, 1681; [Rich. Drake and Margaret Drake, 1704, 1676 (obliterated)]; Sir G. Hungerford and Margaret his wife, 1684/5, 1711 (arms obliterated, Hungerford crest); [H.M. Hungerford, 1808]; Hen. Stephens, 1803; J.S., 1780; M.S., 1779; Anne Wickens, 1850; James Wickens, 1827.

In S aisle: [?Hill, 1694–5, (Hill)]; Rowland Laugharne, 1691; Alex. Ballantyne, [1783] (Ballantyne); Anne Russell, 1671; Edw. Colman, 1664; Thomas Brent, 1664; Edw. Lynch, 1669 (obliterated); John St. Barbe, 1683 (St. Barbe imp. ?Snow); [Henry Gresley, 1679]; Francis Robertes, 1668; John St. Barbe, 1722 (St. Barbe imp. Beckett); Punchardon Robertes, 1687; [Coles, Gen ?]; Maria Robertes, 1725; Alex Hyde, 1667; [Anne Lambert, 1698]; Helena Lowe, 1661; Mary Parker, 1666, Henry Hyde; Catherine Hyde, 1661; Lawrence Hyde, 1641; obliterated; [Amphillis Hyde, 1631]; Fredk. Colman, 1711 (Colman); [Anna Pope, 1751]; Mary Miller, 1698 (lozenge, Miller); [Eliz. Pink, 1708 (lozenge, Pink)].

In cloisters, in E walk: Richard Guy, 1846; Louisa Haydon Chicheley Chapeau, 1848; Louisa Elizabeth Chapeau, 1843; William Posthumous Chapeau, 1833; Eliz^h. Coleridge, 1794; Rich^d. Turner, 1794; M.F., 1791; Alex^r. Forcyth, 1795; William Dodsworth, 1826, verger of this cathedral; [Francis] Price, 1753, architect; E.P., 1776; Mrs Ann Burch, 1792; Sarah Todd, 1797; Sarah Cane, [1803]; Daniel Macdonald, 1794; H.A.M., 1790; B.O., 1811; Richard Oakley, 1816; Anne Stook, 1839; Anthony Lewis Layard, 1823. *In N walk:* Maria (Hancock) [Robinson], 1827; Saml. Rogers, 1790. *In S walk:* Betty Lesh, 1831; Mary Neale, 1812; John Young, 1823; [Thomas Lawes, 1640]; [Mary Dennis] Hibbard, 1811; Harriet Ekins?, 1827; Frances Coree, 1842?; Catherine Davies, 1799; Ann Davies, 1843; Mary Ann Coree, 1849; Daniel Eyre, 1836; Charles John [Wapshare], 1833. *In W walk:* [William Hinton, 1662]; [Edward Houghton, 1666]. *In garth:* E.C.S. King, 1841; William Gould,

121 *Bishop de Wyville's brass. Originally installed c 1375 in the choir, the brass was moved in 1684 to a position before the altar in St Catherine's chapel [BB73/7510]*

1826; Mary Mee, 1835; H. Morgan, 1833; Jane (Nowell) Watkins, 1827; Henry Jacob, 1842; Louisa Mary Denison, 1841; Louisa Macdonald, 1834; Richard Brassey Hole, 1849; Mary Pleydell Bouverie, 1849; Jane Anne Fitzgerald, 1849; Sarah Lucas, 1849; Mary Razley, 1842; Eliz. Ann Titball, 1848.

Brasses and indents

It is clear from Symonds's testimony that many brasses had been lost by the middle of the 17th century [Long 1859, 140], but the following remain.

On the N side of the chancel, forming part of the monument of Bishop Roger de Martival (d 1330), (13), is a tomb slab with indents for brasses comprising a floriate cross on which is imposed a demi-figure, mitred and bearing a crosier, surrounded by four lozenge-shaped indents, perhaps for Evangelists' emblems. On the S side of the chancel, forming part of the monument to Bishop Simon de Gandavo (d 1315) (146), is a similar slab with an indent for a mitred demi-figure only.

In the pavement of the NE transept, near the eastern crossing, is an indent in a floor slab for head and shoulders of a figure and an oblong plate. Opposite St Catherine's chapel is a large slab (4.2 m x 1.4 m), with brass and indents of Bishop Robert de Wyville (d 1375), which was originally located in the chancel. It was moved to a central position before St Catherine's altar in 1684 (see p 38 and Gough plan, Fig 15), and to its present position, 1.21 metres further S, in 1789. The brass depicts a demi-figure of de Wyville inside the castle of Sherborne, recovered for the See in 1337. The process originally involved trial by combat, and the bishop's champion, Robert (or Richard) Shawell, wielding the double-pick appropriate to combat, is depicted in the gateway. A cash settlement was eventually agreed. The grassy foreground inhabited by rabbits is thought to represent Bere Chace, also restored to the See through de Wyville's efforts. Of the five shields, only two survive. The brass has also lost the symbols of the Evangelists that once decorated the corners of the marginal fillet; that of St Luke is preserved in the British Museum. The brass has been attributed to the London 'Series A' workshop [Alexander and Binski 1987, cat 98, 231]. The marginal fillet contains a long inscription, partially lost, but recorded (eg by Richard Symonds [Long 1859, 136–7]):

> (Hic iacet bone memorie Robtus Wyvell huius ecclīe Salisburie Epus qui eccliam istam quatraginta quinque annos & amplius pacifice & laudabilit' rexit, dispsa eiusdm ecclīe prudenter) congregavit & congregata vt pastor vigilans conseruauit Int[er] enim alia beficia sua minima • Castrum dce ecclīe de Schirebon p[er] ducentos annos et amplius manu militari violent (occupatum eidem ecclīe ut pugil) intrepidus recup[er]auit ac ipi ecclīe chaceam suam de la Bere restitui p[ro]curauit qui quarto die Septembz anno dni millio CCCmo.lxxvto et anno consecr sue xlvjto sicut altissimo placuit in dco castro debitum reddidit (humane natur' Cujus aie ppiciet' ille in quo sp'avit & credidit cuncta potens).

Adjacent, on the N, are brasses of Bishop Edmund Gheast (d 1577), with a figure and large oblong plate with black-letter inscription, together with indents for a smaller plate and four shields. They were in the choir until 1684 (see p 38). Also in the NE transept is a floor slab with an indent for demi-figure and oblong plate, and, on the same slab, a rectangular brass with an epitaph of Thomas Whyte (d 1588), chancellor of the Cathedral, archdeacon of Berkshire and sometime Warden of New College.

On the E wall of the N transept, in the chapel of St Thomas, is a brass to George Jackson Christian and his wife, killed in the Mutiny of the Sepoys, 1857. On the N wall of the N transept a brass wall plaque to Eleanor, widow of Dean Hamilton, commemorates her gift of the stained glass in the window above, given in memory of her parents by Dame Katherine Jane Hulse in 1895. Immediately below is a wall plaque to Alan Wyldbore Bosworth Smith (d 1901). The NE corner of the N wall of the N transept has a plaque commemorating the gift of the clock in the tower above by the officers and men of the 62nd Wiltshire Regiment, in memory of the fallen in India 1868–82, the plaque is by Hart, Son, Peard & Co (London).

On the W wall of the N transept are a brass to John Britton (d 1857), by John Hardman & Co, and a wall plaque to Grace Mary Phillips (d 1918).

In the N aisle of the nave, in the second bay of the N arcade, on two former floor slabs, cut down in 1779 (when the railings of the Hungerford chantry were moved to the choir) and reset to form the top of a table tomb (52), are worn indents of Sir Walter Hungerford and his wife, Catherine (Peverell), surrounded by sickles. On the E end of the same table tomb, a brass plate with an inscription records alterations in 1779. In the adjoining pavement are a slab with two rectangular inscription plates of Sir Giles Hungerford (d 1684) and his wife Margarite (d 1711), and a worn rectangular plate with an obliterated shield of arms with helm and mantling. On the N wall of the nave, in the fifth bay, a large brass plaque commemorates the dead of the Wiltshire Regiment in the South African campaign of 1899–1902.

In the pavement of the S aisle of the choir are a slab with cement filled indents and dowels for brasses, and, adjacent, a slab to Mary Strachan (d 1825), with a later brass shield of arms, Strachan quartering Leigh and twelve other coats. On the wall of the S-choir aisle, in the second bay from the E, is a brass of foliate canopy on slate slab, to John Fulford, RN, d 1888, and, in the third bay from the E, a large cross brass on marble tablet to Henry Parry Liddon, d 1890. Both are by Hart, Son, Peard and Co. Further W, between the Medford and Mompesson monuments (123 and 125), a large brass on red marble slab, commemorates Douglas Hamilton Gordon, d 1901. It is by John Hardman and Co.

In the pavement of the S aisle of the nave, in the second bay from the E, are indents of a small robed figure and an inscription plate; in the third bay, two copper plates with a shield of arms of the See impaling Hyde and a Latin epitaph of Bishop Hyde (d 1667); in the fourth bay, on a plinth, largely hidden by a monument superimposed in 1789, Purbeck floor slabs with

indents for four shields and for a figure in 14th-century armour, with crested helm; in the fifth bay, on a plinth, partly hidden by a monument, an indent for a crocketed canopy, medieval.

On the S wall of the S transept is a brass plaque to Frances Elizabeth, Lady Poore (d 1896), with, immediately below, a brass plaque to Roger Poore (d 1915), in fine lettering. A plaque mounted on a wooden slab, with armorials at the upper corners, is to Robert Harold Oliver (d 1914).

On the wall of the S-choir aisle, immediately W of the Mompesson tomb (125), is a brass set into a red marble slab to Douglas Hamilton Gordon (d 1901), by John Hardman and Co. Immediately below, a plaque records the restoration of the stained-glass Tree of Jesse (now in window s33) in memory of Ellen Susan Hamilton Gordon (d 1914, wife of the above) and other members of the family, given by their surviving daughter.

In the E walk of the cloister is a brass to Bishop Edward Denison (d 1854).

122   *Brass of Bishop Gheast (d 1577), removed from the choir in 1684*
[BB73/7509]

123   *The nave vault, with traces of 13th-century ashlar pattern and foliage decoration largely obscured by 18th-century overpainting [BB93/15963]*

Paintings, Tiles and Textiles

Paintings

The medieval mural and vault decoration of Salisbury Cathedral has suffered considerably; in the mid 18th century the pigment on the choir vault was already in a very fragile condition [Price 1753, 53]. In 1790 the vaults throughout the Cathedral were overpainted with a buff wash, and 19th-century attempts to replace the lost scheme in the eastern arm with accurate copies were only partially successful. The precise dating and stylistic analysis of the original 13th-century figurative paintings in the choir and eastern transepts are therefore extremely difficult, although there seems to be no evidence for the assertion made in the 18th century that they are any later in date than the underlying ashlaring [Dodsworth 1792]. Examination of the original paint beneath the 18th-century wash in the third bay from the W of the N-choir aisle and the uncovering of paint in the N-choir aisle in the 1980s has revealed that here, at least, the pigment survives, and examination has also yielded traces of gilding on the vault bosses. No more extensive restoration has yet been attempted. Ultra-violet examination of the vault paintings beneath the limewash in the NE transept revealed strong outlines of 13th-century painting; upon removing the wash it was discovered that the original pigment had not survived, only a shadow of the oil that had soaked into the plaster [Spring 1987a, 77]. Shadows of painted medallions are also visible through the wash in the SE transept.

The original painted scheme
The decorative painting

Throughout the Cathedral there are considerable traces of the original painted 'skin' that covered the interior masonry. The simplest form of painting consisted of the common 13th-century imitation of ashlar, painted in red, employed throughout the church, including the high vaults, where in the choir it underlies the figurative roundels (see p 15). The mouldings of the vault ribs were picked out in alternating red and green paint, which in the eastern arm at least was decorated with nebuly and bezanty patterns. At the intersections of the lateral and transverse ribs of the vaults of the Trinity Chapel, choir, choir aisles, and western transepts this simple ashlaring was augmented and enriched with triangular wedges of foliage ornament, still visible in many places as triangular shadows beneath the 18th-century wash. This foliage decoration continued along the vault of the main vessel of the nave, creating a fictive ridge rib. In the nave aisles, however, this decorative scheme diminished to ashlaring alone. In addition, the mouldings of the main and triforium arcades and of the clerestory windows in the choir and eastern transepts, except where restored, have extensive traces of red and green paint. The decoration of the Trinity Chapel vault, repainted in the 1870s by Clayton and Bell, did not meet with Scott's approval, but comparison with similar decoration on the vault of the Chapter House vestibule, still in excellent condition, suggests that this repainting is reasonably accurate; it is the vault of the Chapter House vestibule which offers the clearest impression of the original character of the Cathedral's decorative scheme.

The decorative painting within the choir and eastern transepts was apparently of a richer and more complex order. In the choir and NE transept, the spandrels of the main arcade and triforium preserve traces of the foliage tendrils noted by Price in the 18th century [Price 1753, 52]. At clerestory level the walls bear simple masonry lines. It has been suggested that this ornament may have been displayed against a red background [Armfield 1878, 135], although Wyatt's overpainting makes this difficult to assess. Spandrel ornament was recreated on the terminal wall of the choir and in its SW bay as part of Clayton and Bell's 1872 restoration, although against a white rather than a red ground.

Elsewhere in the Cathedral, a second, and probably slightly later, form of simple painted ornament survives from the 13th century. The walls of the treasury and its vestibule, the Muniment Room on the first floor (now the choir school) and the Parvis chamber above the N porch all retain fragmentary remains of ashlaring with upper friezes of trefoiled rinceau. Similar decoration is found in a number of the 13th-century canonries [RCHME 1993b].

The historiated painting of the choir

Within the choir and eastern transept, the decorative painting was accompanied by a rich figural scheme which retained the power to impress even in the late 17th century; Celia Fiennes recorded that 'the top of

124   *Decorative 13th-century rinceau painted on the upper wall of the Muniment Room [BB69/5185]*

the Quoire is exactly painted and it looks as fresh as if but new done though of 300 yeares standing' [Morris 1995, 37]. Defoe was rather less complimentary, in the 1748 edition of his *Tour of the Whole Island of Britain* deriding the 'paltry old Painting in and over the Choir'. In 1789 Jacob Schnebbelie was employed by the Society of Antiquaries to record these paintings, receiving 20 guineas for the work in December 1789 [Horlbeck 1960, 116]. His original sketches are preserved in the Society's archives [MS 263], while the more finished drawings have been rediscovered in the Gough collections in the Bodleian Library [MS Gough Maps, vol 32]. Schnebbelie's drawings, although of limited value for a stylistic analysis, confirm the iconographic programme. The figures are all set in medallions. The focus of the scheme, at the crossing with the eastern transepts, was Christ in Majesty within a vesica, with the Evangelists in small medallions at his feet, contained in the easternmost compartment, with the Apostles in larger medallions occupying the other three (see Fig 9). To the W

of the Majesty were twenty-four medallions containing the major and minor prophets (including Elizabeth and a sibyl), seated and holding inscribed scrolls, some named and some identifiable from their texts, all of which relate to the Incarnation. The vaults of the eastern transepts were occupied by smaller medallions containing demi-angels holding crowns, chalices, suns, moons, stars, palms and musical instruments. The scheme as it now appears as a result of the 1872 restoration by Clayton and Bell is accurate in some respects, although no reference could be made to Schnebbelie's drawings. Tracings of the faintly visible originals were made and the positioning of the figures of Joel (in the western bay), Moses, Daniel and Zephaniah (in the central bay) and Isaiah, Jeremiah, Haggai, Malachi and Obadiah (in the eastern bay) correspond to Schnebbelie's evidence, suggesting that they were still clearly discernible. Other figures do not correspond to Schnebbelie's plan, and presumably were indecipherable. Further E, in the three bays of the presbytery, the vault is decorated with the Labours of the Months,

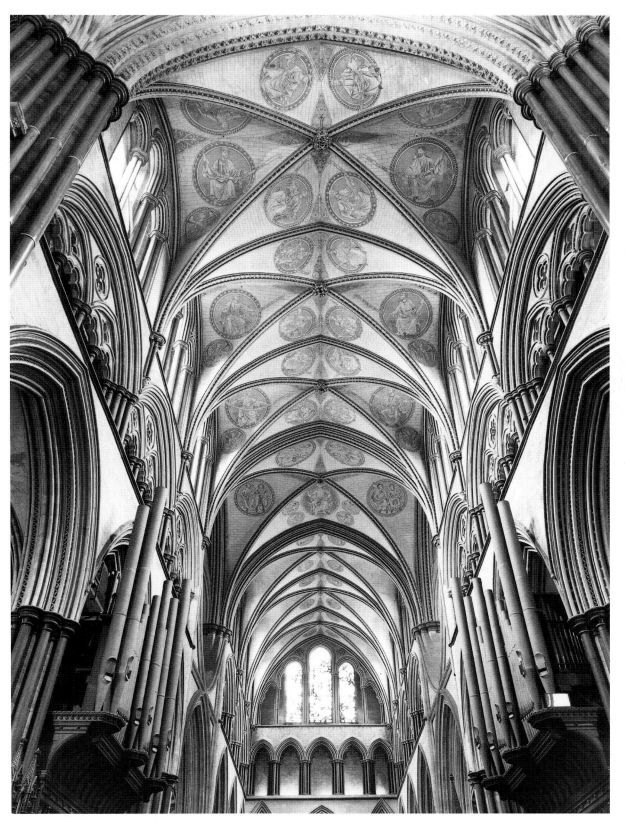

125   *The presbytery vault – a 19th-century re-creation of the 13th-century scheme [BB71/3263]*

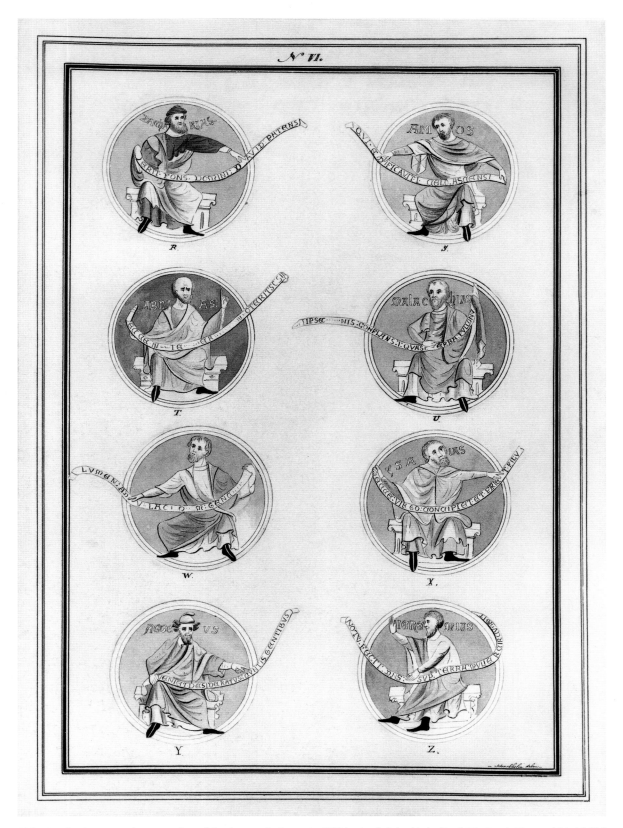

126   *Prophet figures on the eastern bay of the choir vault. Drawn in 1789 by Jacob Schnebbelie [Bodl MS Gough Maps, vol 32, fol 59ʳ]*

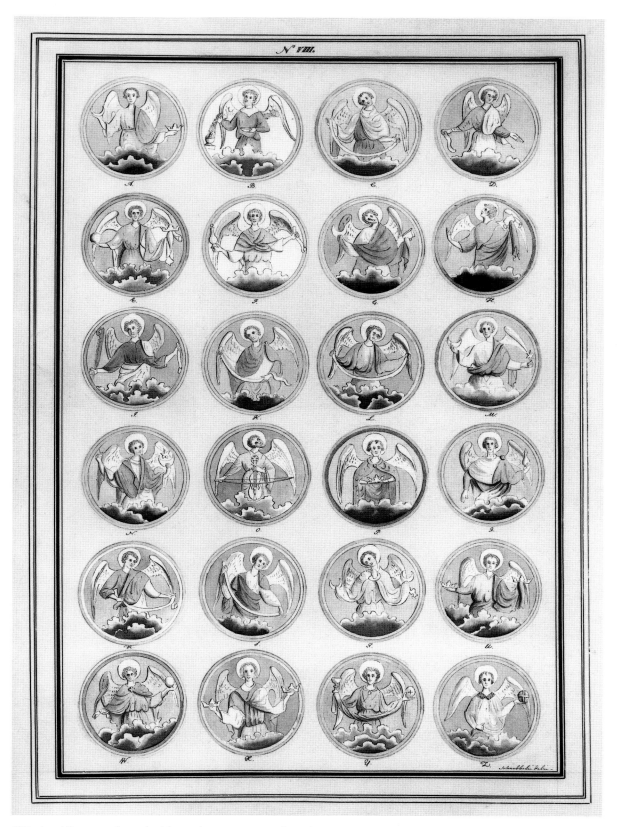

127 *Angel figures on the vault of the south-east transept, as drawn by Jacob Schnebbelie in 1789 [Bodl MS Gough Maps, vol 32, fol 61ʳ]*

the presence of which has fired much debate as to the original position of the high altar [Armfield 1878]. The present scheme of *c* 1870 bears very little relationship to the cycle recorded by Schnebbelie. By the 19th century, the labels recorded by him were no longer clearly visible and some of the tracings of the shadow images discernible through the 18th-century wash were, as a result, wrongly labelled. Five of the Labours were missing from the tracings altogether and new versions of the medallions were supplied by the restorers, using English 13th-century manuscript calendars as a source, although the models used appear to have been less typical than the original cycle, as re-corded by Schnebbelie [Horlbeck 1960, 119]. No attempt was made to restore the eastern transept paintings.

Scott, under whose aegis Clayton and Bell undertook the restoration, was disappointed with the results: 'Messrs. Clayton and Bell made a tentative restoration of some parts, but not (as I now find) very accurately' [Stamp 1995, 305]. Regrettably, the tracings they made in preparation for the work, exhibited at the Society of Antiquaries in 1876, have now been lost. A single tracing, labelled 'No 4 South Side' was reproduced in an article published in 1932 and offers the closest impression of the style of the originals, not readily conveyed by the Schnebbelie drawings [Borenius 1932, fig 1]. In terms of its general decorative characteristics, the scheme can be compared with that in the chapel of the Guardian Angels (c 1240) at Winchester Cathedral and the Chapter House at Oxford (third quarter of the 13th century). In the treatment of the foliage forms in the roundels of the Labours, comparison has been made with the Chertsey tiles in the Westminster Chapter House (dated 1253–8), while in the treatment of some of the architectural features Horlbeck suggested a general affinity with the manuscripts of the Sarum Master [Horlbeck 1960, 129], although the tracing reproduced in 1932 suggests a more naturalistic interpretation of the Sarum figure style. Those who examined the full set of Clayton and Bell tracings exhibited at a meeting of the Society of Antiquaries in 1876 were of the opinion that they were roughly coeval with the date of the consecration [Society of Antiquaries 1873–6]. It seems highly unlikely that they are any later than the completion of the choir, for the painters would doubtlessly have used the masons' scaffolding before it was struck. Recent reconsideration of the chronology of the church would therefore suggest a date in the early 1240s for the scheme [Simpson 1996, 10–20].

At lower level, the wall behind the choir stalls may also have been painted with figurative scenes. It is extremely unlikely that such an expanse of wall would have been left blank, although at Westminster decoration was provided in the form of tapestries rather than paintings [Binski 1991]. However, neither Price nor Scott recorded any traces of painted decoration.

Other painting in the church

Figurative painting at ground level in the eastern arm may have been provided by a series of painted retables in the individual chapels. Traces of a mid 13th-century Crucifixion survive on the E wall of St Martin's chapel. Further colour was provided by the series of consecration crosses (see pp 186–188), inset with brass and enlivened with paint.

The pulpitum, effectively shielding the splendour of the chancel from the eyes of the congregation in the nave, provided some hint of the richness within; traces of paint and gilding can still be discerned on the surviving fragments (see Plate 1), and, in its repetition of the theme of demi-angels in the spandrels of the arcade, the pulpitum echoes one of the prominent iconographic elements of the chancel vault beyond. The surviving paint traces suggest that a naturalistic effect was sought; the angels' cheeks have a rosy blush on them. The figures of kings of England that once filled the niches no doubt were also painted.

The Chapter House and its vestibule

The least restored area of 13th-century painting is probably that to be found on the vault of the vestibule of the Chapter House, conserved in 1981. Wedges of tendril ornament, similar to that found in the Cathedral, are preserved along the principal ribs of the vault, while the hollows of the vaulting bosses retain traces of dark red paint. When examined by Burges in 1855, prior to their restoration, the figures of the Virtues and Vices adorning the Chapter House entrance preserved considerable traces of bright colour; the presence of yellow, red, green, blue and 'chocolate' were all meticulously noted. Some of the figures had already lost their polychromy, however, as a result of casts being taken by Cottingham [Burges 1859, 8], and today the vestiges of paint are slight, more paint no doubt having been lost when the figures were restored in 1856 [Green 1968, 148]. Within the Chapter House itself, extensive traces of polychromy survived until 1855 on both vault and wall sculpture, despite the damage suffered by the latter [BL Add MS 29,939, fol 80[r], Carter drawings; Burges 1859, 11–20, 22–3]. The webs of the vault had been 'ashlared', with the vault ribs painted red, with red and white nebuly ornament. The gilded bosses were relieved in red with wedges of foliage in green and yellow against a red ground radiating from them. The 1855 restoration (executed by Octavius Hudson) introduced blue to the scheme, although Burges claimed to find no evidence for this colour on the vault [Burges 1859, 23]. The sculpted frieze had been richly coloured and gilded, although by 1855 all gilding had been scraped off. G F Sargent's watercolour of 1852 gives some impression of its appearance immediately prior to restoration (Plate 4). The restorers went about recreating both the sculpture and the polychromy, although Burges's detailed examination of the pigment traces no doubt ensured that the restored painting was at least in part an accurate re-creation of the original effect. Unfortunately the rapid and severe deterioration of the 19th-century paint, leading to its complete removal, has also had the effect of removing all but slight traces of medieval colour. Burges's notes, published in 1859, remain an invaluable record, detailing a varied palette, displayed against alternating red and blue grounds.

The cloisters

Like the interior wall surfaces of the church, the cloister walls were originally decorated with red lines in imitation of ashlar. This type of decoration is best preserved in the N walk, where ashlaring above the blind arcade is capped by a red line following the curve of the wall arches, also surviving on the vault arches. The principal panels of the blind arcade, below the ashlaring, have traces of ochre or green colouring, possibly contemporary. Above the door leading from the cloister into the SW transept are traces of a late medieval painting (15th century?), with traces of figures, one bearing a long scroll, while on the W wall of the former Consistory Court is a shield of Lovel, also depicted in red – possibly for Canon Gilbert Lovel, who held prebends from 1298 or before until at least 1311 and was granted the Leadenhall as his house in 1305 [Rich Jones 1881, 381].

The Hungerford chantry

The most extensive late medieval painted scheme was that in the destroyed chantry chapel of Robert, Lord Hungerford (built 1464–71), a monument which greatly impressed Symonds, who described it in some detail – the Annunciation with dedicatory inscription, St Christopher, Death and the Gallant (Fig 17) and a quantity of heraldry. Once again, it was Schnebbelie who

128   Original 13th-century foliage decoration on the vault of the Chapter House vestibule [BB82/11181]

most usefully recorded its appearance, and, despite its already dilapidated condition (demolition was already in progress), it was evidently a scheme of considerable quality and iconographic interest [Shortt 1970]. There is otherwise little late medieval wall painting surviving.

The monuments
Finally, of course, it should be remembered that many of the monuments were once brightly coloured. The tomb chest of William Longespee, the effigy of Robert Hungerford, the tomb of Richard Medford (see Plate 2) and the chantry of Bishop Audley all retain considerable traces of colour. The monument of Thomas Bennett included a painted reredos recorded by Schnebbelie and Trotter and now lost (Plate 3). The post-medieval monuments, notably the Hertford and Mompesson tombs, were also intended to be coloured, although their present bright decoration is of recent vintage.

The exterior
Little is known of the use of colour on the exterior, although the central western portal was known as the Blue Porch in the Middle Ages and in 1878 colour traces were said to be less clear than they had been before Scott's restoration [Armfield 1878, 129]. Current conservation work has identified medieval polychromy. Some slight traces of colour have also been noted in the north porch.

Tiles
The Cathedral was once richly tiled throughout its eastern arm and in the Chapter House, in a programme spanning the period *c* 1225-66 [Norton 1996]. By the middle of the 18th century many of the chapels still preserved traces of their tiled floors [Price 1753, 65].

The only tiles to remain in the Cathedral are *ex situ* in the chapel of St Peter (originally in the Chapter House), and the *in situ* pavement in the Muniment Room, together with the landing at the top of the staircase up to the room, the window sill on the stair and a few tiles at the base of the stair. Despite the renewal of the roof and central timber pier and the supporting floor timbers in the 1930s [FOSC 1961, 22], this scheme is exceptionally well preserved and one of the most important medieval pavements in Europe.

Of the tiles from the earliest phase of tiling activity in the Cathedral, in the Trinity Chapel and retrochoir, nothing survives *in situ*. John Carter drew one small tiled area in October 1781 [BL Add MS 29,925, fol 129], but it is unlikely that this represents original paving. The recent identification of small fragments of a plain greenglazed mosaic tile suggests the nature of the earliest phase of tiling activity in the Cathedral [Norton 1996, 91]. All medieval floors in the Trinity Chapel and retrochoir were swept away by Wyatt.

The great pavements of the choir and Chapter House have likewise disappeared, although, in the case of the latter, not without considerable documentation. The tiles in the choir suffered as a result of successive postmedieval flooring campaigns, particularly that of 1671, when the area under the choir stalls was renewed [Pope 1697, 66], to be more extensively repaved in 1684, when white marble was laid in the choir, and a number of ledger stones and Bishop de Wyville's brass were moved (see p 158). A small number of tiles in the collection of material in the Cathedral and in the Salisbury Museum suggest that the choir pavement was a roundel of inlaid tiles very similar to that ordered in 1244 by Henry III for the King's Chapel at Clarendon Palace [Norton 1996; Eames 1963; 1972; 1988].

The Chapter House pavement survived far longer. It is shown in perfect condition in Britton's somewhat inaccurate view of 1801, although by 1852 G F Sargent's watercolour shows large areas, particularly near the central column, to be disturbed (Plate 4). John Carter prepared a sketch plan and details of some areas of it in 1781 [BL Add MS 29,939, fols 70^r, 71^r, 72^r]. In 1849 the Revd. Lord Alwyn Compton read a paper [Compton 1851] which included a sketch plan of the pavement, made before its destruction, with details of its principal decorative elements, and in 1858 Henry Shaw published a complete and accurate scale plan based on it [Shaw 1858](Plate 6). By this time the pavement itself had been taken up by the restorers, to be replaced by a Minton copy. The medieval tiles have largely disappeared. Some are now preserved in the British Museum [Eames 1980], in the Compton Collection at the Society of Antiquaries and in Salisbury Museum [Saunders and Saunders 1991]. A small number remain within the Cathedral itself, in small tiled areas either side of the Gorges monument in the chapel of St Peter.

The tiles of the Chapter House pavement were arranged in a radiating design, based on only six basic patterns separated by borders, some patterned (with three motifs) and the rest plain. In this respect the Chapter House pavement differs from that of 1252 in the Queen's chamber at Clarendon [Eames 1957-8; 1988, 143-7], where the decorative zones are separated by plain borders. The Chapter House patterns are developed in a series of radiating chevrons, perfectly adapted to fit the octagonal space available.

The same tilers were responsible for the perfectly preserved radiating pavement surviving in the Muniment Room. This has been boarded over for protection while in use for choir practice since the 1970s,

129 Tiles from the Chapter House resited in St Peter's chapel
[BB93/22082]

130   Tile pavement in the Muniment Room [BB69/5180]

131   Tiles around the central column [BB69/5182]

but was photographed by the RCHME in 1961. The general layout is almost identical to the lost Chapter House pavement, made up of chevrons of radiating decoration, but with plain borders. The range of motifs is greater than that of the Chapter House, however, despite its smaller size, encompassing ten or eleven designs, some of which appear to be reused tiles from an earlier campaign. The repertoire is further extended by the tiles on the landing, on the window ledge and at the foot of the stairs.

132   Upper landing, Muniment Room stair [BB69/5183]

133   Window sill, Muniment Room stair [BB93/15940]

134   *Chasuble with apparel, c 1500 (back) [BB73/7418]*

135   *Spanish or Italian altar frontal with scenes from the life of St Theresa of Avila, 17th century [BB73/7489]*

136   *The* Te Deum *Frontal designed by Sir Sidney Gambier Parry and embroidered by Jane Morris Weighall [BB95/5304]*

Textiles

Textiles include a chasuble with embroidered apparels of the Crucifixion and Apostles, with the inscription '*orate p. aia Johann Baldwini*', *c* 1500. Its provenance is unknown.

Displayed in St Margaret's chapel, is a 17th-century embroidered frontal with scenes from the life of St Theresa of Avila. This is perhaps Spanish or Italian. It was purchased in 1946.

The *Te Deum* frontal, 3.65 metres long, designed by Sidney Gambier Parry and embroidered by Jane Morris Weighall, is displayed in a case on the N wall of the NE transept.

In the choir the embroidered cushions for the canons' stalls, the dean and sub-dean's stalls, the choristers' benches and the Bishop's Throne, all on the theme of Wiltshire flowers, are the work of the Salisbury Cathedral Embroiderers Guild, founded in 1937.

There are also the bench cushions in the baptistry and the kneelers in the NE transept.

*137   Mitred corbel head
in the east side, south
transept [AA72/674]*

*138   Male corbel head
in the nave south arcade
[AA72/626]*

Sculpture, Decorated Masonry and Architectural Features

Sculpture

Compared to other 13th-century English cathedrals and great churches (Wells and Lincoln Cathedrals and Westminster Abbey spring to mind), the interior of Salisbury Cathedral is not rich in architectural sculpture. It is, none the less, work of impressive quality.

Capitals, label stops and corbel heads

Decoration of capitals throughout is restrained, confined to stiff-leaf foliage decoration, without the addition of figurative detail which is characteristic of the capitals at Wells, for example. There is a noticeable degree of sculptural enrichment in the presbytery, where the spandrels of the clerestory windows are decorated with roundels of tightly curling stiff-leaf foliage. The capitals in the choir and presbytery are unadorned, with the exception of those immediately east of the crossing with the eastern transepts which are distinguished by the use of stiff leaf, marking the entry into the presbytery. The label stops of the nave are decorated by small quantities of stiff leaf.

Figurative sculpture is to be found, however, in an impressive series of corbel heads which extends throughout the presbytery, choir, and transepts and runs the length of the nave. Only the Trinity Chapel and retrochoir have no figurative architectural sculpture. The heads are listed by Whittingham [1979], although a head of a beardless youth surmounted by foliage in the NE bay of the SE transept, carved on a smaller scale than the other corbel heads, seems to have escaped his notice. The largest number of corbel heads (41) are in Chilmark stone, with a smaller number (22) in Purbeck marble, all to be found in the transepts.

The Salisbury corbel heads explore a wide range of naturalistic expressions, displaying an astonishing naturalism and a degree of characterisation that could be described as 'portraiture'. Five of the heads are crowned and six wear mitres, prompting attempts to identify those depicted [Whittingham 1979]. These identifications must remain speculative, however.

Naturalistic facial expression in sculpture was first explored in the Île de France in the period c 1220 and was taken up at Westminster Abbey (via Rheims

Cathedral) in the 1240s and 1250s. The animation of the face by a smile was of particular interest and demonstrably intrigued King Henry III, who, in 1241, ordered smiling angels to go either side of a rood for the church of St Martin le Grand [Alexander and Binski 1987, 322]. The Salisbury pulpitum of c 1236 already expresses this new interest in the gently smiling faces of the spandrel angels. A similarly calmly joyful expression is found on a number of the faces of the corbel heads, notably on that of the bishop in the south transept (Fig 137). A small number of heads express more extreme emotions comparable to the anguished head of a youth of c 1246–56 found on the site of the King's apartments at nearby Clarendon Palace [Alexander and Binski 1987, 323, cat. 295]. A wide-eyed smiling male head with furrowed brow and corkscrew curls in the south nave arcade of the cathedral (Fig 138) could even serve as the joyful companion presumed to have once partnered the sorrowful Clarendon boy.

Pulpitum

The pulpitum, shown in its original position in Biddlecombe's view of 1754 (Fig 19), projected a little to the W of the eastern piers of the central crossing; the E responds of the 15th-century reinforcing arches rested on top of it. The choir was entered through a double door with coupled lintels or flat arches supported by clustered shafts with foliate capitals and moulded bases. By September 1779 this doorway had apparently been removed in order to enlarge the vista into the choir [SJ, 27 Sept 1779] as part of the work supervised by Edmund Lush between 1777 and 1779. The lower arcade of ten bays was surmounted by a zone of trefoil-headed panels, possibly of stone, but more probably of wood. The top of the pulpitum, from which the Gospel and Epistle were intoned during mass, was gained by a double stair marked on Gough's plan. A late 14th-century manuscript fragment describes fourteen royal figures on its western face, seven on the left side of the entrance to the choir and seven on the right side [Wordsworth 1914, 551–66]. It is not made clear exactly what form these figures took, although it has been assumed that they were statues filling the niches in the pulpitum, presenting a chrono-

139   *The southern half of the pulpitum of* c 1236, *now located on the west wall of the north-east transept, to which it was moved in 1789 [BB71/3248]*

logical sequence from King Edgar on the N side to King Henry III on the S [Hope 1917*a*, 505–6]. It is not clear how these fourteen figures were arranged across ten niches; they would have fitted into the upper tier of small panels, although a reference to flooding in the Cathedral in 1309 states that the water came 'up to the feet of the kings, which stand at the west door of the choir' [Wordsworth 1917, 505], making it more likely that they were located at the lower level. This problem remains unresolved. The pulpitum must have been in place *c* 1236, when the timber for the choir stalls which abut it was provided by the king (see p 74).

An awareness of French sculptural developments can also be discerned in the treatment of the architectural sculpture on the Salisbury pulpitum. The use of angels with outstretched wings to decorate spandrels has recently been compared to the treatment of the wall arcades at the Sainte-Chapelle in Paris [Williamson 1995, 202], and, in their gentle demeanour and sweet-

ness of expression, the pulpitum angels and corbel heads of *c* 1236 are a precocious precursor to the angels in the spandrels of the interior of the N transept of Westminster Abbey (*c* 1250). The loss of the full-length figures of kings from the niches of the pulpitum is all the more to be regretted.

The remains of the 13th-century pulpitum were relocated against the W wall of the NE transept in 1789. There were two groups of five niches, with sculpted decoration; each niche has a segmental recess of roughly dressed ashlar, presumably once rendered, flanked by vertical bands of undercut leaf carving. Between niches, lobed shafts of polished Purbeck marble have moulded Purbeck bases and Chilmark capitals with elaborate foliage below roll-moulded Purbeck abaci. These support a Chilmark arcade in which each arch has two moulded orders, the inner trefoil and overhanging, the outer two-centred; each order has its own label, respectively straight-sided with foliate ball-stops

140   *Detail of the north side of the pulpitum [BB71/3283]*

and concentric with head-stops. The spandrels of the outer order are filled by angels, some defaced, but others supporting a scroll, a censer, a wavy star and a harp respectively. There are plentiful traces of colour and gilding, intended to give the figures a naturalistic appearance (Plate 1). Above, a hollow-chamfered and roll-moulded stringcourse is composed partly of reused material, probably from Old Sarum. The central opening is derived from the demolished Beauchamp chantry chapel (see p 189).

141 Detail of the north side of the pulpitum [BB71/3280]

The west front

The greatest display of figure sculpture was reserved for the screen-like W front, presumed to be complete by 1266, if not by 1258, although on stylistic grounds it would seem that the sculpted figures were only installed c 1290–1300. The façade, including the return of the elevation, has niches sufficient for 203 standing figures on five principal levels. Thacker's sketch view of the W front of c 1671 shows twenty-eight figures *in situ*. Eight medieval figures remain in the positions indicated in early 19th-century views [eg Dodsworth 1814; Britton 1836]. John Carter's drawings of 1802 [BL Add MS 29,939, fols 39^r and 40^r] record a ninth figure, of St James the Great, which survived until 1851, when C R Cockerell described it [Cockerell 1851], but it has since disappeared. The niches on the façade are comparatively shallow and the relative exposure of the slender figures has contributed to their corrosion, particularly in the course of this century.

The W front at Salisbury has been compared to that of Wells and certainly shared some liturgical features with it (see pp 3–4). The treatment of the entrances is different, however, with the Salisbury design, with three gabled portals, indicating a greater awareness of French practice. Despite their increased size and the greater depth of the central portal at Salisbury when compared to that at Wells, the portals were not treated as a great sculptural opportunity, in the French manner. There is no evidence of any jamb sculpture, although the tympanum over the central door no doubt contained sculpture – probably of the Virgin and Child, a subject appropriate to both the dedication of the Cathedral and the Marian imagery at a higher level on the façade. The voussoirs were adorned with a frieze of stiff-leaf foliage apparently inhabited by figures and beasts. Small fragments of the original carving were carefully incorporated in the Victorian restoration. Traces of polychromy survive on the portal, confirmation of its medieval designation as

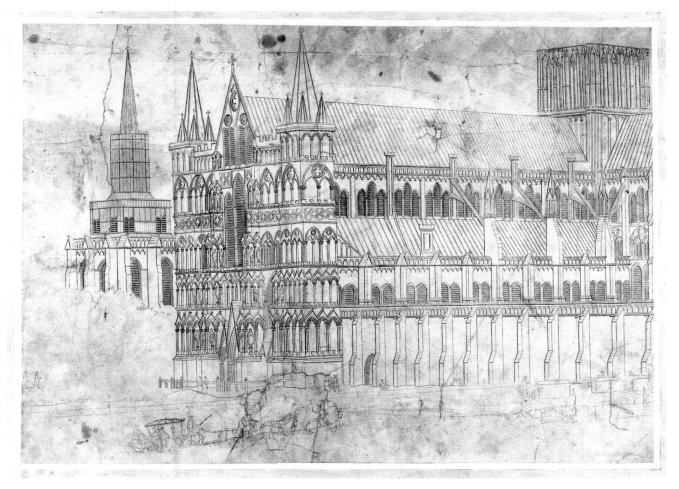

142   South-west prospect of the Cathedral. Anonymous and undated drawing (late 17th century) [BB76/4149, Society of Antiquaries of London]

the Blue Porch. The grotesque head-stops decorating the porches are weathered but original.

The surviving medieval figures are: in the uppermost niches of the buttresses flanking the centre bay, second stage, the Virgin Mary (?), St John the Baptist; third stage, St Peter, St Paul; top stage, two angels, in the niches of the NW tower, in the lowest stage, a robed figure facing N and a bishop facing W. All are heavily weathered and restored. A relief of the Pelican in her Piety above the medallion containing the 19th-century figure of Christ in Majesty in the gable also appears to be original. The original iconography cannot be recovered with any precision, although the Coronation of the Virgin was plausibly suggested by Cockerell for the culmination of the programme and a figure of the Virgin is probably one of those medieval figures to survive.

Left: 143   13th-century head-stop over western portal

Below left: 144   13th-century figure of St Peter from the west front

Below: 145   13th-century figure of St Paul from the west front

[Photographs on this page: Courtauld Institute of Art]

The 19th-century restoration, directed by Scott, sought to recreate what was believed to be the lost scheme, and does at least recapture the density of the original display. Recent conservation work is revealing the careful nature of the work. For the execution of the new sculptural programme and the restoration of the medieval figures from 1867 onwards, Scott chose one of his favourite collaborators, James Redfern (1838–76), a fine-art sculptor who also worked on a number of Scott's architectural projects, notably the Albert Memorial, for which he created the figures of Prudence, Humility and Temperance. He also worked for Scott at Ely, Gloucester and on the N transept of Westminster Abbey [Read 1982, 103, 266]. He was one of the most prolific and successful sculptors of his day. In all, seventy-one new figures were installed, together with new heads for some of the medieval figures (eg St Peter, Fig 144). By January 1869 thirty-one statues together with a Majesty, two choral angels and two archangels had been modelled [*Sarum D&C*, Scott Papers, bundle 8]. The actual carving of the statues was done locally from Redfern's models. The niches now contain seventy-one standing figures, mainly of 1867 and later, designed by Redfern in accordance with what was the supposed original scheme, the *Te Deum*: top stage, angels; second stage, Old Testament prophets and patriarchs; third stage, Apostles and Evangelists; fourth stage, Confessors of the Faith and Martyrs; lowest stage, bishops, martyrs and other worthies of the English Church [Cockerell 1851; Fletcher 1938].

The Chapter House vestibule

In niches forming the outer order of the archway to the Chapter House are fourteen small statue groups, formed by a female figure standing on a recumbent figure, dating from the third quarter of the 13th century. As early as 1851 these figures attracted the attention of C R Cockerell [Cockerell 1851], and they were drawn by his son Frederick Pepys Cockerell [RIBA Drawings Collection, Box H, 10], providing an invaluable record of their condition prior to restoration in 1856. Of the missing tympanum group no trace survives, although a figure of the Virgin Mary probably filled this space.

The figures have been identified as one of the most extensive depictions of the Virtues and Vices in European art in the 13th century [Green 1968], far more extensive than any contemporary English scheme (eg the Painted Chamber at Westminster). The figure groups were originally richly coloured. Traces of the polychrome can be seen in J M W Turner's watercolour of the vestibule of 1796–7 [V&A, Inv No. 503–1883; RCHME 1993a, frontispiece]. Burges recorded surviving traces of naturalistic colour in considerable detail in 1855 [Burges 1859, 7–8], although the taking of casts by

Cottingham [Burges 1859, 8] had already removed some paint. The restoration of 1856, when John Birnie Philip supplied those missing parts of the figures, also effectively removed vestigial traces of medieval colour.

The scheme was carefully structured to depict the four cardinal and theological Virtues on the S side, with the seven deadly sins and their Virtuous remedies on the N (identifications follow Green [1968]):

South side (bottom to top):
1. Fortitude and Infortitude (*Fortitudo/Infortitudo*), head of Fortitude 1856; 2. Temperance and Intemperance (*Temperantia/Intemperantia*), head of Temperance 1856; 3. Charity and Poverty (*Caritas/Paupertas*), upper half of Charity 1856; 4. Prudence and Imprudence (*Prudentia/Imprudentia*), head of Prudence 1856; 5. Patience and Anger (*Patientia/Ira*), no restorations; 6. Hope and Despair (*Spes/Desperatio*), head of Hope 1856; 7. Justice and Injustice (*Justitia/Injustitia*), no restorations.

North side (bottom to top):
1. Humility overcoming Pride (*Humilitas/Superbia*), head of Humility 1856; 2. Bounty overcoming Avarice (*Largitas/Avaritia*), head of Bounty 1856; 3. Chastity overcoming Dissipation (*Castitas/Luxuria*), head of Chastity 1856; 4. Sobriety overcoming Gluttony? (*Sobrietas/Gula?*), no restorations; 5. Faith overcoming Unbelief (*Fides/Infidelitas*), minor restoration; 6. Wisdom overcoming Jealousy (*Misericordia/Invidia*), no restorations; 7. Gladness overcoming Sloth (*Laetitia/Accidia*), no restorations.

The Chapter House

In the spandrels of the main arcade, a frieze of great iconographic interest, depicting sixty Old Testament scenes from the Creation to the giving of the Ten Commandments on Sinai. Proceeding clockwise from the entrance, they depict the seven days of Creation (7 scenes); Adam and Eve (5); Cain and Abel (3); Noah (4); the Tower of Babel (1); Abraham and Lot (6); Jacob (8); Joseph (21) and Moses (5). The extensive Joseph cycle has been shown to have been derived from a 13th-century Middle English poem [Blum 1969]. The sculpture was badly damaged during the Civil War, when the Chapter House was used for meetings of Parliamentary commissioners [Gilpin 1798, sect 5, 66]. Only the scene depicting Pharoah's dream is perfect, although in that of Noah entering the ark, only the dove and the raven's foot are broken. Most other scenes have lost heads and arms. In 1855 Burges described the scenes in detail and recorded original traces of polychromy [Burges 1859]; the scenes were painted mainly in light colours with

146 The entrance to the Chapter House from the vestibule [A F Kersting H 5461]

147   *North side of the Chapter House door decorated with figures of the Virtues overcoming the Vices [AA66/643]*

148   Chapter House sculpture; the Flood (seventh spandrel, north side) [BB71/2567]

149   Chapter House sculpture; Abraham entertaining the angels (fourth spandrel, north-east bay) [BB71/2572]

150   *Carved slab, perhaps brought from Old Sarum, reused in the capping of the pulpitum in the north-east transept [BB73/7488]*

diapering on many draperies. The painted narrative was offset by alternating blue and red grounds. The frieze was restored and repainted soon after. John Birnie Philip undertook the sculptural work, and Octavius Hudson renewed the painting. The original sculpture is in Chilmark stone, with restoration in Caen stone, a composite stone made of pulverised Chilmark and a mastic [Blum 1996, 69]. By the end of the century Hudson's polychromy had deteriorated so badly that it was removed in 1905 [Blum 1996, 70–1], an operation which also removed remaining medieval pigment beneath.

The tympanum over the W door was also restored in the 19th century and now contains a large quatrefoil with Evangelist symbols at the angles and a seated figure of Christ at the centre. Large spandrels flanking the quatrefoil may once have contained censing angels.

The cusps of the large roundels in the Chapter House windows contain 13th-century portrait head-stops depicting nun, monk, merchant, countryman, sailor, etc.

The base of the central pillar was reconstructed *c* 1855 and is now decorated with the story of Reynard the fox, reconstructed under Burges's supervision [Burges 1859]. The original base, much weathered, is among the loose sculptural and architectural fragments in the Cathedral's lapidarium.

The differing views as to the chronology of the Chapter House have resulted in equally divergent views as to the stylistic milieu to which the sculptures belong. Dr Blum, favouring the later date of *c* 1280 [Blum 1996, 75–6], has compared the Salisbury Chapter House figures to Parisian ivories of the second half of the 13th century. A recent survey [Williamson 1995, 212] places the Salisbury scheme at the end of a series of mid-13th

century English sculptural friezes, comparing the handling of the Salisbury Chapter House reliefs to the treatment of the wall arcade at the E end of Worcester Cathedral and the earliest parts of Westminster Abbey. A comparison with a source even closer to home can also usefully be made – namely, with the treatment of the narrative reliefs on the spandrels of the Bridport monument in the Cathedral of *c* 1262.

Carved slab

In the NE transept, the moulded capping of the former pulpitum includes a reused stone slab with abraded carving on the upper face (45 x 75 cm), showing four figures in relief, on a red-coloured background. It is 12th century, possibly from the cathedral at Old Sarum [RCHME 1980, 15].

20th-century additions

In the 1940s a series of figures of saints were introduced to niches on the southern face of the choir wall, flanking the door into the choir, and at the crossing on the strainer arches. All but one are naturalistically painted.

On the south wall of the choir enclosure, facing the S-choir aisle, are the following figures (E to W): St Monica (in memory of Evelyn Lovett, d 1937); St Nicholas (in memory of Kenneth Robert Balfour, d 1936); St Francis (in memory of Christopher Wordsworth); St Aldhelm (in memory of Henry William Carpenter).

At the crossing the following figures have been introduced. NE pier, N side: Richard Poore (in memory of Brig General Robert Montagu Poore, d 1938); S side: Thomas Becket? (in memory of Alfred Cecil Parr, d 1943). NW pier, N side: Elias de Dereham (given in 1946 by the Freemasons); S side: St Edwin King and Martyr (in memory of Edwin CL Parker). SW pier, N side: Archangel Michael (in memory of Hugh Trenchard, d 1943); S side: unpainted figure of 'Fortitude' signed by R Garbes RA (in memory of Edith Maud Hulse, d 1937).

Decorated masonry

Consecration crosses

There were originally twenty-four consecration crosses, of which ten external and nine internal examples remain (one is no longer visible). It has been suggested that they date from the reconsecration of 1280.

Externally there are ten in all, counting two in the gables of the aisle doors. An eleventh may be hidden by the W wall of the treasury vestibule, on a buttress of the SE transept. All are of 13th-century date, positioned 2.1–2.7 m from the ground. All but one comprise deep (9 mm) indents for a metal equal-armed foliate cross,

151   Exterior consecration cross, 13th century, east wall of the south-east transept [BB77/10042]

152   13th-century interior consecration cross, north wall of the north transept [BB71/2251]

63 cm across, with square central bosses; each indent is set in a quatrefoil stone panel to which the former cross, probably of brass, was attached by an elaborate lead fastening. The exception is an elaborate foliated cross carved in high relief on a square stone set diagonally, on the S transept, badly decayed.

Internally there are eight similar indents for metal crosses, below windows and in spandrels above the W doorways of the nave. Metal inlays were held in place with iron dowels set into wooden pegs. Each is surrounded by a painted quatrefoil, repainted with white foliage on a red and green ground in 1954, probably following the original scheme. Centrally below the E window of the Trinity Chapel is a similar cross, but painted, with no indent for a metal inlay. Stumps of iron spikes in masonry some 7.5 cm below most indents may mark the position of original lamp or candle brackets.

All of the internal crosses have been repainted, except for the ones behind the altar in the Trinity Chapel and the one in the N transept.[20]

Inscriptions and Graffiti

Externally there are two inscriptions. On the S face of the SW buttress of St Stephen's chapel, formerly protected by masonry of St Stephen's porch, but revealed in 1789, when the porch was demolished, and drawn by Jacob Schnebbelie [1789, 1002] is an indulgence of thirteen days in well-formed Lombardic letters, 10.2 cm high, from the 13th century:

:X:I:I:I:D[IES:VE]NIE:OR
ACION[EM: DO]INICA[M]
DICEN[TIBUS:]CV[M]:SAL
VTAC[IONE:BE]ATE:V
IRGIN[IS:PRO A(N)I(M)A:A
GNET[IS:REQ]VIES
CENT[IS: HIC]

This transcription was made by C A R Radford, communicated 8 July 1976. For a variant transcription, see Wordsworth [1913, 23–4]. At the time of writing the inscription has been rendered almost illegible through weathering.

On the E face of the SW buttress of the ambulatory, low down, is a black-letter Latin epitaph relating to music and musical instruments, attributed to Precentor Adam Mottram (d 1415). The inscription, described as 'sumwhat defacid', was noticed by Leland, although he did not attempt to transcribe it [Toulmin Smith 1964, 265]. A transcription is suggested in Malden [1908, 347–40]:

HAC IA[CET IN] TUMA FIDEI TUBA TIBIA MOTT[RAM]
MUSICA MENDICAT MUTA VIOLLA DOLET
PSALTERIUM CITHARE LIRA SISTRA SALES LITUORUM
CONTINUERE SUO FUNERE MESTA IACENT
INSTRUMENTA...
QUI (or QUE)

and variant readings are listed.

153 13th-century indulgence inscription, offering thirteen days' indulgence for those offering prayers for the soul of Agnes. Cut into the south face of the south-west buttress of St Stephen's chapel [BB76/3740]

Internally, there is an inscription in the NE transept, on a tablet on the W wall: 'The three gravestones underneath thise place of Jo. Jewel, Robert Wyvill and Edmund Gheast, bishops of this church of Sarum, were removed out of the choir upon the paving thereof with white marble which was done at the charges of the Rev. Dr Robert Townson, the sone of Robert Townson, formerly bishop of this church, Anno Dom. 1684'. In the SE transept, at the NW corner of the clerestory, is the inscription: 'J Compton French Polished this Bay July 1874'.

There are graffiti throughout the Cathedral.

On the N face of the SE buttress of Trinity Chapel, 'IR 1632'.

In the S-choir aisle, on the stonework of the tomb of Simon de Gandavo, 'W Boyer 1673, EG 1674'; also some illegible black-letter, probably medieval.

In the S-choir aisle, on the SW pier of the eastern crossing, 'IB 20 May 1620', with a symbol similar to a merchant's mark. On the tomb of John Capon, 'WH 1620, IR 1622' in a lozenge, and 'Roger Gory 1681, WG 1696'.

In the N transept, on the tomb of John Blythe, 'HN 1585'. In the nave, on the effigy of Sir John Cheney, 'Iohn Spring 1580, ES 1646', in a lozenge.

In the N triforium gallery of the nave, painted on a spandrel of the flying buttress, near the doorway to the porch chamber, 'Biddlecomb 1792'; on the jamb of the W window, 'HI 1647'.

At the W end of the S aisle, in the passage from the SW stair to the window embrasure, 'WS 1671'.

In the N porch, on the responds of the archway, on the E side, '1628 IM'; on the W side, 'IR 1629'.

In the central tower, in the SE corner, at the level of the lower window sills, 'AP 1689'; on the jamb of the E window, 'H. Stocker, glazier, 1745'.

Inside the spire, on the E side, 'RC 1664'.

Externally, near the apex of the spire, 'GE Roche, 1578', 'FWC 1696', and others later.

Throughout the Cathedral, numerous other 18th- and 19th-century dated initials.

Architectural features

Doorway

Reset in 1789 against the W wall of the NE transept, in the middle of relocated 13th-century pulpitum, is a doorway of 1481, formerly in the N side of the Beauchamp chantry chapel, where it was recorded *in situ* by Jacob Schnebbelie and was illustrated in Gough's *Sepulchral Monuments in Great Britain* of 1796 [Gough 1796, II, pt 2, pl LXXI]. The doorway has a moulded four-centred head and continuous jambs; above, a foliate spandrel encloses a gartered shield of arms of Beauchamp under a mitre, surrounded by a casement-moulded ogee outer head with crockets; the foliate finials and cinquefoil-headed stone panels are also probably from the Beauchamp chapel, but rearranged.

Font

The medieval font, mentioned in a number of documents, was located at the W end of the nave [Malden 1904, 32]. This has since disappeared. A 17th-century font, probably that brought from London in 1661 at a cost of £2 12*s* [Sarum D & C, Everett MS U52] was also sited at the W end of the nave and can be seen in this position in Biddlecombe's view of the nave of 1754 (see Fig 19). Biddlecombe's detailed engraving (Fig 25) shows it to have had a gadrooned bowl, surmounted by a swagged octagonal cover with a flame finial. It was removed *c* 1850, and in 1877 was taken to Australia [Shortt 1964, 168–9].

The present font is located in St Catherine's chapel. It is in 13th-century style, with an arcaded bowl with stiff-leaf foliage in spandrels resting on a pedestal of clustered shafts with intervening foliate and zig-zag decoration. It was given as a memorial to Dean Francis Lear (d 1850).

Lavatory

The lavatory is reset against the E wall of St Catherine's chapel, in two tiers to accommodate the main bench seat of the E wall of the chapel. Its oblong stone basin, 1.45 m x 0.6 m x 0.9 m, has a moulded rim enriched at the corners with carved bosses and a large circular outlet hole (which may have been dressed with lead). The plinth has trefoil-headed arcading. Above, the foliate frieze supports a shelf in the recess, flanked by panelled uprights. The canopy is carved to represent groin-vaulting fronted by sub-cusped trefoil-ogee head with crocketed enrichment culminating in a large finial. Over all, is trefoil-headed stone panelling with embattled cresting. The lavatory is probably late 14th or early 15th century, and is said by Carter to have been moved to its present location by Wyatt, from 'the South East angle of the second South transept' [Carter 1803, 1023].

Niche

In the vestibule inside the W doorway of the N aisle, in the S wall, is a shallow recess with a chamfered two-centred head, continuous jambs and splayed stops, perhaps made for a stoup. The lower part has subsequently been rebuilt. It is probably 14th century.

154   19th-century font in St Catherine's chapel, given in memory of Dean Francis Lear (d 1850) [BB74/2734]

155   Late 14th/early 15th-century lavatory reset in St Catherine's chapel [BB73/4684]

Piscinae and aumbries

In the N wall of St Peter's chapel is a double aumbry of polished Purbeck with a roll-moulded frame supporting two triangular heads with fleur-de-lis finials; the jambs are rebated for doors and retaining iron hinges; *c* 1225.

In the S wall of St Stephen's chapel is a double piscina of Chilmark and Purbeck with a roll-moulded rectangular frame enclosing coupled trefoil-headed arches with

156   Piscinae in St Stephen's chapel [BB74/4686]

shafts with moulded caps and bases; sill formerly had two plain bowls (one obliterated, one with central drain); *c* 1225. In the N wall of St Martin's chapel is a double aumbry similar to that in St Peter's chapel, but retaining oak doors hung on iron strap-hinges; two doors are probably original; *c* 1225–36. In the S screen wall of St Catherine's chapel is a coupled piscina and aumbry with keeled roll-moulded trefoil heads of Chilmark, under roll labels which meet at a foliate stop, rising from Purbeck shafts with moulded caps and bases; the basin is of Purbeck with a roll-moulded lip projecting on a semicircular pedestal, with a stone shelf above; the aumbry has a stone shelf and chamfered rebated surround with iron hinge-pins (the doors are gone); *c* 1225–36.

In the N screen wall of St Mary Magdalene's chapel is a double aumbry, nearly uniform with that in St Catherine's chapel; *c* 1225–36. In the S wall of St Nicholas's chapel is a double piscina, resembling that in St Stephen's chapel; *c* 1225–36. In the S wall of St

Michael's chapel is a similar double piscina, but with shorter jambs and roll-moulded labels with cross-roll stops; it retains two bowls with drains; *c* 1225–36.

Pulpit

In the NE corner of the nave is a pulpit designed by Scott and executed by Farmer and Brindley of London in 1877. The base and shafting are of Purbeck marble, the body of Chilmark with Purbeck details. It is decorated with figures standing within recessed canopied niches: Noah, Elijah, Jonah, St John the Baptist. There are Chilmark steps with a handrail and balustrade by Skidmore of Coventry. Scott's choir pulpit has been destroyed; photographs show it to have been a more modest version of that surviving in the nave. The present choir pulpit is by Randol Blacking. It is wooden, of a wine-glass shape, with armorial decoration on panelled sides, and partially gilded. It was erected in memory of Bishop Lunt (1946–9).

157   Double aumbry in St Martin's chapel [BB71/3162]

158   Piscina and aumbry in St Catherine's chapel [BB71/2391]

159   The nave pulpit of 1877. Designed by Scott and made by Farmer and Brindley, with handrail and balustrade by Skidmore [BB93/22081]

Notes to Part II

1. This entry was written by Tim Tatton-Brown, Consultant Archaeologist to Salisbury Cathedral. The RCHME is grateful to him for permission to publish this material.

2. This account is based on Matthews [1983].

3. Neither Rickert [1965] nor Brieger [1968] considers Salisbury's stained glass at all.

4. Nicholas Charles, BL Lansdowne MS 874, fol 32; Richard Symonds published in Long [1859]; Celia Fiennes published in Morris [1995].

5. Thomas Gray's observations are unpublished – verbal communication by Dr Marion Roberts, British Archaeological Association Conference, Salisbury, 1991.

6. John Carter's drawings. BL Add MS 29,939, fols 57, 81–3; C A Buckler sketches, BL Add MS 37,138, nos 32, 33, 35, 36, 37 and 40; the Gwilt drawings are in the collection of Chapel Studio, Kings Langley, Hertfordshire, with photographs in the National Monuments Record; Octavius Hudson drawings, V&A, Dept of Prints and Drawings, B3a and CG65b; Charles Winston watercolours, BL Add MS 35,211, III (nos 177–186) and IV (nos 187–203) and Add MS 33,851, fol 74; Clayton and Bell album, V&A, Dept of Prints and Drawings, B4a; drawings in the Cathedral archives are nos 192–5.

7. I am grateful to Professor Marks for drawing this to my attention.

8. The references to grisaille types follow the typology published by Richard Marks [Marks 1996].

9. The only surviving Cistercian example, from Abbey Dore in Herefordshire, was destroyed by careless restoration. The glass had been excavated and its date and the authenticity of its design could not be established beyond question [Marks 1986]. It appears to have been very similar to the Salisbury 'fishscale' design.

10. Unpainted grisaille survives in parish churches at Brabourne and Hastingleigh in Kent and at Marston in Oxfordshire. A panel of unknown provenance from the collection of Alfred Fisher is on loan to the Stained Glass Museum at Ely (no. 90/4).

11. The unpainted grisaille in York Minster was installed in the nave clerestory in the early 14th century. Its date cannot be proved beyond question, but it is likely to be of late 12th-century origin, reused in the 14th century, together with late 12th-century historiated panels.

12. See n4.

13. Recent unpublished research on the glass of Wells Cathedral by Dr T Ayers has reassigned the surviving labels bearing the names of a number of late 13th-century canons now in the Lady Chapel windows to the windows of the Chapter House.

14. Post-war excavations in areas around the Cathedral and Chapter House have recovered fragments of painted glass. Some are now in windows in the retrochoir of Winchester Cathedral and a number of local parish churches, but their heavily corroded and largely opaque condition after burial means that they add little information to the corpus of Salisbury material.

15. Notably in the V&A, C.278–1911; the Glencairn Museum, Bryn Athyn, Pennsylvania, no. 0.03.SG.218; the Toledo Museum of Art, Toledo, Ohio, nos 35.38, 35.39, 35.41; small panels of grisaille fragments recently donated to the Stained Glass Museum at Ely, made up by the firm of Lowndes and Drury during their restoration of 1922.

16. I am grateful to G F Fisher of the Courtauld Institute for these as yet unpublished attributions. The other major monuments attributed by him to this Salisbury workshop are the Ashley Monuments (1627–80) at Wimborne St Giles (Dorset), John Evelyn (d 1627), West Dean (Wilts), Lady Mompesson (d 1633), Lydiard Tregoze (Wilts) and Lady Gorges (erected 1634), Maidwell (Northants).

17. This information supplied by R O C Spring.

18. Attribution by G F Fisher.

19. Attribution by G F Fisher.

20. This entry is based on a description prepared for RCHME by W J Blair, subsequently published as Blair [1981]. The RCHME is grateful to Mr Blair for his assistance.

Appendix 1

The Bishops of Salisbury, 1220–1998

Richard Poore 1217–28

Robert de Bingham 1229–46

William of York 1247–56

Giles de Bridport 1257–62

Walter de la Wyle 1263–71

Robert de Wickhampton 1274–84 (elected 1271)

Walter de Scammel 1284–6

Henry de Braunstone 1287–8

William de la Corner 1289–91

Nicholas Longespee 1292–7

Simon de Gandavo 1297–1315

Roger de Martival 1315–30

Robert de Wyville 1330–75

Ralph Erghum 1375–88

John de Waltham 1388–95

Richard Medford 1395–1407

Nicholas Bubwith 1407

Robert de Hallum 1407–17

John Chaundeler 1417–26

Robert Neville 1427–38

William Aiscough 1438–50

Richard Beauchamp 1450–81

Lionel Woodville 1482–4

Thomas Langton 1485–93

John Blythe 1493–9

Henry Dean 1500–1

Edmund Audley 1502–24

Lawrence Campeggio 1524–34

Nicholas Shaxton 1535–9

John Capon or Salcote 1539–57

John Jewel 1559–71

Edmund Gheast 1571–7

John Piers 1577–89

John Coldwell 1591–6

Henry Cotton 1598–1615

Robert Abbot 1616–18

Martin Fotherby 1618–20

Robert Tounson 1620–1

John Davenant 1621–41

Brian Duppa 1641–60

Humphrey Henchman 1660–3

John Earles 1663–5

Alexander Hyde 1665–7

Seth Ward 1667–89

Gilbert Burnet 1689–1715

William Talbot 1715–21

Richard Willis 1721–3

Benjamin Hoadley 1723–34

Thomas Sherlock 1734–48

John Gilbert 1748–57

John Thomas 1757–61

Robert Hay Drummond 1761

John Thomas 1761–6

John Hume 1766–82

Shute Barrington 1782–91

John Douglas 1791–1807

John Fisher 1807–25

Thomas Burgess 1825–37

Edward Denison 1837–54

Walter Kerr Hamilton 1854–69

George Moberly 1869–85

John Wordsworth 1885–1911

Frederick Ridgeway 1911–21

St Clair Donaldson 1921–36

Neville Lovat 1936–46

Geoffrey Lunt 1946–9

William Anderson 1949–63

Joseph Fison 1963–73

George Reindorp 1973–82

John Austin Baker 1982–93

David Stancliffe 1993–

Appendix 2

Deans of Salisbury, 1220-1998

Adam 1215-20

William de Waude 1220-38

Robert de Hertford 1238-57

Robert de Wickhampton 1258-71

Walter de Scammel 1271-84

Henry de Braunstone 1285-7

Simon de Micham 1287-97

Peter of Savoy ?-1308

William Ruffati 1308-11

Raymond de Fargis 1311-46

Bertrand de Fargis 1346-7

Raynald Ursinus 1347-?

James Ursinus ?-1379

Robert de Braybrooke 1379-81

Thomas Montacute 1382-1404

John Chaundeler 1404-17

Simon Sydenham 1418-31

Thomas Brouns 1431-5

Nicholas Bildeston 1435-41

Adam Moleyns 1441-5

Richard Leyot 1446-9

Gilbert Kymer 1449-63

James Goldwell 1463-72

John Davyson 1473-85

Edward Cheyne 1486-1502

Thomas Ruthall 1502-9

William Atwater 1509-14

John Longland 1514-21

Cuthbert Tunstal 1521-2

Richard Pace 1523-36

Peter Vannes 1536-63

William Bradbridge 1563-71

Edmund Freake 1571-2

John Piers 1572-7

John Bridges 1577-1604

John Gordon 1604-19

John Williams 1619-20

John Bowle 1620-30

Edmund Mason 1630-5

Richard Bayley 1635-67

Ralph Brideoke (Brideoak) 1667-75

Thomas Pierce 1675-91

Robert Woodward 1691-1702

Edward Young 1702-5

John Younger 1705-28

John Clark 1728-57

Thomas Greene 1757-80

Rowney Noel 1780-6

John Ekins 1786-1808

Charles Talbot 1809-23

Hugh Nicholas Pearson 1823-46

Francis Lear 1846-50

Henry Parr Hamilton 1850-80

George David Boyle 1880-1901

Allan Beecher Webb 1901-7

William Page Roberts 1907-20

Andrew Ewbank Burn 1920-8

John Hugh Granville Randolph 1928-36

Edward Lowry Henderson 1936-43

Henry Charles Robins 1943-52

Robert Hamilton Moberly 1952-60

Kenneth William Howarth 1960-71

William Fenton Morley 1971-7

Sydney Hall Evans 1977-86

Hugh Geoffrey Dickinson 1986-96

Derek Richard Watson 1996-

Appendices compiled from Greenaway [1991], Horne [1962; 1986] and Spring [1987*a*].

Unpublished sources

Devizes
Devizes Museum

Wiltshire Archaeological Society Library
  'The Antiquities of Salisbury', watercolours by
    J Buckler, vol IX
  A series of original drawings and sketches
    made for Britton [1836] by F Nash, F Mackenzie,
    G and R Cattermole, Prints and Drawings
    Catalogue, Press Mark S
  Thomas Trotter, album of watercolours, c 1798

London
British Library

Add MS 5,833
Add MS 27,349 (Smart Lethieullier and Charles
  Frederick)
Add MS 29,925 (John Carter)
Add MS 29,928 (John Carter)
Add MS 29,939 (John Carter)
Add MS 34,866 (Thomas Willement)
Add MS 33,851 (Charles Winston)
Add MS 35,211 vols III and IV (Charles Winston)
Add MS 36,980 (Charles Buckler)
Add MS 37,138 (Charles Buckler)
King's Top Coll XLIII
Lansdowne MS 874 (Nicholas Charles)
Lansdowne MS 968

Public Record Office

SC 6/1119/9

Royal Institute of British Architects Drawings Collection

Box H, 10 (Frederick Pepys Cockerell)

Society of Antiquaries of London

MS 263 (Jacob Schnebbelie)

Victoria and Albert Museum

Department of Prints and Drawings
B3a (Octavius Hudson)
CG65b (Octavius Hudson)
B4a (Clayton and Bell)
93.E.1 (William Burges)
93.E.5 (William Burges)

Oxford
Bodleian Library
MS Douce G Subt 25 (2), page 1
MS Gough Eccl Top 55 (Frances Godwin)
MS Gough Maps, vol 32
MS Gough Misc Antiq 4
MS Gough Wilts 3

Salisbury
Dean and Chapter Muniments

Chapter Acts
Everett MSS
Fabric Accounts
Liber Evidentiarum B
Scott Papers

Bibliography

ADDLESHAW, G W O and ETCHELLS, F 1948. *The Architectural Setting of Anglican Worship*. London.

ALEXANDER, J J G and BINSKI, P 1987 (eds). *The Age of Chivalry: Art in Plantagenet England*. London.

ARMFIELD, H T 1873. Note on the choir vault paintings. *Proceedings of the Society of Antiquaries*, 2nd ser, VI, 477–9.

   1878. 'The ancient roof paintings in Salisbury Cathedral'. *WAM* XVII, 129–35.

ASTON, M 1988. *England's Iconoclasts. Laws against Images*. Oxford.

BAILEY, H 1978. 'Salisbury Cathedral Library'. *Hatcher Review* 5, 27–32.

BEDDARD, R 1971. 'Cathedral furnishings of the Restoration Period'. *WAM* LXVI, 147–55.

BEER, E J 1956. *Die Glasmalereien der Schweiz vom 12. bis zum Beginn des 14. Jahrhunderts*. Corpus Vitrearum Medii Aevi, Switzerland. I. Basle.

BEESON, C F C 1971. *English Church Clocks 1280–1850*. London and Chichester.

BENSON, R and HATCHER, H 1843. *The History of Old and New Sarum* (constituting vol VI of R C Hoare, *History of Modern Wiltshire*). London.

BINSKI, P 1986. *The Painted Chamber at Westminster*. London.

   1991. 'Abbot Berkyng's tapestries and Matthew Paris's Life of St Edward The Confessor'. *Archaeologia* CIX, 85–100.

   1995. *Westminster Abbey and the Plantagenets. Kingship and the Representation of Power 1200–1400*. New Haven and London.

BLAIR, W J 1981, 'The consecration-cross indents of Salisbury Cathedral'. *Transactions of the Monumental Brass Society* XII, 16–21.

BLUM, P Z 1969. 'The Middle English Romance "Iacob and Iosep" and the Joseph Cycle of the Salisbury Chapter House'. *Gesta* VIII, 18–34.

   1978. '*The Salisbury Chapter House and its Old Testament Cycle*', PhD thesis, Yale University (thesis available as Ann Arbor UMI, 1978, No. 8121401).

   1986. 'Liturgical influences on the design of the west front at Wells and Salisbury'. *Gesta* XXV, 1, 145–50.

   1991. 'The sequence of building campaigns at Salisbury'. *The Art Bulletin* LXXIII, 1, 6–38.

   1996. 'The sculptures of the Salisbury Chapter House', in Keen and Cocke 1996.

BOND, F 1908. *Screens and Galleries*. London.

BOOKER, C and DUNLOP I 1990. *Laurence Whistler. The Glass Engravings in Salisbury Cathedral*. FOSC Publication. Salisbury.

BORENIUS, T 1932. 'A destroyed cycle of wall paintings in a church in Wiltshire'. *Antiquaries Journal* XII, 393–406 and fig 1.

BRIEGER, P 1968. *English Art 1216–1307*. Oxford.

BRITTON, J 1801. *The Beauties of Wiltshire* vol 1. London

   1836. *The History and Antiquities of the Cathedral Church of Salisbury*. London.

BROWN (Brown & Co Publishers) 1871. *Stranger's Handbook to Salisbury Cathedral*. Salisbury.

   1882. *Stranger's Handbook to Salisbury Cathedral*. Rev edn. Salisbury.

BROWN, S 1992. 'The thirteenth-century stained glass of Salisbury Cathedral'. *Council for British Archaeology, Wessex Newsletter* (Nov), 4–8.

   and O'CONNOR, D 1991 *Medieval Craftsmen. Glass Painters*. London.

BUILDER, THE 1868. XXVI, 473–4.

BUMPUS, T F 1907. *The Cathedrals of England and Wales*. London.

BURGES, W 1859. 'The iconography of the Chapter-House, Salisbury'. *The Ecclesiologist* XX, 109–14, 147–62.

CAL CLOSE 1234-7. *Calendar of Close Rolls. Henry III, iii. 1234–1237*. London 1909.

CAL CLOSE 1247-51. *Calendar of Close Rolls. Henry III, vi. 1247–1251*. London 1922.

CAL CLOSE 1251-53. *Calendar of Close Rolls. Henry III, vii. 1251–1253*. London 1928.

CAL CLOSE 1256-59. *Calendar of Close Rolls. Henry III, x. 1256–1259*. London 1932.

CAL CLOSE 1259-61. *Calendar of Close Rolls. Henry III, xi. 1259–1261*. London 1934.

CAL LIB 1240-5. *Calendar of Liberate Rolls. Henry III, ii. 1240–1245*. London 1930.

CAL LIB 1245-51. *Calendar of Liberate Rolls. Henry III, iii. 1245–51*. London 1937.

CARTER, J 1803. 'The pursuits of architectural innovation' by 'An Architect'. *Gentleman's Magazine* LXXIII, 515–17, 642–5, 735–7, 1020–3, 1122–4.

   1845. *The Ancient Architecture of England (1795–1814)*. 2 vols. Revised and edited by J Britton. London.

CAVINESS, M H 1981. *The Windows of Christ Church Cathedral Canterbury*. Corpus Vitrearum Medii Aevi, Great Britain. II. London.

CHANDLER, J 1993. *Travels in Tudor England*. Stroud.

CHERRY, B 1984. 'An early 16th-century London tomb design'. *Architectural History* 27, 86–94.

1990. 'Some new types of late medieval tombs in the London area', in Lindy Grant (ed), *Medieval Art, Architecture and Archaeology in London*. British Archaeological Association Conference Transactions. London.

CHEW, H M 1963 (ed). *Hemingby's Register*. Wiltshire Record Society. XVIII. Devizes.

COBB, G 1980. *English Cathedrals, the Forgotten Centuries*. London.

COCKE, T 1993. 'Historical summary', in RCHME 1993*a*.

COCKERELL, C R 1851. *The Iconography of the West Front of Wells Cathedral, with an Appendix on the Sculptures of other Medieval Churches in England*. Appendix N, 95–100. London and Oxford.

COLE, D 1980. *The Work of Sir Gilbert Scott*. London.

COLVIN, H M 1978. *A Biographical Dictionary of British Architects 1600–1840*. 2nd edn. London.

COMPTON, Lord Alwyne 1851. 'On tile pavements, especially that at Higham Ferrers Church'. *Associated Architectural Societies Reports and Papers* I, 1850–1, 6–12.

CORMACK, P 1980. *Christopher Whall 1849–1924*: Arts and Crafts Stained Glass Worker. London.

1989. *Henry Holiday 1839–1927*. London.

CORPUS VITREARUM CHECKLIST II, 1987. *Stained Glass before 1700 in American Collections: Mid-Atlantic and Southeastern Seaboard States*. Washington.

CORPUS VITREARUM CHECKLIST III, 1989. *Stained Glass before 1700 in American Collections: Midwestern and Western States*. Washington.

CROOK, J MORDAUNT 1981. *William Burges and the High Victorian Dream*. London.

1995. *John Carter and the Mind of the Gothic Revival*. London.

CROOK, J 1990. 'The typology of medieval shrines – a previously misidentified "tomb-shrine" panel from Winchester Cathedral'. *The Antiquaries Journal* LXXX, pt 1, 49–64.

1993*a* (ed). *Winchester Cathedral. Nine Hundred Years*. Chichester.

1993*b* 'St Swithun of Winchester', in Crook 1993*a*, 57–68.

DAY, L F 1897. *Windows: A Book about Stained and Painted Glass*. London.

DEFOE, DANIEL 1928. *A Tour through England and Wales*. London.

DODSWORTH, W 1792. *Guide to the Cathedral Church of Salisbury. With a particular account of the late Great Improvements made therein under the direction of James Wyatt, Esq*. Salisbury.

DODSWORTH, W [and Hatcher, H] 1814. *Historical Account of Cathedral Church of Salisbury*. London.

DORLING, E E 1894. 'Hatchment in Salisbury Cathedral'. *WAM* XXVII, 314–6.

1895. 'Barnston monument in Salisbury Cathedral'. *WAM* XXVIII, 171.

1896. 'Notes on the heraldry of Salisbury Cathedral'. *WAM* XXIX, 113–22.

1903*a*. 'Notes on the Montagu monument in Salisbury Cathedral'. *The Ancestor* IV, 46–8.

1903*b*. 'Notes on some armorial glass in Salisbury Cathedral'. *The Ancestor* IV, 120–6.

1905. 'Fifteenth century heraldry'. *The Ancestor* XII, 146–8.

DRAKE, M 1922. 'War Memorial windows'. *Architectural Review* LII (July–Dec), 117–21.

DRAPER, P 1987. 'Architecture and liturgy', in Alexander and Binski 1987, 83–91.

1996. 'Salisbury Cathedral: paradigm or maverick?', in Keen and Cocke 1996, 21–31.

and Morris, R K, 1993. 'The development of the east end of Winchester Cathedral from the 13th to the 16th century', in Crook 1993*a*, 177–92.

DUFFY, E 1992. *The Stripping of the Altars. Traditional Religion in England 1400–1580*. New Haven and London.

DULEY, A J 1989. *The Medieval Clock at Salisbury Cathedral*. Salisbury.

DUNLOP, I 1980. 'Prisoners of Conscience commemorated: new stained glass for Salisbury Cathedral'. *Country Life* (3 July), 12–13.

EAMES, E S 1957–58. 'A tile pavement from the Queen's Chamber, Clarendon Palace, dated 1250–2'. *JBAA* XX–XXI, 95–106.

1963. 'A thirteenth-century tiled pavement from the King's Chapel, Clarendon Palace'. *JBAA* XXVI, 40–50.

1972. 'Further notes on a thirteenth-century tiled pavement from the King's chapel of Clarendon Palace'. *JBAA* XXXV, 71–6.

1980. *Catalogue of Medieval Lead-Glazed Earthenware Tiles in the Department of Medieval and Later Antiquities, British Museum*. London.

1988. 'The tile kiln and floor tiles', in T B James and A M Robinson (eds), *Clarendon Palace*. London.

1991. 'Tiles', in P and E Saunders (eds), *Salisbury Museum Medieval Catalogue*. Part 1. Salisbury.

EASTON, E 1771 *Antiquitates Sarisburiensis*. Salisbury.

EASTON, J 1825. *The History of the Cathedral Church of Sarum or Salisbury*. London.

EDWARDS, K 1949. *English Secular Cathedrals in the Middle Ages*. Manchester.

ELTRINGHAM, G J 1958. 'Alexander Fort and Salisbury Cathedral'. *WAM* LVII, 56–63.

ESDAILE, K A 1942. 'The Gorges monument in Salisbury Cathedral'. *WAM* CLXXVII, 53–62.

EVANS, J 1956. *A History of the Society of Antiquaries*. London.

EVERETT, C R 1943. 'An episcopal visitation of the Cathedral Church of Sarum in 1607'. *WAM* L, 170–87.

EWARD, S M 1983. 'Vistas – and vandals'. *FOSC 23rd Annual Report*, 15–19.

FERRIDAY, P 1953. 'Francis Price, Carpenter', *Architectural Review* 114 (July–Dec), 327–8.

FINUCANE, R C 1977. *Miracles and Pilgrims. Popular Beliefs in Medieval England*. London.

FIRTH, C H 1894. *The Memoirs of Edmund Ludlow, 1625–72.* 2 vols. Oxford.

FLETCHER, J M J 1927. *The Hertford Monument in Salisbury Cathedral* (A lecture given in the Cathedral 25 Oct 1927 and published in the *Wiltshire Gazette*). Reprinted by George Simpson and Co, Devizes.

1930*a*. 'The stained glass in Salisbury Cathedral'. *WAM* XLV, 235–53.

1930*b*. *The Statues on the West Front of Salisbury Cathedral with a Note on the Gargoyles.* Salisbury.

1932. 'The Gorges monument in Salisbury Cathedral'. *WAM* XLVI, 16–34.

1936*a*. 'The tomb of Lord Walter Hungerford KG'. *WAM* XLVII, 447–56.

1936*b*. 'The monument of Robert Lord Hungerford'. *WAM* XLVII, 457–65.

1937. 'The old belfry in the Close of Salisbury'. *WAM* XXXVII, 608–16.

1938. 'Bishop Richard Beauchamp'. *WAM* XLVIII, 161–73.

1939. 'The cloister of Salisbury Cathedral'. *FOSC 9th Annual Report*, 9–19.

1940. 'Seth Ward, bishop of Salisbury 1667–1689'. *WAM* LXIX, 1–16.

FOSC 1953. *FOSC 23rd Annual Report*, 8.

1954. *FOSC 24th Annual Report*, 21.

1961. 'The Muniment Room and its pavement'. *FOSC 31st Annual Report*, 21–4.

1971. *FOSC 41st Annual Report*, 8–10.

1973. *FOSC 43rd Annual Report*, 7.

1979. *FOSC 49th Annual Report*, 22–4.

1989. *FOSC 59th Annual Report*, 24.

FRANKL, P 1962. *Gothic Architecture.* Harmondsworth.

FRERE, W H 1894 (ed). *Graduale Sarisburiensis.* London.

1902 (ed). *Antiphonale Sarisburiensis.* London.

1910*a* (ed). *Visitation Articles and Injunctions of the Period of Reformation. Volume 1 Historical Introduction.* Alcuin Club Collections XIV. London.

1910*b*. *Visitation Articles and Injunctions of the Period of the Reformation. Volume 2 1536–1558.* Alcuin Club Collections XV. London.

1910*c*. *Visitation Articles and Injunctions of the Period of the Reformation. Volume 3 1559–1575.* Alcuin Club Collections XVI. London.

FREW, J 1979. 'Richard Gough, James Wyatt and late 18th-century preservation'. *Journal of the Society of Architectural Historians* XXXVIII, 366–74.

1984. 'James Wyatt's choir screen at Salisbury Cathedral reconsidered'. *Architectural History* 27, 481–7.

GARLAND, R and MOULE, T 1838. *Winkle's Architectural and Picturesque Illustrations of the Cathedral Churches of England & Wales, with Drawings by R Garland and Descriptions by Thos Moule.* Vol 1. London.

GEM, R 1990. 'The first Romanesque Cathedral of Old Sarum', in Eric Fernie and Paul Crossley (eds), *Medieval Architecture and its Intellectual Context. Studies in Honour of Peter Kidson.* London and Ronceverte.

GENTLEMAN'S MAGAZINE 1789. Letters to Mr Urban from 'RG' (Richard Gough). *Gentleman's Magazine* LIX, 873–5 and 1194.

1790. Letters to Mr Urban. *Gentleman's Magazine* LX, 692 (from J Elderton), 787–8 (from 'Indoctus') and 908 (from 'Indoctior').

1830. Contributions on the choir of the Cathedral. *Gentleman's Magazine* C, pt 1, 405–6; pt 2, 8–9.

1833. Contribution on 'Ancient Table in Salisbury Cathedral Chapter House' by 'An Architectural Antiquary'. *Gentleman's Magazine* CIII, 297–99.

GILPIN, W 1798. *Observations on the Western Parts of England.* London.

GOODISON, N 1969. *English Barometers 1680–1860.* London.

GOUGH, R 1770. 'Conjectures on an ancient tomb in Salisbury Cathedral'. *Archaeologia* II (1770), 188–93.

1796. *Sepulchral Monuments in Great Britain.* Vol II, Parts 1 and 2. London.

GREEN, R B 1968. 'Virtues and Vices in the Chapter House vestibule in Salisbury'. *Journal of Warburg and Courtauld Institutes* XXX, 148–58.

GREENAWAY, D E 1991 (ed). *John Le Neve. Fasti Ecclesiae Anglicanae 1066–1300.* Vol IV. Salisbury. London.

1996. '1091, St Osmund and the Constitution of the Cathedral', in Keen and Cocke 1996, 1–9.

GRODECKI, L 1976, *Les Vitraux de Saint-Denis. Étude sur le Vitrail du XII*e *Siècle.* Corpus Vitrearum Medii Aevi, France. Études Vol I. Paris.

GUNNIS, R 1980. *Dictionary of British Sculptors 1660–1851.* London.

HADLEY D and HADLEY J, 1991. 'Henry Holiday 1839–1927'. *The Journal of Stained Glass* XIX, 1, 1989–90 (publ 1991), 48–75.

HALL P 1834. *Picturesque Memorials of Salisbury.* Salisbury.

HAMMOND, J J 1929. 'Three inventories of plate and furniture belonging to Salisbury Cathedral'. *WAM* XLIV, 407–10.

HARDING, J 1895. 'The Belfry formerly in the Close and its bells'. *WAM* XXVIII, 108–20.

HARRIS J 1825. *Copies of the Epitaphs in Salisbury Cathedral, Cloisters and Cemetery.* Salisbury.

HAWORTH, K W 1973. *The Use of Sarum.* Salisbury.

HAYWARD, J and CAHN, W 1982. *Radiance and Reflection. Medieval Art from the Raymond Pitcairn Collection.* New York.

HEWITT, C 1988 'English Medieval Cope Chests'. *JBAA* CXLI, 105–23.

HOBBS, M 1994 (ed). *Chichester Cathedral. An Historical Survey.* Chichester.

HOLIDAY, H 1896. *Stained Glass as an Art.* London.

HOLLAENDER, A J E 1943. 'The Sarum Illuminator and his School'. *WAM* L (1942–4), 230–62.

1958–9. 'Jacob Pleydell-Bouverie, Second Earl of Radnor

and Wyatt's renovation of Salisbury Cathedral'. *FOSC 28th Annual Report*, 22-6.

HOPE, W St John 1916. 'On the tombs of two bishops in the Cathedral church of Salisbury'. *Proceedings of the Society of Antiquaries* XXVIII, 184-8.

1917a. 'Quire screens in English Churches with special reference to the twelfth century quire screen formerly in the Cathedral Church of Ely'. *Archaeologia* LXVIII, 43-110.

1917b. 'The Sarum consuetudinary and its relation to Cathedral Church of Old Sarum. *Archaeologia* LXVIII, 111-26.

1917c. 'Images of kings in the Cathedral church of Salisbury'. *WAM* XXXIX, 505-6.

HORLBECK, F R 1960. 'The vault paintings of Salisbury Cathedral'. *Archaeological Journal* CXVII, 116-30.

HORNE, J M 1962 (ed). *John Le Neve. Fasti Ecclesiae Anglicanae 1300-1541. III Salisbury Diocese*. London.

1986. *John Le Neve. Fasti Ecclesiae Anglicanae 1541-1857. IV Salisbury Diocese*. London.

HUTCHINS, J 1774. *History of Dorset*, Vol 4, 176 (description of the Hungerford chantry in Salisbury Cathedral). London.

JACKSON, J E 1869. 'An inventory of chantry furniture AD 1472 Hungerford Chapel, Salisbury Cathedral'. *WAM* XI, 334-9.

JACOB, E F 1947. 'The Medieval Chapter of Salisbury Cathedral'. *WAM* LI, 479-95.

JAMES, T B and ROBINSON, A M 1988 (eds). *Clarendon Palace. The History and Archaeology of a Medieval Palace and Hunting Lodge near Salisbury, Wiltshire*. London.

JUDD, L 1990. *Embroideries in Salisbury Cathedral*. Salisbury.

KEEN, L and COCKE, T 1996 (eds). *Medieval Art and Architecture at Salisbury Cathedral*. British Archaeological Association Transactions XVII. London.

KER, N R 1949. 'Salisbury Cathedral manuscripts and Patrick Young's catalogue'. *WAM* LIII, 153-83.

KIDSON, P 1993. 'The historical circumstances and the principles of the design', in RCHME 1993a.

KITE, E 1860. *Monumental Brasses of Wiltshire* (facsimile edn Bath 1969).

KNOWLES, J A 1951-2. 'Exhibitions of stained glass in London'. *Journal of the British Society of Master Glass Painters* XI, 1, 44-50.

LEGG, L G WICKHAM 1936. 'Relation of a short survey of the Western Counties'. *Camden Miscellany* XVI. Camden Society, 3rd ser, LII.

LEHMBERG, STAMFORD E 1988. *The Reformation of Cathedrals. Cathedrals in English Society 1485-1603*. Princeton.

LETHABY, W R 1925. *Westminster Abbey Re-examined*. London.

1926. 'Early thirteenth-century glass at Salisbury'. *Journal of the British Society of Master Glass Painters*. I, 4, 17-18.

LONG, C E 1859 (ed). *Diary of the Marches of the Royal Army during the Great Civil War kept by Richard Symonds*. Camden Society LXXIV.

LUARD, H R 1876 (ed). *Matthew Paris. Chronica Majora* III. Rolls Series 57. London.

LUKIS, N C 1857. *An Account of Church Bells with some Notices of Wiltshire Bells and Bellfounders*. London and Oxford.

MADDEN, F 1866a (ed). *Matthew Paris. Historia Anglorum. I 1067-1189*. Rolls Series 44. London.

1866b. *Matthew Paris. Historia Anglorum. II 1189-1245*. Rolls Series 44. London.

1869. *Matthew Paris. Historia Anglorum. III 1246-1253*. London.

MAGALOTTI, Count Lorenzo 1821. *Travels of Cosmo III through England*. London.

MALDEN, A R 1901. *The Canonisation of St Osmund from the Manuscript Records in the Muniment Room of Salisbury Cathedral*. Wiltshire Record Society. Salisbury.

1904. 'A Salisbury fifteenth century death register', *The Ancestor* IX, 28-35.

1908. 'Note on an inscription on a buttress of Salisbury Cathedral'. *WAM* XXXV, 347-40.

1912. 'The burial places of the bishops of Salisbury'. *WAM* XXXVII, 339-52.

MARKHAM, SARAH 1984 (ed). *The Diary of John Loveday of Caversham (1711-1789)*. Salisbury.

MARKS, R 1986. 'Cistercian window glass in England and Wales', in C Norton and D Park (eds), *Cistercian Art and Architecture in the British Isles*. Cambridge, 211-27.

1988. 'Window Glass', in James and Robinson 1988, 229-33.

1993. *Stained Glass in England during the Middle Ages*. London.

1996. 'The thirteenth-century glazing of Salisbury Cathedral', in Keen and Cocke 1996, 106-20.

MATTHEWS, B 1983. *The Organs and Organists of Salisbury Cathedral*. Salisbury.

1989. *The Organs and Organists of Salisbury Cathedral 1480-1983*. 4th edn. Salisbury.

MIDDLETON, J H 1885. 'On consecration crosses with some English examples'. *Archaeologia* XLVIII, 456-64.

MILNER, J 1798. *Dissertation on the Modern Style of Altering Cathedrals as Exemplified in the Cathedral of Salisbury*. London.

1798-1801. *The History, Civil and Ecclesiastical, and Survey of the Antiquities of Winchester*. 2 vols. Winchester.

MORGAN, N J 1982. *Early Gothic Manuscripts (I). 1190-1250*. London.

1983. *The Medieval Glass of Lincoln Cathedral*. Corpus Vitrearum Medii Aevi, Great Britain, Occasional Papers 3. London.

1988. *Early Gothic manuscripts (II). 1250-1285*. London.

1990. *The Lambeth Apocalypse. Manuscript 209 in Lambeth Palace Library. A Critical Study*. London.

MORRIS, C 1995. *The Illustrated Journeys of Celia Fiennes*. Stroud.

MOUNT, R 1960. 'Screens or vistas in cathedrals'. *Country Life* (29 Sept), 672-3 (written by G U S Corbett and C A R Radford).

MURRAY (John Murray Publishers) 1861. *Handbook to the Cathedrals of England. Southern Division Part I*. London.

NICOLAS, N H 1826. *Testamenta Vetusta*. London.

NIGHTINGALE, J E 1881. 'Letter to the Editor' (Concerning John Berry, glazier of Harnham). *WAM* XIX, 226–7.

1891. *The Church Plate of The County of Wilts* [*sic*]. Salisbury.

NORTON, C 1996. 'The decorative pavements of Salisbury Cathedral and Old Sarum', in Keen and Cocke 1996, 90–105.

PARRY, L 1996. *William Morris*, London.

PEVSNER, N and METCALF, P 1985. *The Cathedrals of England: Southern England*. London.

PLANCHE, J R 1859. 'On the sepulchral effigies in Salisbury Cathedral'. *JBAA* XV, 115–30.

POPE, W 1697. *The Life of Seth, Lord Bishop of Salisbury*. Luttrell Society Reprints 21 (ed J B Bambrough). Oxford.

PRICE, F 1753. *A Series of Particular and Useful Observations made with Great Diligence and Care, upon that Admirable Structure, the Cathedral Church of Salisbury*. London.

1774 *A Description of that Admirable Structure the Cathedral Church of Salisbury* (2nd edn of Price 1753). London.

QUIRK, R 1948. 'Note on the Salisbury Cathedral muniments'. *Archaeological Journal* CIV, 1947 (publ 1948), 148–9.

RABY, F J E 1948. 'The tomb of St Osmund at Salisbury'. *Archaeological Journal* CIV, 1947 (publ 1948), 146–8.

RADNOR, HELEN, DOWAGER COUNTESS 1927. *From a Great-Grandmother's Armchair*. London.

RAWLINSON, R 1723. *History and Antiquities of the Cathedral-Church of Salisbury and Abbey-Church of Bath*. London.

RCHME 1924. *London Vol I. Westminster Abbey*. London.

1931. *Herefordshire. Vol I*. London.

1977. *The Town of Stamford*. London.

1980. *City of Salisbury. Vol I. Ancient and Historical Monuments*. London.

1993a. *Salisbury Cathedral. Perspectives on the Architectural History*. London.

1993b. *Salisbury: The Houses of the Close*. London.

READ, B 1982. *Victorian Sculpture*. New Haven and London.

RICH JONES, W H 1878. 'On the original position of the high altar at Salisbury Cathedral'. *WAM* xvii, 136–46.

1879. *Fasti Ecclesiae Sarisberiensis*, part I. London.

1881. *Fasti Ecclesiae Sarisberiensis*, part II. London.

1883. *Vetus Registrum Sarisberiense; The Register of St Osmund. Volume 1*. Rolls Series 78. London.

1884. *Vetus Registrum Sarisberiense; The Register of St Osmund. Volume 2*. Rolls Series 78. London.

and Dunn Macray, W 1891 (eds). *Charters and Documents Illustrating the History of Salisbury in the 12th and 13th Centuries*. Rolls Series 97. London.

RICKERT, M 1965. *Painting in Britain. The Middle Ages*. Harmondsworth.

ROBERTS, M 1983. 'The tomb of Giles de Bridport in Salisbury Cathedral'. *The Art Bulletin* LXV, 4, 559–86.

1993. 'Thomas Gray's contribution to the study of medieval architecture'. *Architectural History* 36, 49–68.

ROBINSON, J M 1979. *The Wyatts. An Architectural Dynasty*. London.

ROGERS, H 1982. 'Bishop Brodie and Bishop Salcot'. *Hatcher Review* 13, 141–2.

RUFFINIÈRE DU PREY, P DE LA 1982. 'Giannantonio Selva in England'. *Architectural History* 25, 20–34.

SANDELL, R E 1976. 'Two medieval bishops and their wanderings'. *Hatcher Review* 1, 19–25.

SAUNDERS, P AND SAUNDERS E 1991. *Salisbury Museum Medieval Catalogue*. Parts 1 and 2. Salisbury.

SCHNEBBELIE, J 1789. Note on an inscription on the buttress, with drawing. *Gentleman's Magazine* LIX, 1002.

1791. *The Antiquaries Museum* XII. London.

SCOTT, G G 1870. *Bishop Hamilton's Memorial. Report on the Restoration of the choir*. Salisbury.

1876. *Salisbury Cathedral. Report upon the Position of the High Altar*. Salisbury.

SEWTER, A C 1975. *The Stained Glass of William Morris and his Circle – a Catalogue*. Newhaven and London.

SHAW, H 1858. *Specimens of Tile Pavements*. London.

SHORTT, H DE S 1958. '13th century heraldry from the Chapter House'. *FOSC 28th Annual Report*, 16–21.

1964. 'Two Wiltshire fonts in South Australia'. *WAM* LIX, 168–9.

1970. *The Hungerford and Beauchamp Chantry Chapels*. Salisbury.

1971. *The Three Bishops' Tombs Moved to Salisbury Cathedral from Old Sarum*. Salisbury.

1972. *No History – No Mystery*. Salisbury.

1973. *Salisbury Cathedral and Indications of Sarum Use*. Salisbury.

SIMPSON, G 1996. 'Documentary and dendrochronological evidence for the building of Salisbury Cathedral', in Keen and Cocke 1996, 10–20.

SLATTER, D 1965. 'The diary of Thomas Naish'. *Wiltshire Record Society*. Devizes.

SMITH, P L 1980 (ed). 'The recollections of John Harding as a chorister at Salisbury 1826–32'. *Hatcher Review* 10, 3–22.

SOCIETY OF ANTIQUARIES 1873–6. *Proceedings of the Society of Antiquaries*. VI, 477–9.

1913. *Proceedings of the Society of Antiquaries*. XXV, 93–104.

1914. *Proceedings of the Society of Antiquaries*. XXVI, 100–19.

1915. *Proceedings of the Society of Antiquaries*. XXVII, 230–40.

1916. *Proceedings of the Society of Antiquaries*. XXVIII, 174–83.

SPRING, R O C 1979. 'Recent discoveries in some of the tombs in the nave of Salisbury Cathedral'. *Hatcher Review* 8, 3–14.

1987a. *Salisbury Cathedral*. London.

1987*b*. *The Stained Glass of Salisbury Cathedral*. Salisbury.

STALLEY, R A 1971. 'A 12th-century patron of architecture'. *JBAA* XXXV, 62–83.

STAMP, G 1995 (ed). *Personal and Professional Recollections. The Autobiography of Sir George Gilbert Scott*. Stamford.

STEPHENS, F 1981–2. Book review. *Journal of the British Society of Master Glass Painters*, XVII, 2, 72–5.

STEVENS, F 1936. 'The inlaid paving tiles of Wilts'. *WAM* XLVII, 358–78.

STONE, L 1955. *Sculpture in Britain, the Middle Ages*. Harmondsworth.

STORER, J (undated, *c* 1820). *History and Antiquities of Salisbury Cathedral*. Salisbury.

STOTHARD, C A 1876. *The Monumental Effigies of Great Britain*. 2nd edn. London.

STREET, A E 1881. *Memoir of G E Street 1824–81*. London.

STROUD, D 1984. 'The cult and tombs of St Osmund at Salisbury'. *WAM* LXXVIII, 50–4.

1993. 'A 12th-century effigy in Salisbury Cathedral'. *WAM* LXXVI, 113–17.

TATTON-BROWN, T 1995*a*. 'The tombs of the two bishops who built the tower and spire of Salisbury Cathedral'. *WAM* LXXXVIII, 134–37.

1995*b*. 'The cloisters of Salisbury Cathedral'. *FOSC 65th Annual Report*, 6–10.

1996. 'Hidden masterpieces'. *Salisbury Cathedral News* 194 (Feb), 8–10.

TOKE, N E 1930. 'The *Opus Alexandrinum* and sculpted stone roundels in the retro-choir of Canterbury Cathedral'. *Archaeologia Cantiana* XLII, 189–221.

TORRANCE, W J 1978. *The Story of St Osmund*. Salisbury.

TOULMIN SMITH, L 1964. *The Itinerary of John Leland 1535–43*. I. London.

TRACY, C 1984. 'Choir stalls at Salisbury Cathedral'. *Country Life* (29 Nov), 1720–2.

1987. *English Gothic Choir Stalls 1200–1400*. Woodbridge.

1992. 'The St Albans Abbey watching chamber: a reassessment'. *JBAA* CXLV, 104–111.

VALLANCE, A 1947. *Greater English Church Screens*. London.

Vernacular Architecture 1996. 'Tree-ring dates. List 65'. *Vernacular Architecture* 27.

VICTORIA AND ALBERT MUSEUM 1971. *Victorian Church Art*. Exhibition Catalogue. London.

VICTORIA History of the Counties of England 1956. *A History of Wiltshire* III.

WAGNER, A 1967. *Aspilogia. Being Materials of Heraldry*. II. London.

WALPOLE SOCIETY 1937–8. 'Vertue Notebook V'. *Walpole Society* XXVI. London.

WALTERS, H B 1927. *The Church Bells of Wiltshire*. Devizes.

WAYLEN, J 1856. 'Who destroyed the images at the west end of Salisbury Cathedral?' *WAM* III, 119–24.

1892. 'The Falstone Day Book'. *WAM* XXVI, 343–91.

WEBB, G 1965. *Architecture in Britain: The Middle Ages*. 2nd

edn. Harmondsworth.

WESTLAKE, N H J 1881. *A History of Design in Painted Glass*. II. London and Oxford.

WHEELER, W A 1889. *Sarum Chronology*. Salisbury.

1901. *Supplemental Sarum Chronology 1881–1900*. Salisbury.

WHITE, A 1989. 'Westminster Abbey in the early seventeenth century: a powerhouse of ideas'. *Church Monuments* IV, 17–53.

1992. 'England *c* 1550–*c* 1660: a hundred years of continental influence'. *Church Monuments* VII, 34–74.

1994. '*The Book of Monuments* reconsidered: Maximilian Colt and William Wright'. *Church Monuments* IX, 62–7.

WHITE, J W G 1921. *Salisbury, The Cathedral and City*. (Bell's Cathedral Series.) Revised edn. London.

WHITTINGHAM, S 1974. *Salisbury Chapter House*. Salisbury.

1979. *A 13th-Century Portrait Gallery in Salisbury Cathedral*. Salisbury.

WILLIAMSON, P 1995. *Gothic Sculpture 1140–1300*. London and New Haven.

WILLIS, R 1849. 'Lecture on the architecture of Salisbury Cathedral, 26 July 1849', in *Architectural History of some English Cathedrals* II. Chicheley (facsimile reprint 1973).

WILSON, C 1977. *The Shrines of St William of York*. York.

1983. 'The original setting of the Apostle and Prophet figures from St Mary's Abbey, York', in F H Thompson (ed), *Studies in Medieval Sculpture*. London.

WINSTON, C 1865. *Memoirs Illustrative of the Art of Glass Painting*. London.

WOODFORDE, C 1954. *English Stained and Painted Glass*. Oxford.

WORDSWORTH, C R 1898. 'On the sites of the medieval altars of Salisbury Cathedral Church'. *Proceedings of the Dorset Natural History and Antiquarian Field Club* XIX, 1–24.

1901. *The Ceremonies and Processions of Salisbury Cathedral*. Cambridge.

1913. 'Wiltshire pardons or indulgences'. *WAM* XXXVIII, 15–33.

1914. 'List of altars in Salisbury Cathedral'. *WAM* XXXVIII, 557–71.

1915. 'Notes on Salisbury Cathedral'. *WAM* XXXIX, 30–57.

1917. 'Salisbury Cathedral: effigies of kings and the flood of 1309'. *WAM* XXXIX, 504–5.

and Macleane, D 1915 (eds). *Statuta et Consuetudines Ecclesiae Cathedralis Beatae Mariae Virginis Sarisberiensis*. London.

and Robertson, D H 1938. 'Salisbury choristers. Their endowments, boy-bishops, music, teachers and head-masters, with the history of the organ'. *WAM* XLVIII, 201–31.

WREN SOCIETY 1934. *Wren Society* XI. London.

ZAKIN, H 1979. *French Cistercian Grisaille Glass*. New York and London.

ZARNECKI, G, HOLT, J and HOLLAND T 1984 (eds). *English Romanesque Art 1066–1200*. London.

Index